IMAGES
of America

FRESH MEADOWS

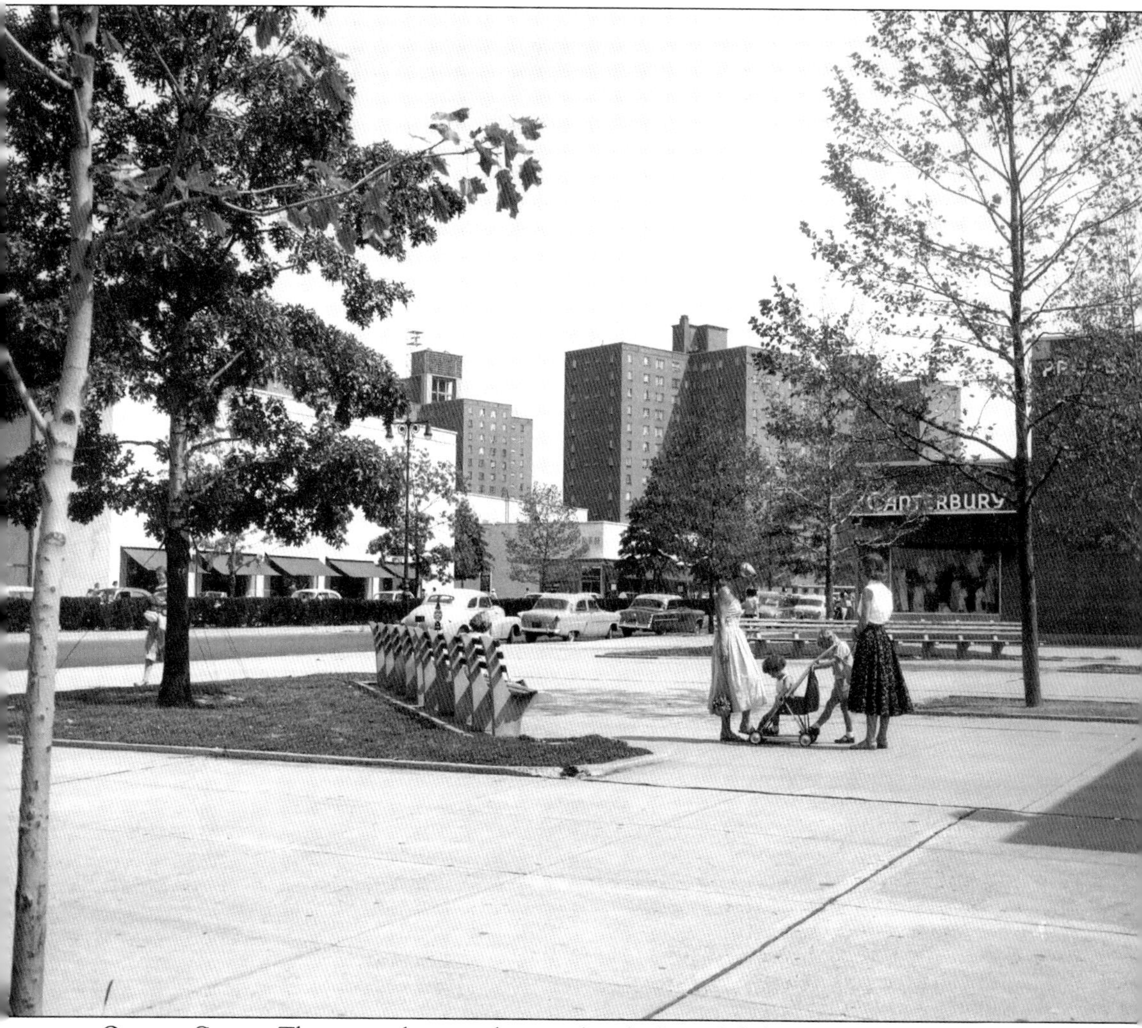

On the Cover: The cover photograph was taken by Jerry Saltsberg & Associates in the small plaza near the southwest corner of 188th Street and Horace Harding Boulevard. The New York Life Insurance Company hired Saltsberg to shoot a variety of photographs of Fresh Meadows, in part for use in materials to help promote the housing development. An accomplished photographer, several of Saltsberg's photographs are in the Archives of American Art, Smithsonian Institution. (Courtesy of Queens Fresh Meadows LLC; photograph by Jerry Saltsberg & Associates.)

IMAGES
of America

FRESH MEADOWS

Fred Cantor and Debra L. Davidson

ARCADIA
PUBLISHING

ISBN 978-0-7385-7572-8

Published by Arcadia Publishing
Charleston, South Carolina

Printed in the United States of America

Library of Congress Control Number: 2011920925

For all general information, please contact Arcadia Publishing:
Telephone 843-853-2070
Fax 843-853-0044
E-mail sales@arcadiapublishing.com
For customer service and orders:
Toll-Free 1-888-313-2665

Visit us on the Internet at www.arcadiapublishing.com

Contents

ACKNOWLEDGMENTS

The authors would like to thank the following individuals and organizations: Pam Sickles at Queens Fresh Meadows LLC and Jennifer Andreola at the History Factory for their help and time in assembling the photographs that originated with the New York Life Insurance Company; New York Life for graciously allowing us to use its photographs; Mitch Kaften for his time and patience in sifting through and scanning the vast trove of photographs and negatives of his father, Douglas Kaften, and for his generosity in sharing his knowledge; Aina Balgalvis for her wonderful photographs; Edna and Bob Harris for their support and help in getting the word out about the book; Mark Inhaber and Alana Hollander at Hillcrest Jewish Center; Erik Huber at the Queens Borough Public Library; the Queens Historical Society; and Erin Vosgien, our editor at Arcadia, for guiding us through the entire process.

This book would not have been possible without the photographs contributed by nearly 40 current and former residents of Fresh Meadows. We would like to offer our sincere thanks to each of them who took the trouble to search their cache of old images and submitted photographs for this book.

Fred Cantor would like to thank his parents for helping create a wonderful home in Fresh Meadows, and his wife, Debbie Silberstein, for picking up where his parents left off. Fred would also like to thank his older brother, Marc, for helping bail him out of the principal's office at PS 179.

Debra Davidson would like to thank her parents, Edna and Sidney Davidson, for settling in Fresh Meadows and enabling her to grow up in a wonderful environment. Debra would also like to thank her friends from childhood, many of whom have remained a part of her life, for making those years in Fresh Meadows so happy and for their support of this project. Finally, Debra thanks her son, Ethan, for his patience and understanding during the writing of this book.

INTRODUCTION

Fresh Meadows is emblematic of postwar America—a time of Americans picking up their lives where they had left off before the war. It was a period of unbridled optimism and prosperity when the American Dream seemed accessible to so many. The postwar years saw the birth of the approximately 76 million Americans who would come to be known as the baby boomers—the most analyzed and influential generation of the 20th century.

The euphoria caused by the end of the war was tempered by some challenges. With little construction activity in the years leading up to World War II because of the Great Depression, and with no construction having taken place during the war, returning veterans and their young families faced an unprecedented housing shortage. Fresh Meadows was one of the communities that came into being in response to this acute need for housing for young families.

Today, Fresh Meadows is defined as the area bordered by Francis Lewis Boulevard to the east, Utopia Parkway/Fresh Meadow Lane to the west, Union Turnpike to the south, and Horace Harding Expressway to the north. The history of this area dates back to colonial times when the area was known as Black Stump. That name was most likely derived from the fact that the local farmers would mark the boundaries of their property with blackened tree stumps. In colonial times, only two roads existed in the area: Black Stump Road (now 73rd Avenue) and Fresh Meadow Lane. During the Revolutionary War, the British Army and the traitor Benedict Arnold were housed in the area.

In the early 20th century, Queens was still very much considered "the country" to residents of tenements in Manhattan. In 1905, the Utopia Land Company was established with the plan to build a cooperative community in Queens for Jewish families from the Lower East Side. The company bought 50 acres of farmland east of 164th Street but was unable to secure sufficient funding and the project was abandoned before any development took place.

While some residential construction took place in the prewar years, it was the development of the Fresh Meadows housing complex by the New York Life Insurance Company that provided the area with its centerpiece. At the time it was erected, only the housing complex itself was known as Fresh Meadows. The areas to the south and west were known at various times as Utopia Estates, Jamaica Estates North, West Cunningham Park, or just Flushing. Today, the entire area is known as Fresh Meadows, a reflection of the importance of the housing development to the entire community.

In 1949, the renowned land-use expert Lewis Mumford hailed the Fresh Meadows housing development as "perhaps the most positive and exhilarating example of large-scale community planning in this country."

More than 30 years later, the Pulitzer Prize-winning critic Paul Goldberger described Fresh Meadows as the "quintessential suburban" housing complex. He also wrote, "What made Fresh Meadows special when it was new was its site planning. There is an enormous amount of landscaped open space, and it is accessible from every one of the apartment units . . . Fresh Meadows has its own school, theater and shopping center; the retail complex was among the first automobile-oriented shopping centers to be built, and this, too, helped earn for the project its place in planning history."

And, most recently, the fifth edition of the *AIA Guide to New York City*, published in 2010, characterized Fresh Meadows as an "avant-garde site plan" at the time of its creation in the 1940s and stated that Fresh Meadows "scores as excellent planning" and that "it is beautifully maintained."

High praise, indeed, throughout six decades, and the acclaim demonstrates that the New York Life Insurance Company unquestionably achieved its goal of creating a model community when it began the process of building Fresh Meadows in 1946.

On March 23, 1946, the *New York Times* reported that New York Life bought the "Fresh Meadow Country Club in Flushing, Queens for $1,075,000." The club was best known for having been the site of the 1932 US Open, which was won by Gene Sarazen, who had served as the club pro. The article stated, "Only about 20 percent of the area will be occupied by buildings, with the remainder given over to roads, park and recreation areas." The *Times* further reported that "rents will be moderate" and that "preference will be given to veterans in accordance with the priority regulations of the Federal Housing Administration."

When completed, the complex succeeded in achieving low density. New York Life initially built two 13-story structures, with the first units available for occupancy in 1947. However, the rest of the housing in the initial plan was composed of two-story and three-story apartment buildings, resulting in only 17 families per acre spread throughout the site of the former golf course. (A 20-story building was later added in 1962.)

As noted above, part of the recognition of Fresh Meadows's place in planning history was the manner in which automobiles were taken into consideration. In addition to having one of the first car-oriented shopping centers, Fresh Meadows had central parking garages for its own residents, and there were curved and angled streets designed to slow down traffic.

But, ironically, perhaps the ultimate feature of Fresh Meadows for many residents accustomed to urban living was that one really did not need a car at all for day-to-day living. It was a self-contained community that provided schools, shopping, a library, post office, and entertainment, all within walking distance. Fresh Meadows combined the best aspects of urban and suburban living.

And it was not just adults who could walk to everything; it was kids as well, which made Fresh Meadows a paradise for children. There were grassy play areas right outside of front doors and behind apartment buildings. There was the Oak Grove, a vestige of Fresh Meadow Country Club, on which the development was built. The abandoned Long Island Motor Parkway provided an ideal bike path, long before the concept of bike paths was common.

Fresh Meadows contains an array of photographs that capture the postwar era in the renowned housing development built by the New York Life Insurance Company as well as the surrounding community, including neighborhood institutions that have changed or vanished.

Visiting Fresh Meadows today, one can readily see that it is still a wonderful place to live and raise a family. It is still well-maintained, and, justifiably, the housing development has been designated a Special Planned Community Preservation District by the City of New York, which should help ensure that Fresh Meadows remains a model community for future generations.

One

A Model Community

Few, if any, of the early residents of the Fresh Meadows housing complex recognized that the community they had moved to would later be held up as a "model community" by urban planners and architects.

Eytan Fichman, who moved to the Fresh Meadows complex at the age of three in 1957 and earned a masters of architecture from Harvard University, recalls, "The parquet-floored rooms of the apartments were well-proportioned and without ornament; the unit designs provided a threshold space at the entry for greeting visitors and gave exposure on two or three sides of the building, affording light and ventilation. Apartments could be reconfigured through breaking open or sealing doorways to rooms that could 'swing' between adjacent units. The 3-story buildings' floors typically had shared landings with a couple of neighbors whose entrance doors were near enough at hand to make it easy, for neighbors who wanted to, to borrow the proverbial cup of sugar and get to know one another."

Fichman goes on to say, "The red brick facades and elevations of the buildings with their periodic rectangular bay windows were mute masks and backdrops for indoor and outdoor life in the neighborhood. The large blocks were not arranged according to a grid—the overall plan was more informal, with major avenues leading to minor streets, crescents and cul-de-sacs. The u-shaped plan of many of the 3-story buildings suggested shared areas more private to the 27 units of each 'u' without enclosing them. The scale was intimate enough that a parent in an apartment could call to a child playing outside. Larger shared outdoor areas beside and behind the buildings were well landscaped with trees, plantings and children's play areas. Lower scale rows of 2-story garden apartments with their lively backyards helped vary the streetscape while defining and softening the edges of some of the outdoor spaces."

The earliest residents, by and large, were simply happy to have found a nice, new apartment. They got much more than they bargained for.

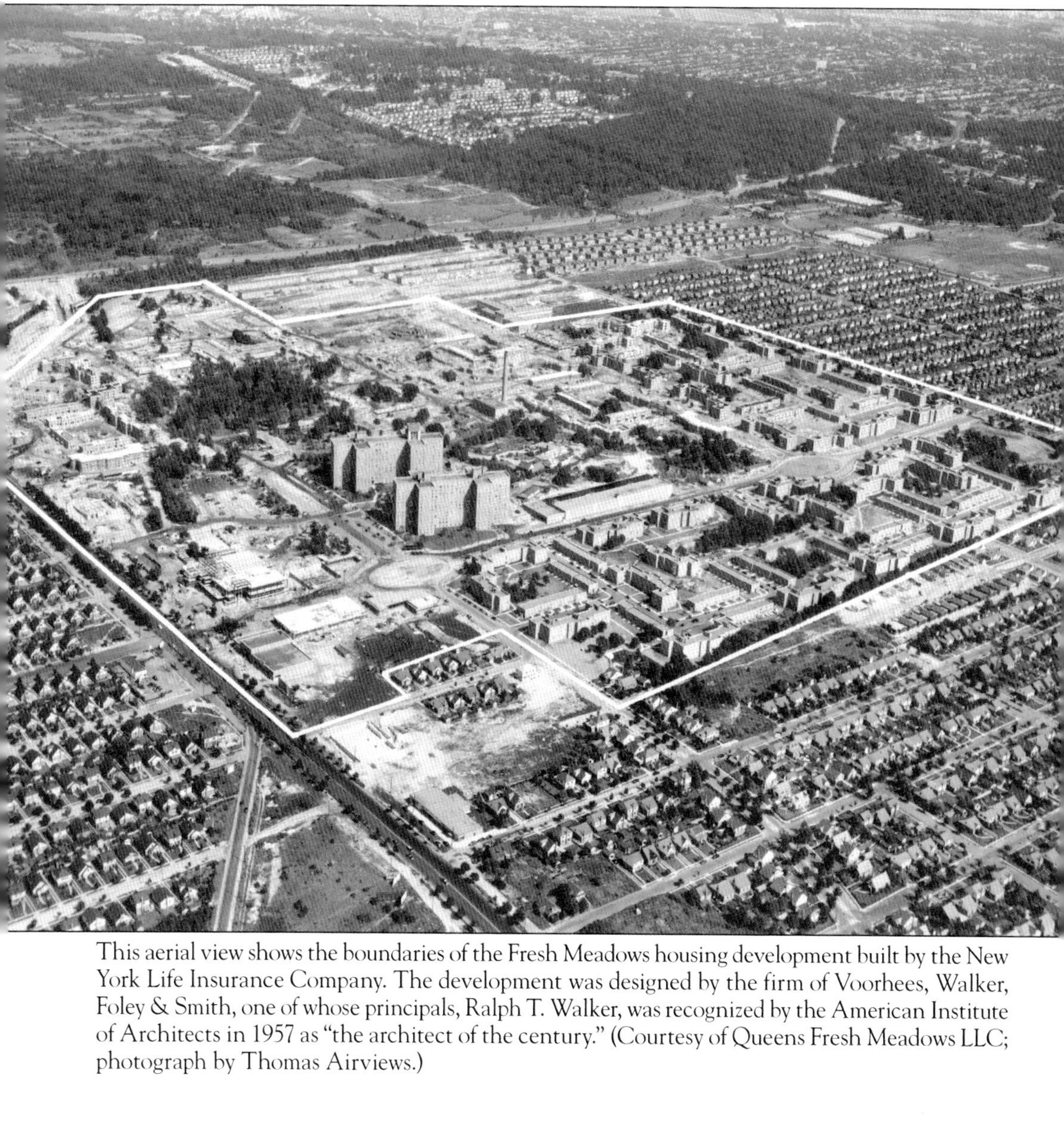

This aerial view shows the boundaries of the Fresh Meadows housing development built by the New York Life Insurance Company. The development was designed by the firm of Voorhees, Walker, Foley & Smith, one of whose principals, Ralph T. Walker, was recognized by the American Institute of Architects in 1957 as "the architect of the century." (Courtesy of Queens Fresh Meadows LLC; photograph by Thomas Airviews.)

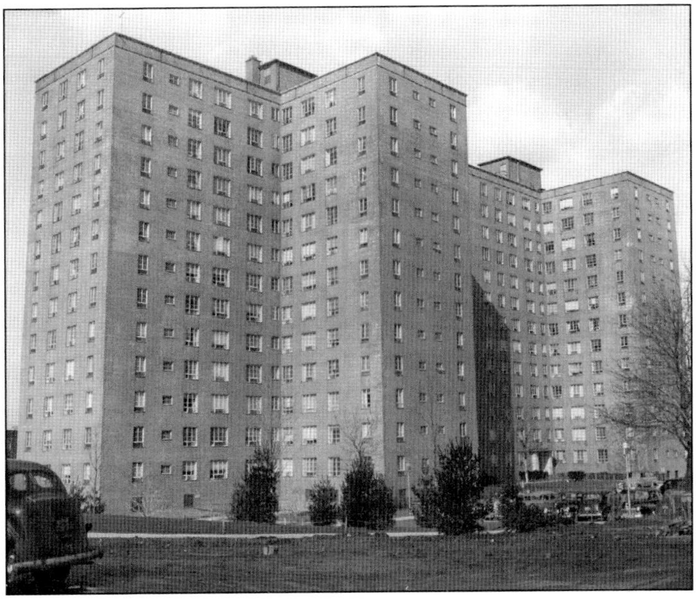

Two 13-story structures were the first apartment buildings completed. The first tenants—20 families, all of whom had at least one World War II veteran—moved in on September 2, 1947. According to the *New York Times*, "All the new tenants had previously searched in vain for suitable living quarters . . . a few of the families had had furniture in storage for three or four years." (Courtesy of Queens Fresh Meadows LLC; photograph by Jerry Saltsberg & Associates.)

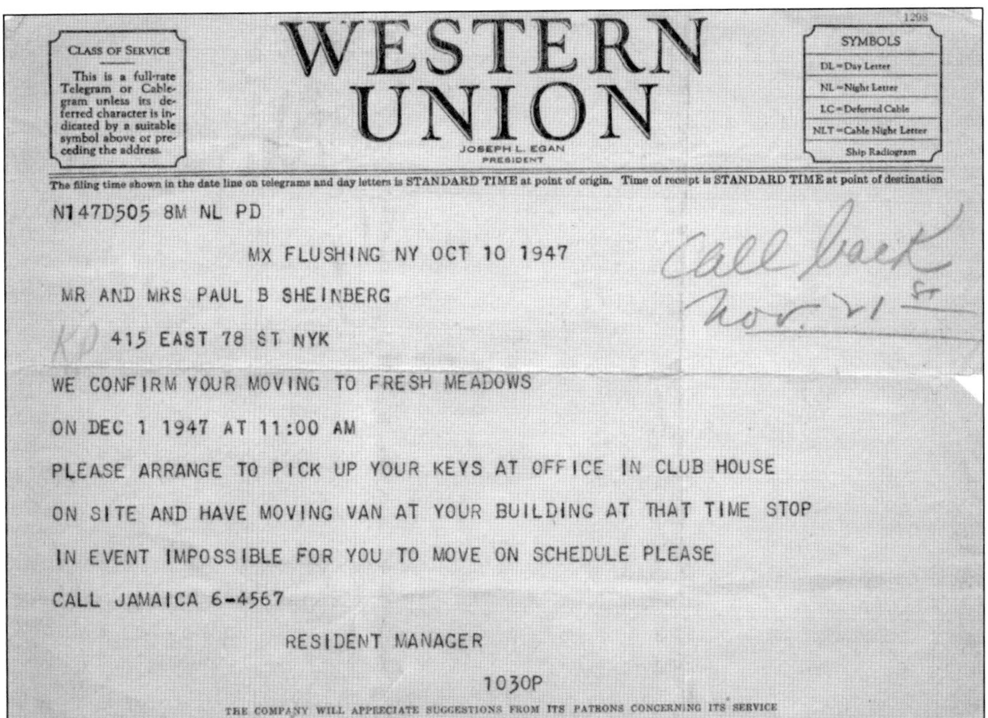

1298

CLASS OF SERVICE

This is a full-rate Telegram or Cablegram unless its deferred character is indicated by a suitable symbol above or preceding the address.

WESTERN UNION

JOSEPH L. EGAN PRESIDENT

SYMBOLS

DL=Day Letter
NL=Night Letter
LC=Deferred Cable
NLT=Cable Night Letter
Ship Radiogram

The filing time shown in the date line on telegrams and day letters is STANDARD TIME at point of origin. Time of receipt is STANDARD TIME at point of destination

N147D505 8M NL PD

MX FLUSHING NY OCT 10 1947

MR AND MRS PAUL B SHEINBERG

415 EAST 78 ST NYK

WE CONFIRM YOUR MOVING TO FRESH MEADOWS
ON DEC 1 1947 AT 11:00 AM
PLEASE ARRANGE TO PICK UP YOUR KEYS AT OFFICE IN CLUB HOUSE
ON SITE AND HAVE MOVING VAN AT YOUR BUILDING AT THAT TIME STOP
IN EVENT IMPOSSIBLE FOR YOU TO MOVE ON SCHEDULE PLEASE
CALL JAMAICA 6-4567

RESIDENT MANAGER

1030P

Call back Nov. 21st

THE COMPANY WILL APPRECIATE SUGGESTIONS FROM ITS PATRONS CONCERNING ITS SERVICE

At least some of the earliest tenants in the Fresh Meadows development received confirmation of their move-in date via telegram. The "club house" referred to in the telegram was the clubhouse of the Fresh Meadow Country Club that was used by the New York Life Insurance Company as a temporary on-site management office. (Courtesy of Donna Sheinberg Gulotta.)

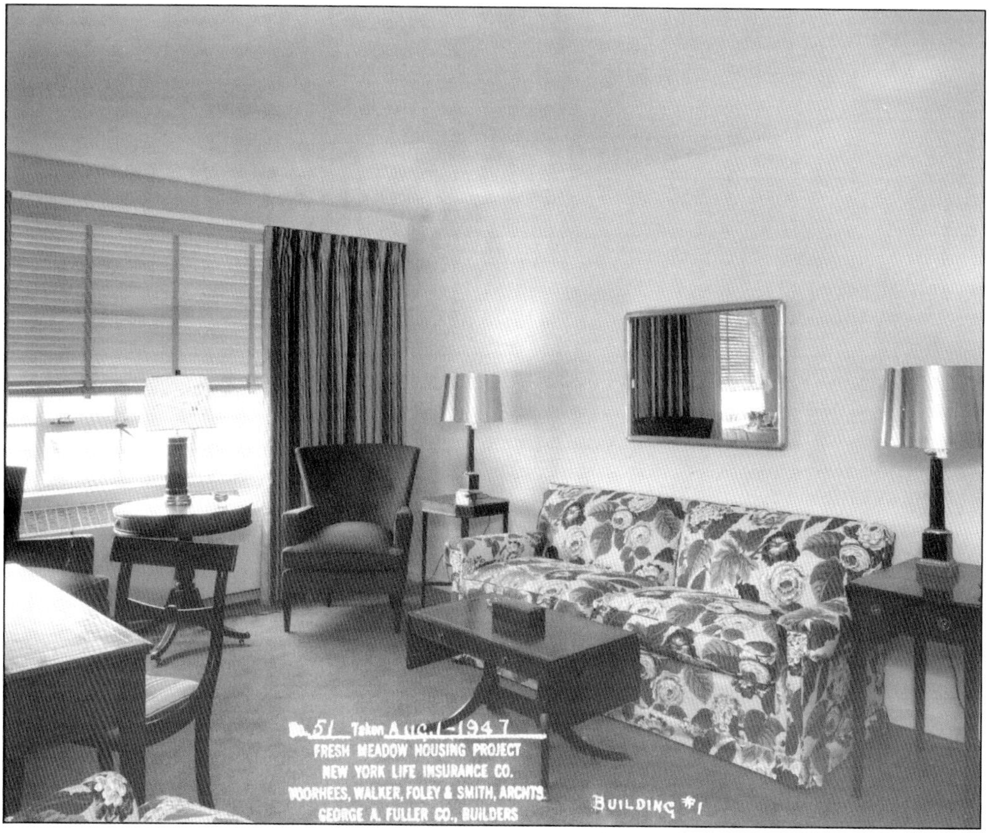

Bloomingdale's decorated the two model apartments that were on display for prospective tenants. The cost of furnishing a two-bedroom unit in the traditional style, as shown in this picture, was roughly $1,600. (Courtesy of New York Life Insurance Company Archives.)

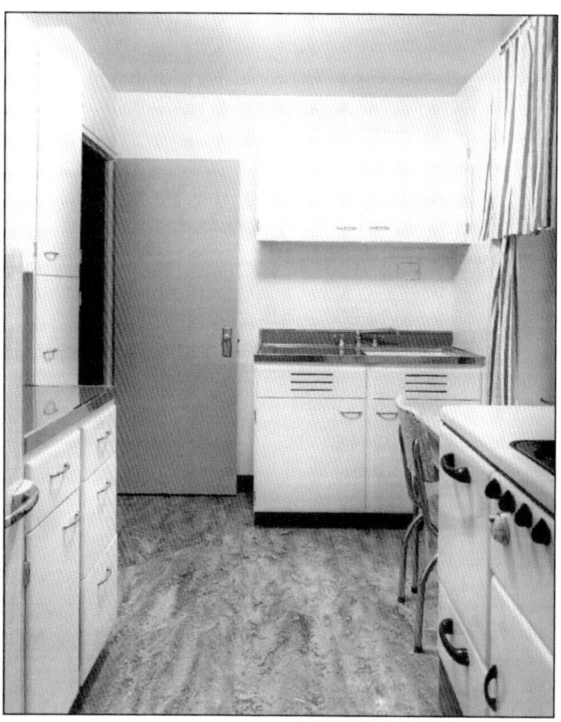

The original kitchens in the apartments featured white cabinetry with chrome fixtures. The monthly rents for the original apartments ranged from $79.50 to $84.50 for three-and-one-half-room units and were $102 for four-and-one-half rooms. Electricity was included. (Courtesy of New York Life Insurance Company Archives; photograph by Jerry Saltsberg & Associates.)

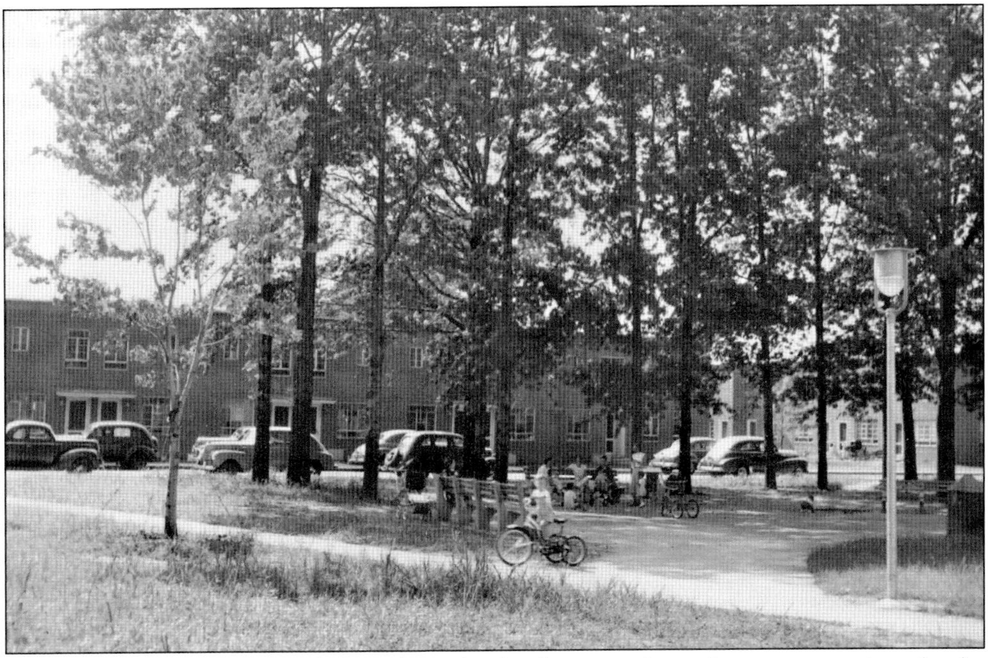

Duplex apartments were spread throughout the development. According to notes written by the New York Life Insurance Company in 1948, "The building sites were selected, so far as possible, to leave trees that existed on the tract when it was owned by the Fresh Meadow Country Club." The photograph below, according to these 1948 notes, depicts a two-story unit "nestled in a grove of oak trees." And, according to architecture critic Lewis Mumford in his book *From the Ground Up*, "The architects have introduced variations in the straight rows of duplex houses by using different entrance porches" such as "slender columns" or "trellises," or by having the small entrance roofs jut out without any support. (Both, courtesy of Queens Fresh Meadows LLC; above, photograph by Jerry Saltsberg.)

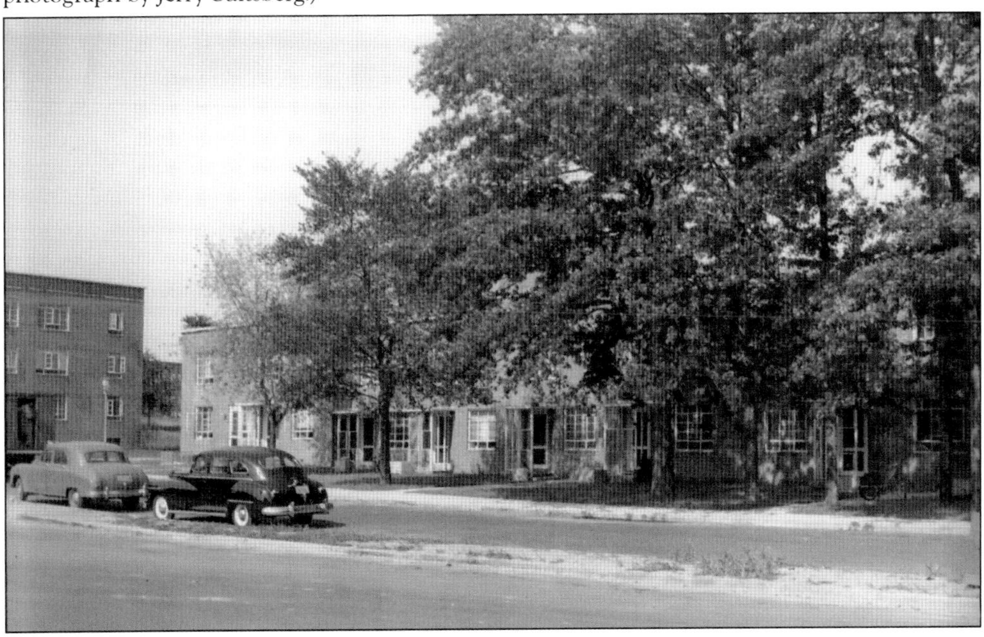

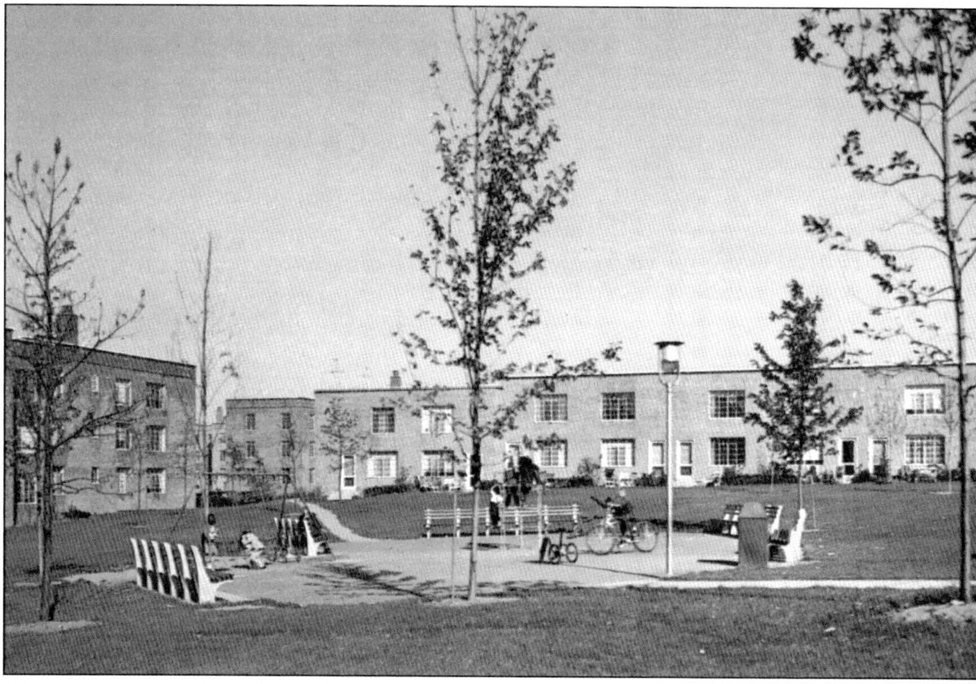

There were a total of 137 garden apartment buildings—a mix of two-story and three-story buildings—in the Fresh Meadows development. There was typically a playground in the backyard areas behind these garden apartments. Some contained a swing set, some had a jungle gym or slide, and some contained a combination of playground equipment. All of the play areas featured park benches for parents to sit and keep an eye on their children. The back of the postcard above stated that the scene depicted was "one of 29 playground areas." (Above, courtesy of Fred Cantor; below, courtesy of New York Life Insurance Company Archives.)

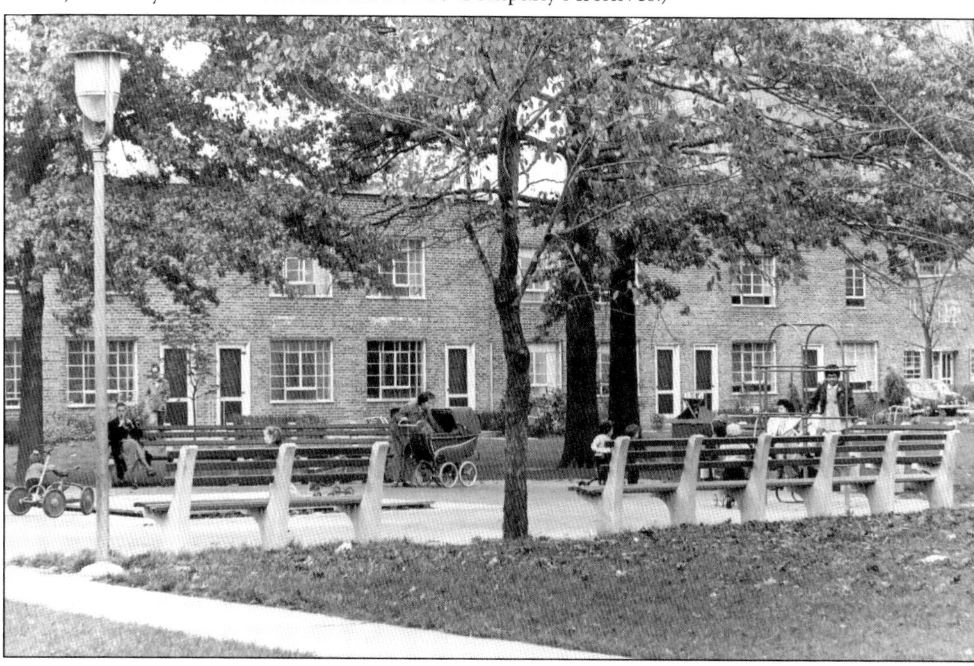

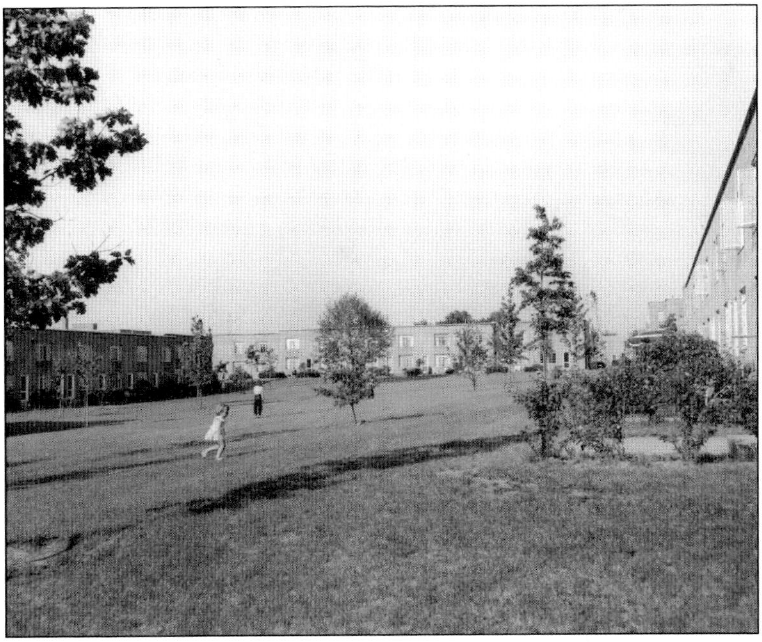

The designers of the Fresh Meadows development also provided some large open grassy areas in the backyards for children to play in. (Courtesy of Queens Fresh Meadows LLC; photograph by Jerry Saltsberg & Associates.)

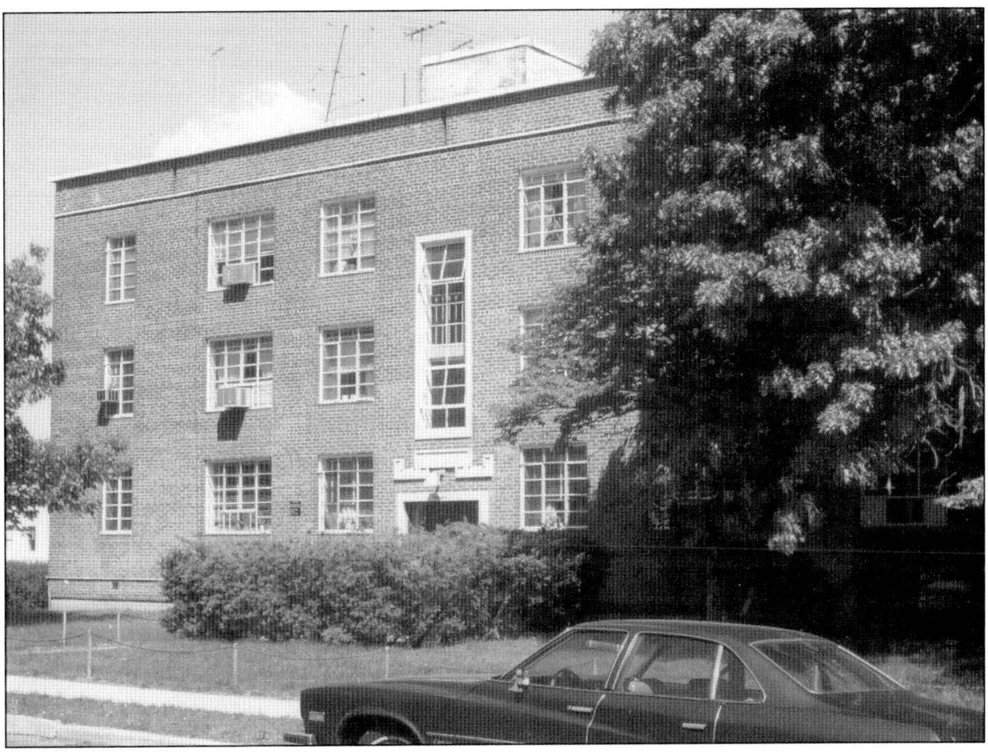

A number of the three-story garden apartment buildings had small grassy areas adjacent to the building entrances that served as front yards for young children to play in. Many of the three-story buildings also featured a large central block of windows that brought natural light to the stairwells and hallways. (Courtesy of Fred Cantor.)

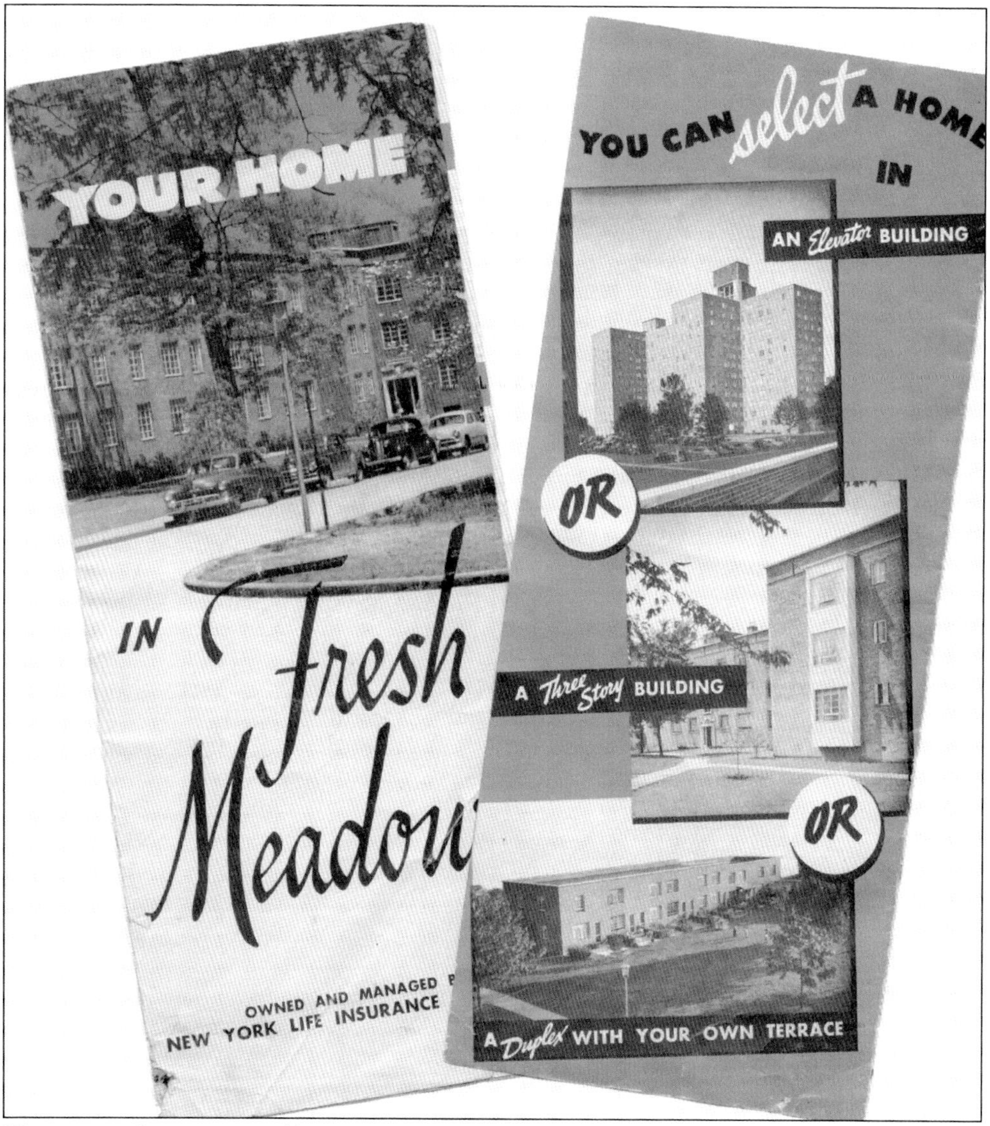

This is part of a promotional brochure created by the New York Life Insurance Company that was distributed to prospective tenants of the Fresh Meadows development in the 1950s. The brochure contained information about a variety of the development's features and proclaimed, "FRESH MEADOWS IS DIFFERENT . . . Architects and city planners have come from the world over to inspect its unusual characteristics." The brochure also noted, "Most of the apartments are the off-foyer arrangement." (Courtesy of Lisa Wessely.)

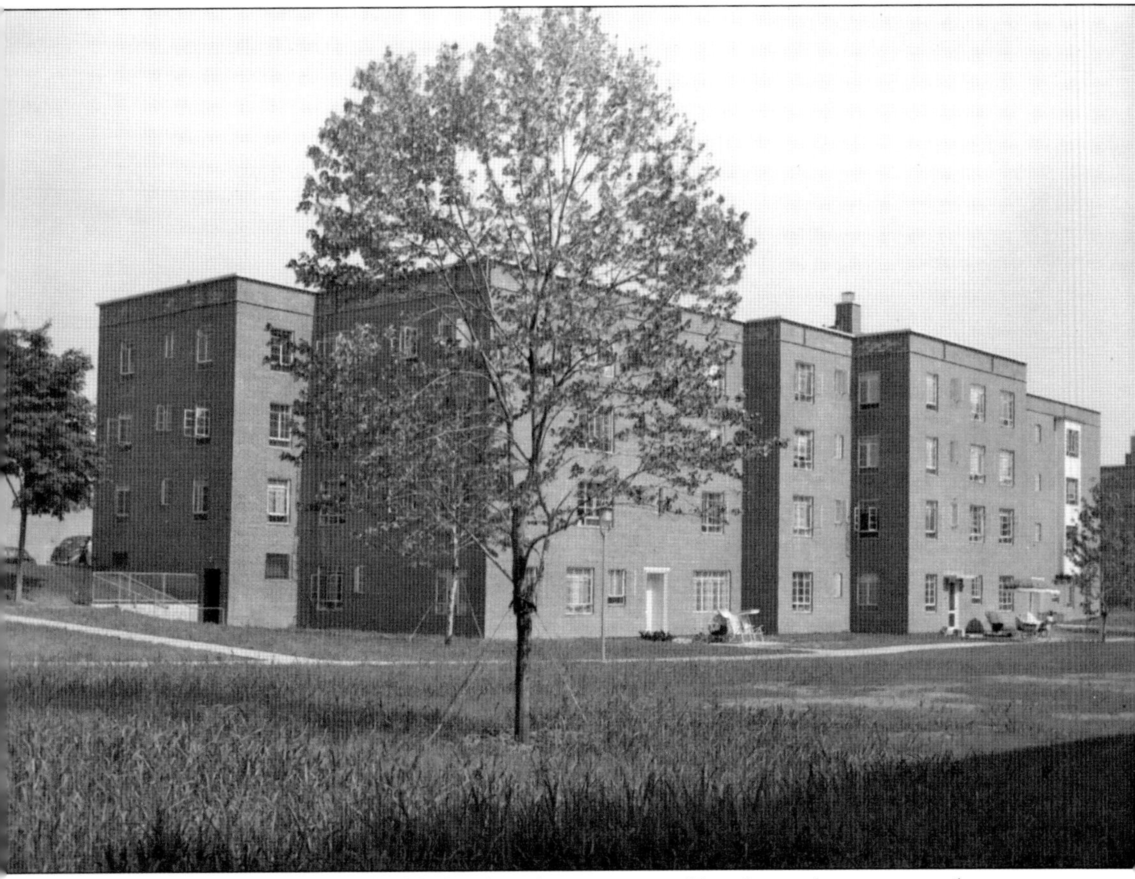

In addition to the apartments highlighted in the promotional brochure, there was another type of apartment that existed in certain buildings. Terrace apartments were located on the back of some three-story buildings that were situated on a slight hill, so that the rear side was, in reality, four stories from the ground up. The terrace apartments had their own entrance and a small private deck. There were 24 such apartments altogether, and they were located on 186th Lane, 188th Street, 71st Crescent, 193rd Lane, 67th Avenue, and 65th Crescent. (Courtesy of Queens Fresh Meadows LLC.)

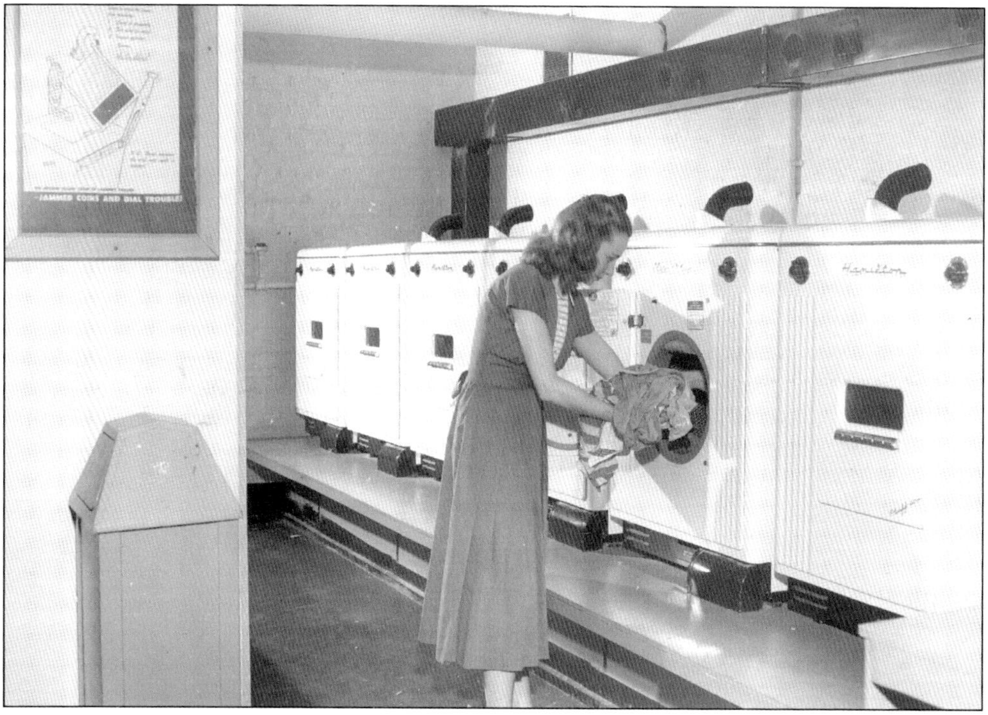

Automatic laundry rooms were situated around the development. The *New York Times* reported on May 17, 1950, "When it was learned that both men and women were using them as community forums and recreation rooms while the laundry whirled, it was decided to improve them further. Now the twenty-five community laundries are equipped with lounging chairs, curtains and chess boards." (Courtesy of New York Life Insurance Company Archives.)

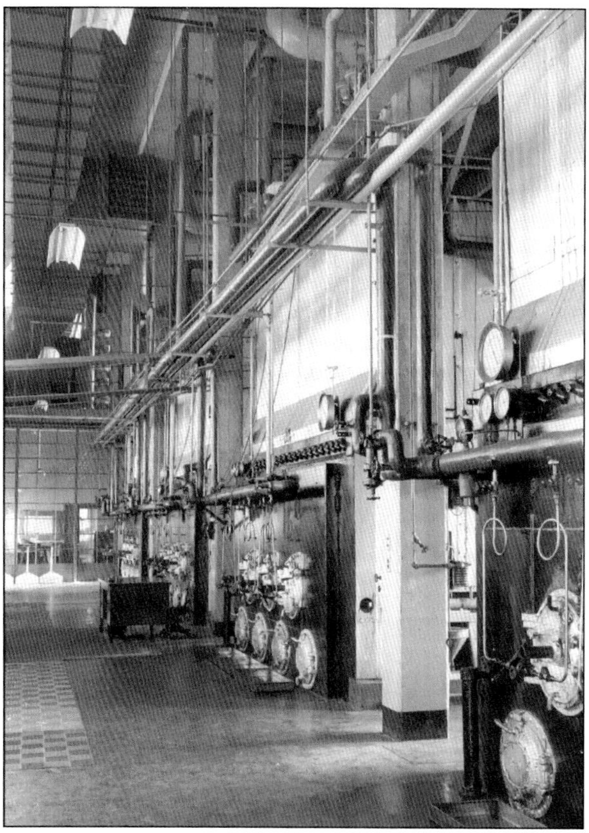

A plant located on 67th Avenue was the focal point of a brand-new central heating system for residents. According to a booklet published by the New York Life Insurance Company in 1966, "The Fresh Meadows heating system is noteworthy because it was the first system of such scope to be controlled from one central point." (Courtesy of New York Life Insurance Company Archives.)

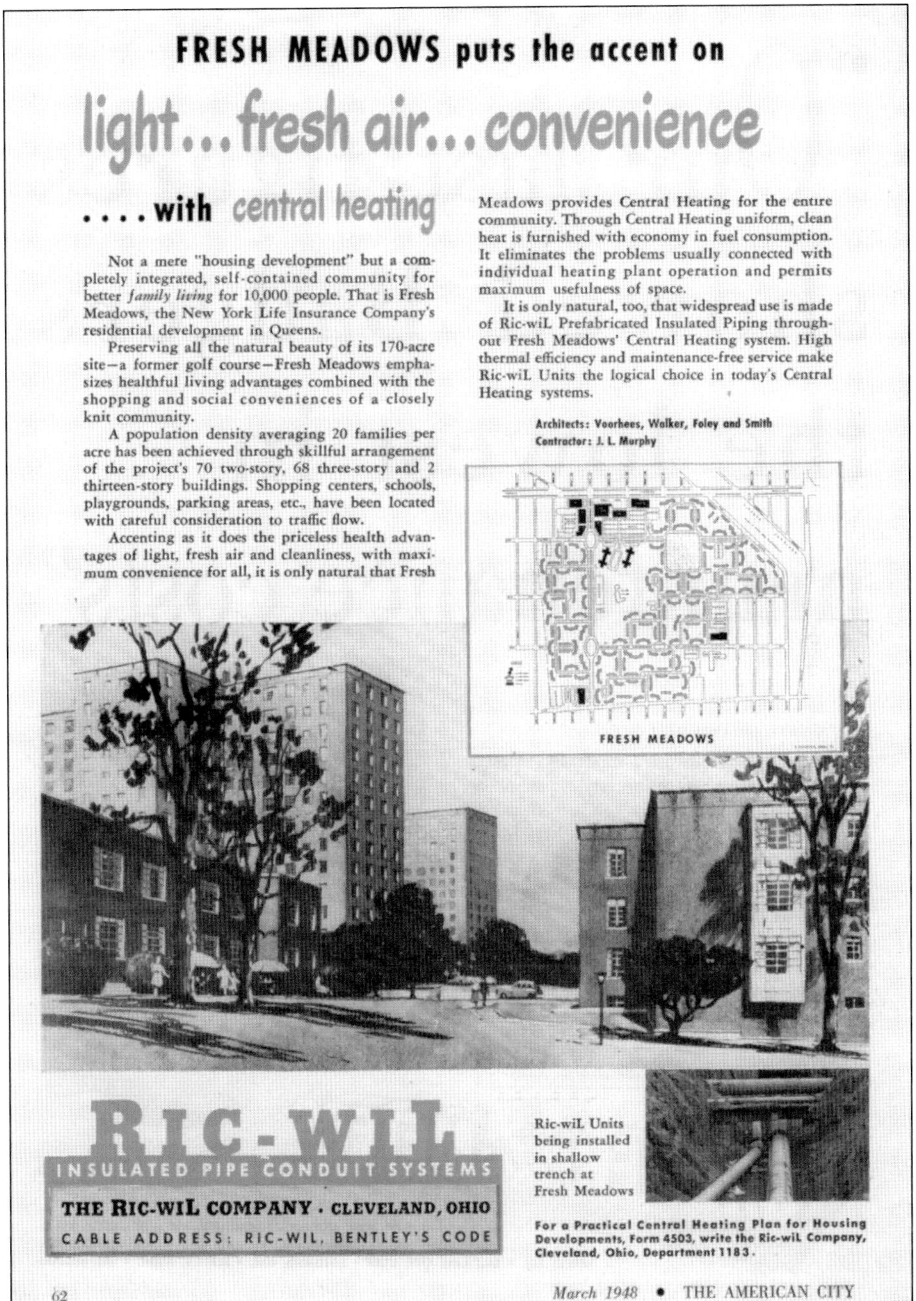

This advertisement, which appeared in the *American City Magazine* in 1948, also lauded the benefits of the new central heating system in Fresh Meadows; however, it was not only the heating operations that generated attention. According to an article in the *New York Times* on August 22, 1948, the central air-conditioning system that was in the process of being installed in the main Fresh Meadows shopping center was "the first installation of its kind . . . central air conditioning such as this was never undertaken before and community planners are watching the results with interest." The system was set up so that chilled water would be "piped through more than a mile of twelve-inch pipe under a 100-pound head pressure." (Courtesy of Fred Cantor.)

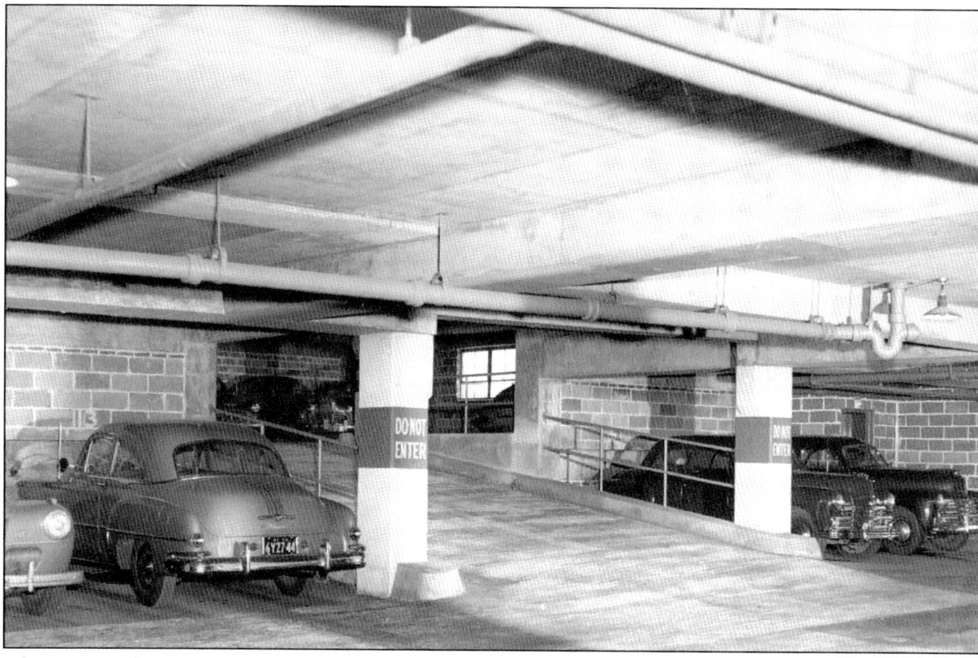

There were four parking garages placed throughout the Fresh Meadows development, designed to offer a total of 1,300 off-street parking spaces for residents and visitors. The garages offered service departments and were open 24 hours a day. (Courtesy of New York Life Insurance Company Archives.)

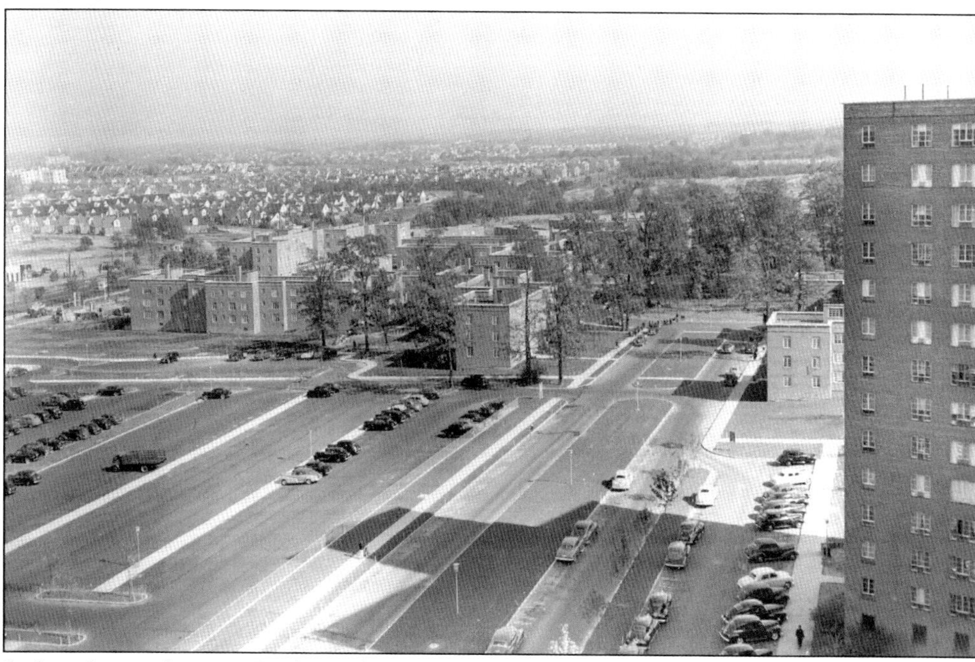

Parking lots in the main Fresh Meadows shopping center provided spaces for approximately 1,000 vehicles. Parking lots were also adjacent to the 13-story buildings. The Oak Grove, situated in the midst of 64th Circle, in the background, was an example of the curved-street pattern featured in the layout of Fresh Meadows. (Courtesy of New York Life Insurance Company Archives.)

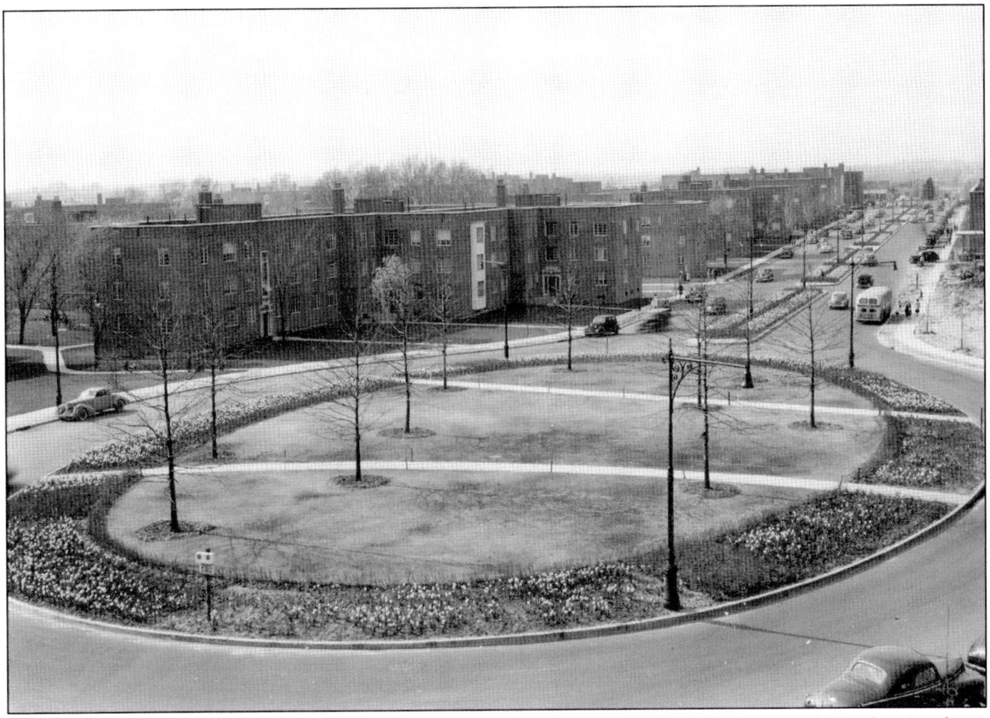

Pictured, 188th Street was the only through street incorporated in the original Fresh Meadows development site plan, and that was done pursuant to a directive from the municipal engineer's office, according to Lewis Mumford. Even then, the designers of the Fresh Meadows site plan inserted two large planted ovals to slow down traffic and create a more aesthetically pleasing thoroughfare. The photograph above shows the view looking north from 69th Avenue in April 1949, and the postcard below depicts the view looking north from closer to 73rd Avenue. (Above, courtesy of Queens Fresh Meadows LLC; photograph by Jerry Saltsberg; below, courtesy of Jeffrey Jonas.)

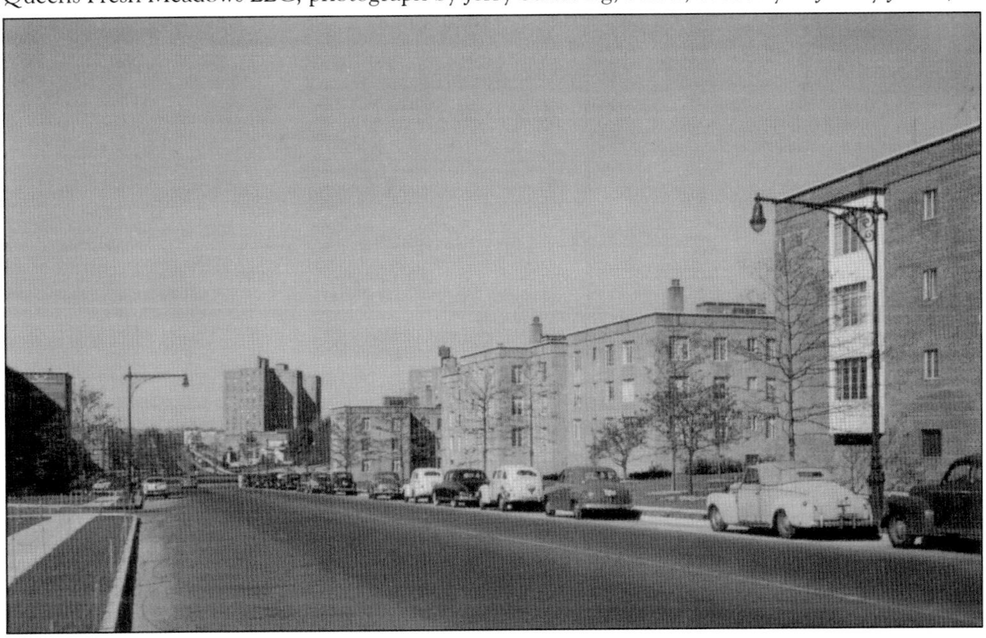

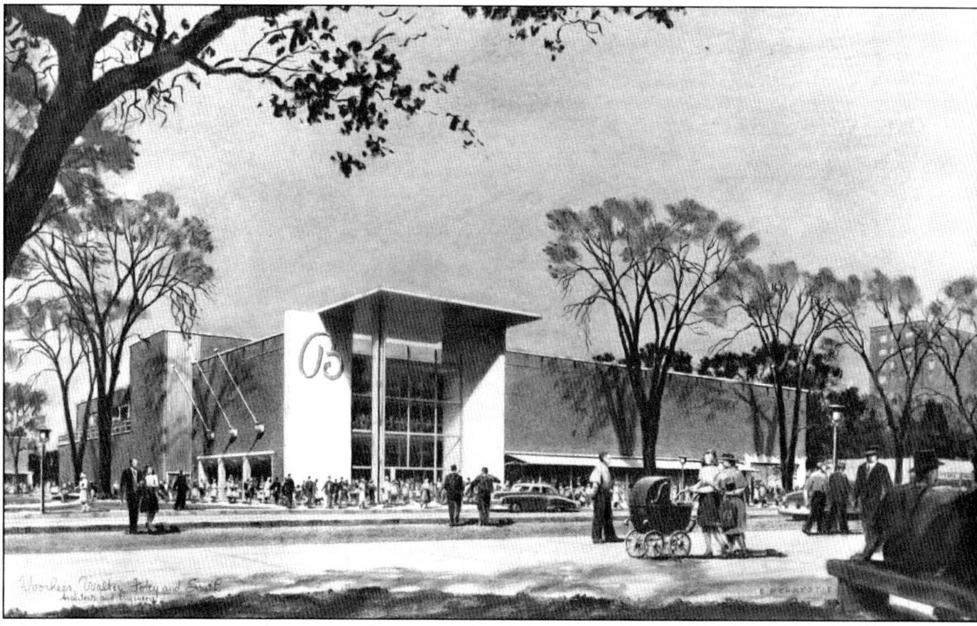

This is an architect's rendering of the main entrance to Bloomingdale's, on 188th Street. This was the first branch store of the famous New York department store, and it opened on May 24, 1949, attracting a crowd of approximately 25,000. The *New York Times* noted, "A covered porch is provided outside the main entrance for mothers to park baby carriages." (Courtesy of Queens Fresh Meadows LLC; photograph by Drix Duryea.)

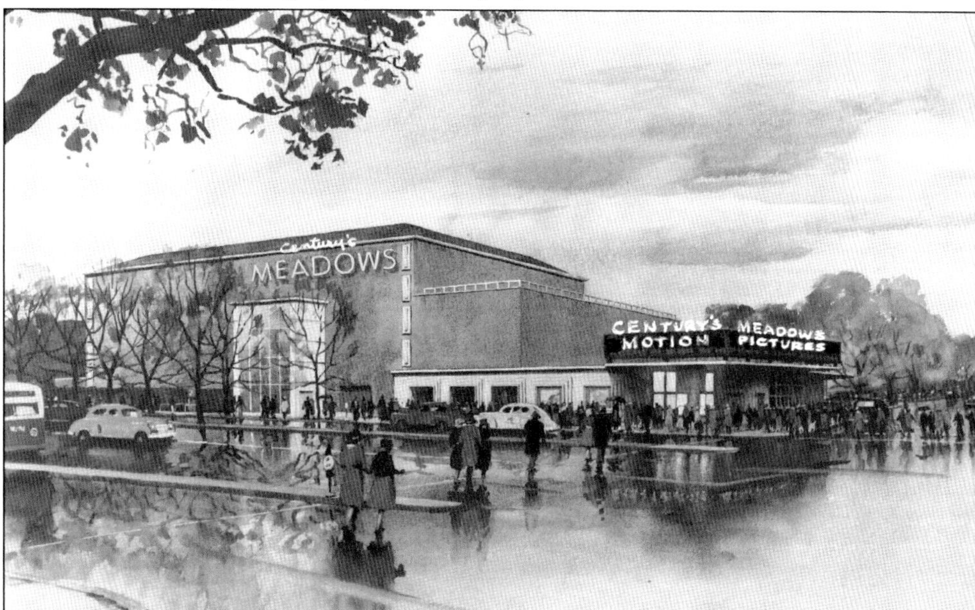

This is an architect's rendering of the Century Meadows Theater and pedestrian traffic—obviously conceived and drawn long before the building of the Long Island Expressway. The New York Life Insurance Company had to seek special approval in 1948 for the theater's construction due to steel shortages and the restrictions at that time on the building of large amusement-related structures. (Courtesy of Queens Fresh Meadows LLC; photograph by Drix Duryea.)

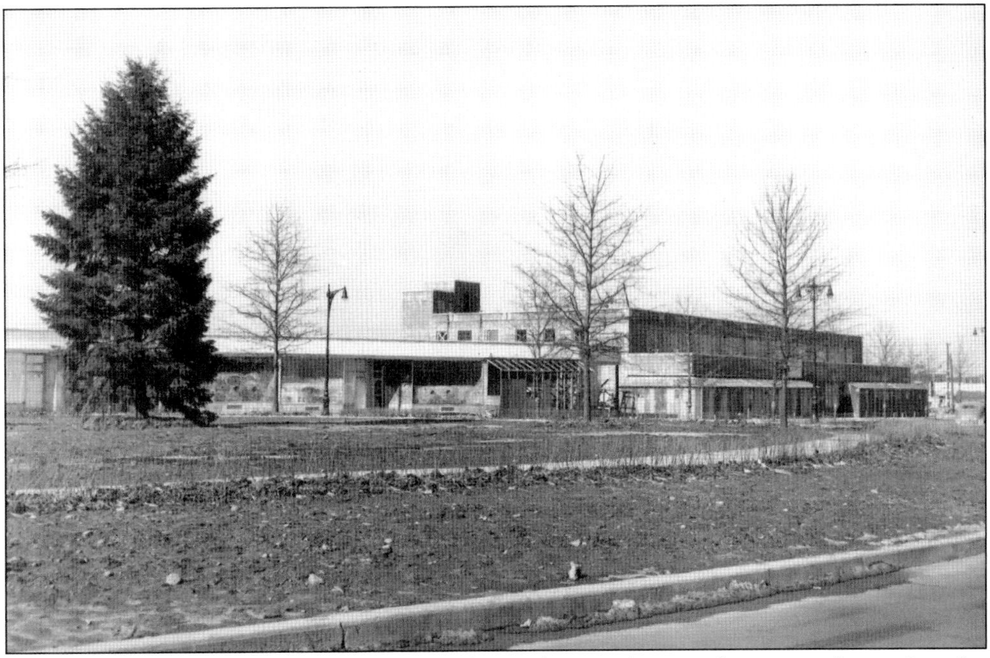

This photograph, taken in February 1949, shows the storefronts, adjacent to the oval at the intersection of 188th Street and 64th Avenue, which were still under construction. Ultimately, considerable landscaping was done in the oval, including the planting of hedges, petunias, and ageratum. (Courtesy of Queens Fresh Meadows LLC; photograph by Jerry Saltsberg.)

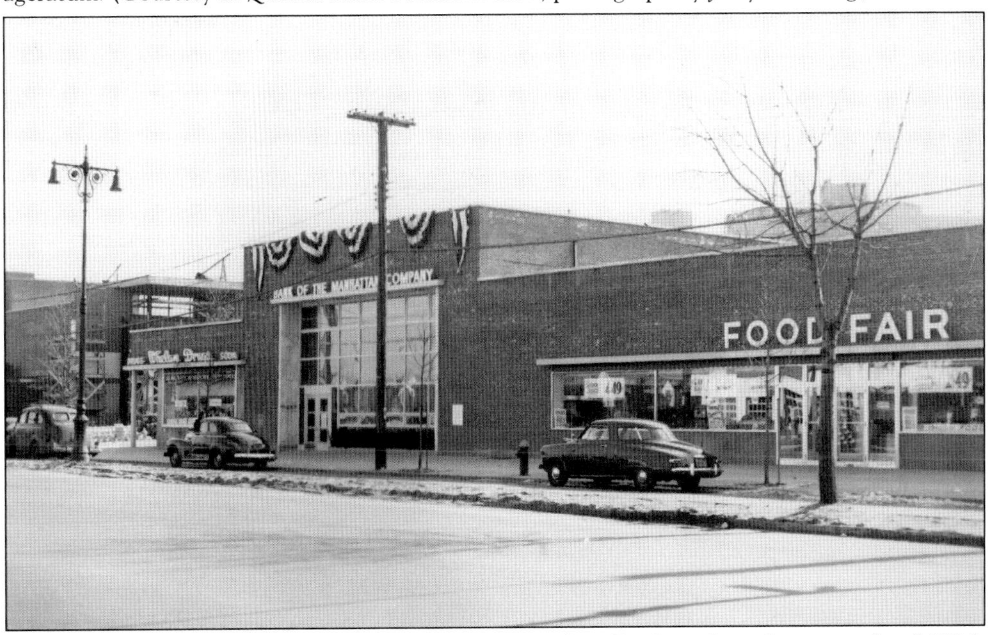

In February 1949, the building bordering Horace Harding Boulevard on the west side of 188th Street was the first commercial complex in the Fresh Meadows shopping center to be fully occupied and open for business. Its tenants included a branch of Bank of the Manhattan Company (a predecessor of the Chase Manhattan Bank), Whelan Drugs, and Food Fair. (Courtesy of Queens Fresh Meadows LLC; photograph by Jerry Saltsberg & Associates.)

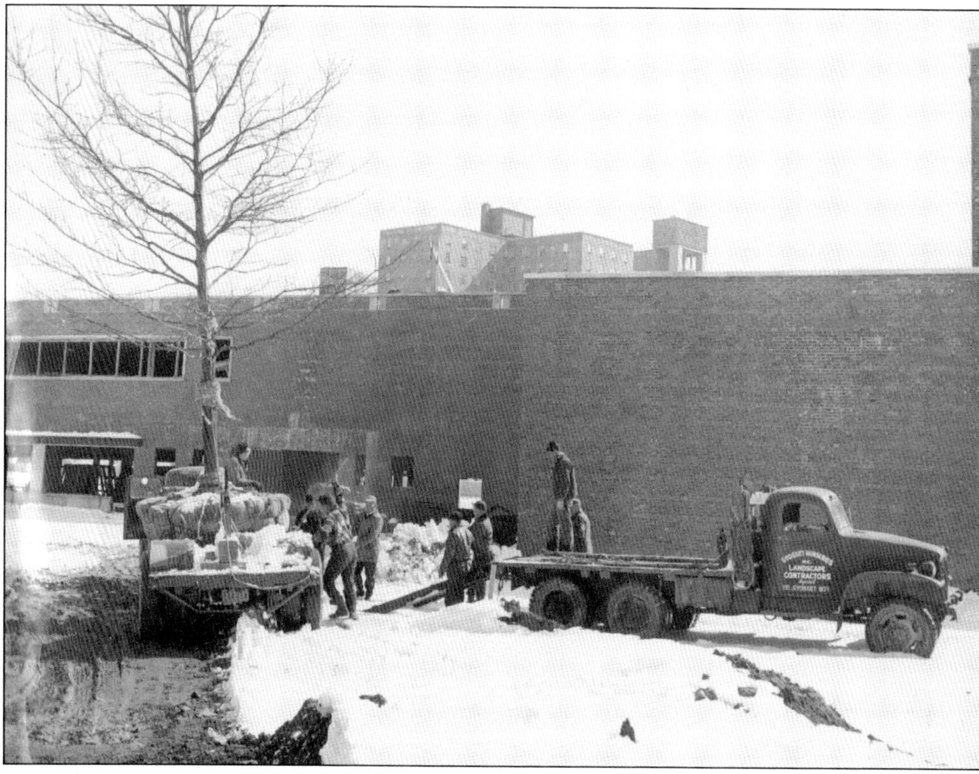

According to notes written by the New York Life Insurance Company in March 1949, gardeners engaged in "'spring planting'... In this picture workmen are unloading one of two 40-foot scarlet oak trees, natives of Long Island, which were planted in the City park on Horace Harding Boulevard at 188th Street. The park will be maintained by New York Life." The photograph below shows the finished park space from the vantage point of the top of the Century Meadows Theater. (Both, courtesy of Queens Fresh Meadows LLC; photographs by Jerry Saltsberg & Associates.)

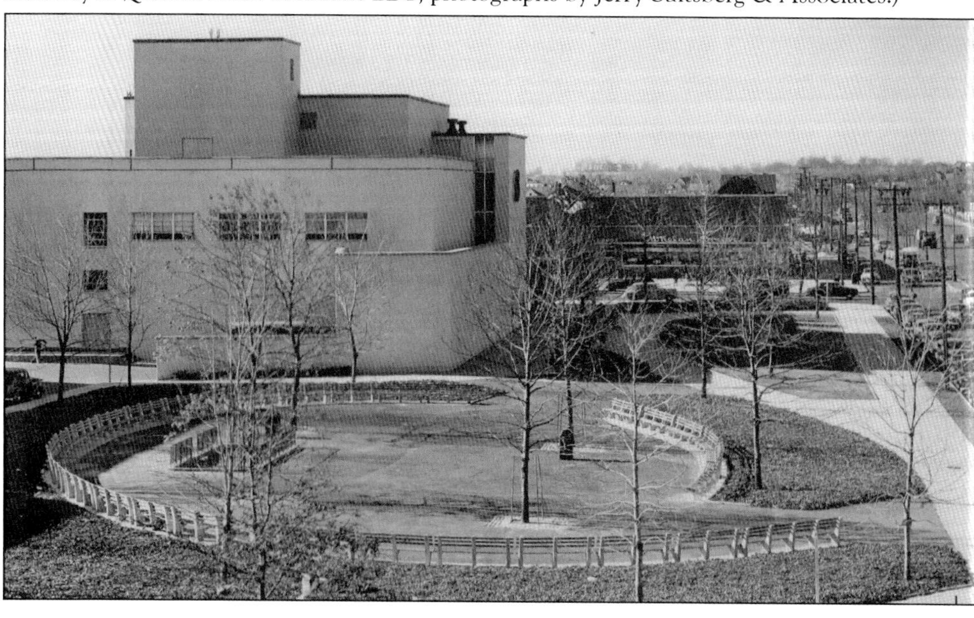

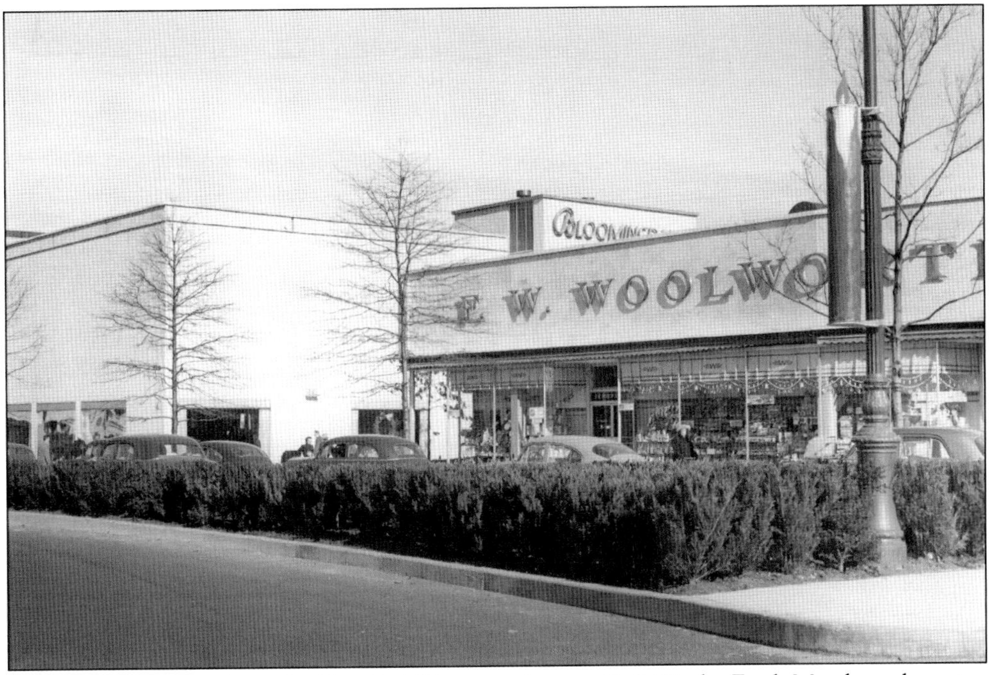

According to an article in the *New York Times* on August 29, 1948, the Fresh Meadows shopping center had entered into a lease for what would become "Woolworth's largest 'suburban' branch." The store ultimately occupied considerable frontage on the east side of a planted median on 188th Street. Among its popular features was a counter where shoppers enjoyed malted milks, and a record department, where young music fans could buy the latest 45-rpm records. On the north side of Woolworth's, adjacent to Bloomingdale's, was a public square that served as a meeting place for shoppers, as well as served as the site of a variety of events, such as a petting zoo during the holidays. (Both, courtesy of Queens Fresh Meadows LLC; photographs by Jerry Saltsberg & Associates.)

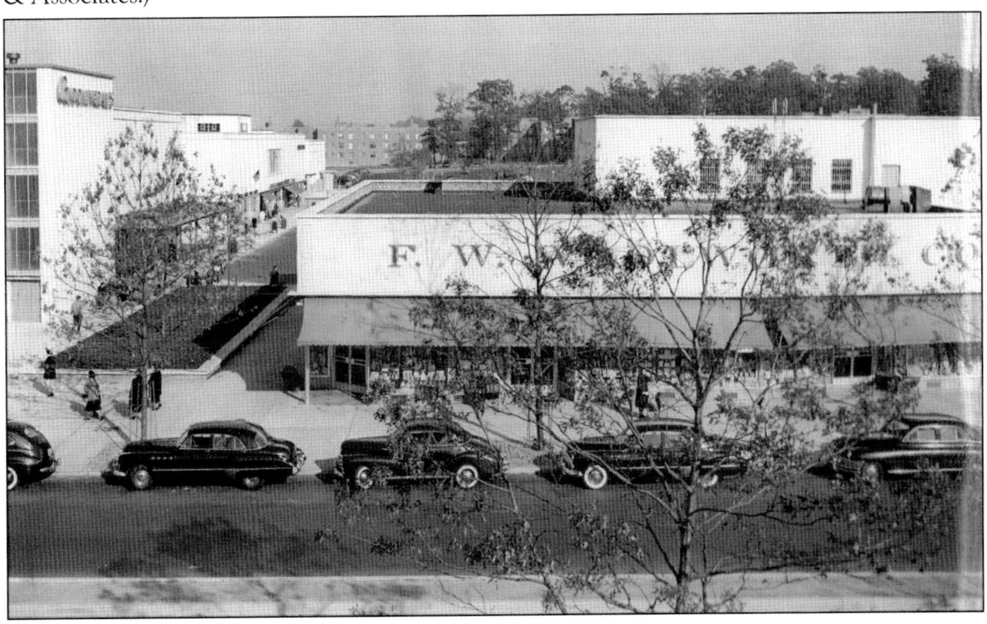

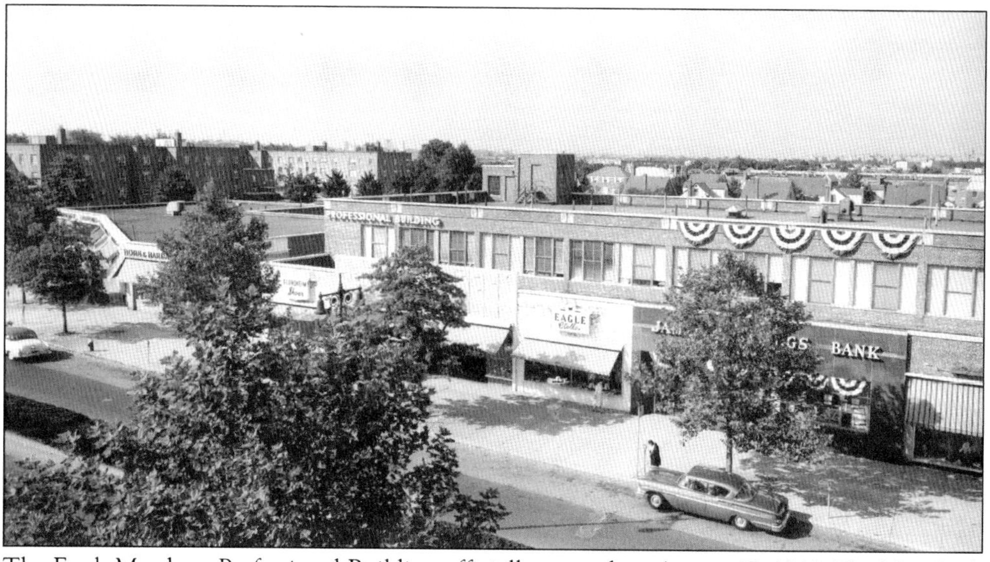

The Fresh Meadows Professional Building officially opened on August 17, 1949. The New York Life Insurance Company conducted a survey to determine both the specialties and the total number of doctors that would be needed to serve the community. The company also screened the applications and selected the doctors and dentists who would rent the professional space. (Above, courtesy of New York Life Insurance Company Archives; below, courtesy of Queens Fresh Meadows LLC.)

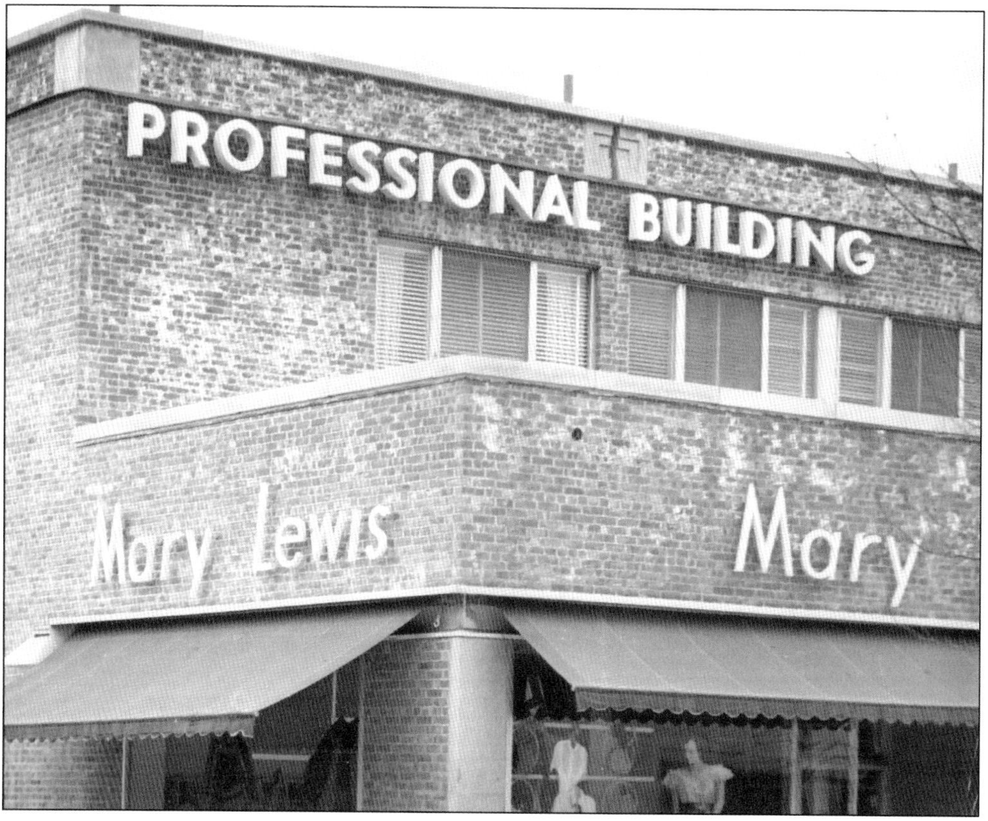

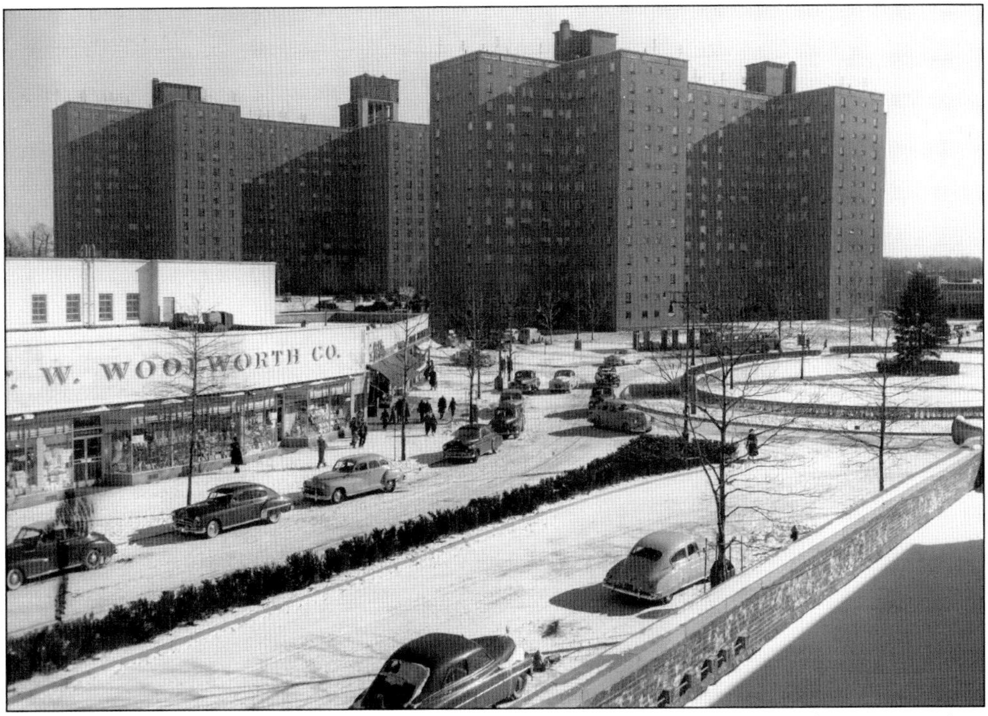

With three shopping centers, stores were within walking distance for most residents. According to the *New York Times*, "Studies were made of the various types of stores required to meet the needs of the neighborhood. The center was then designed and tenants selected according to this definite allocation of space." Among the stores that stayed in business for many years was Womrath's, whose storefront can be seen in the left-center portion of the below photograph. Fresh Meadows residents were able to rent newly published books at Womrath's. (Above, courtesy of Queens Fresh Meadows LLC; photograph by Jerry Saltsberg & Associates. Below, courtesy of New York Life Insurance Company Archives.)

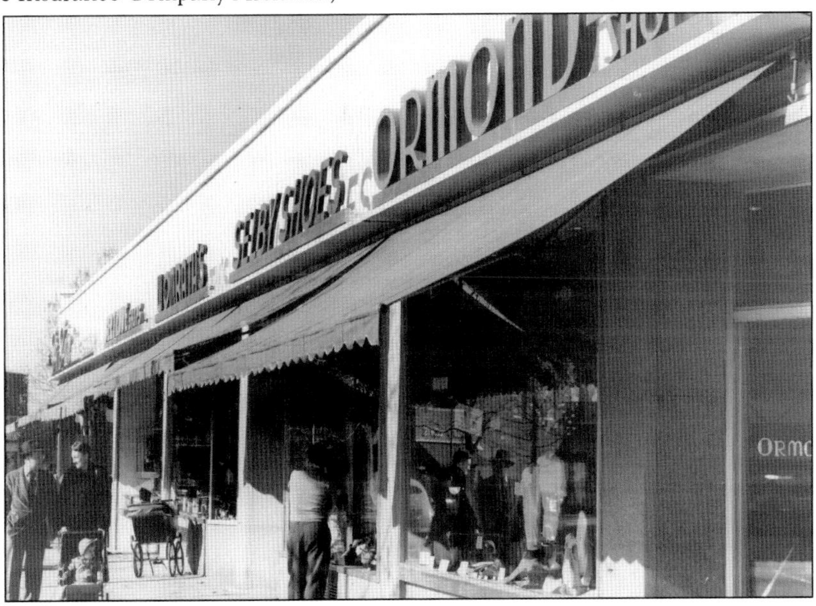

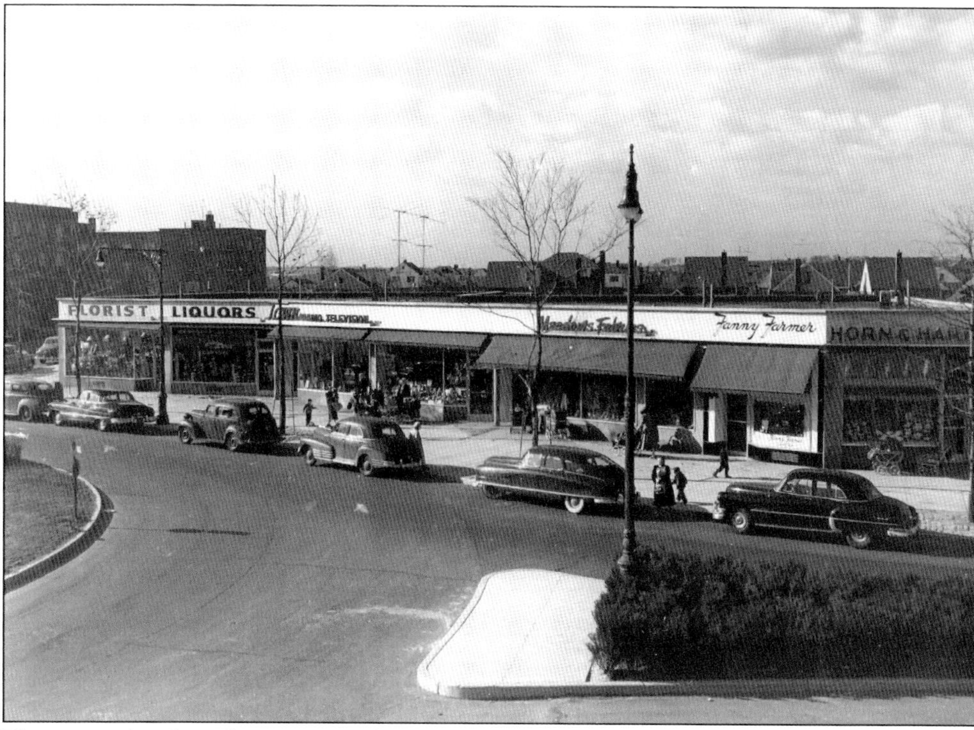

The west side of 188th Street was the locale of a variety of shops, ranging from a local fabric store, Meadows Fabrics, to branches of major chains, including a retail outlet of Horn & Hardart and B & B Lorry's. Many of the commercial tenants signed leases based on a set minimum rental against a percentage of sales. (Above, courtesy of Queens Fresh Meadows LLC, photograph by Jerry Saltsberg & Associates; below, courtesy of Mitchell Kaften, photograph by Douglas Kaften.)

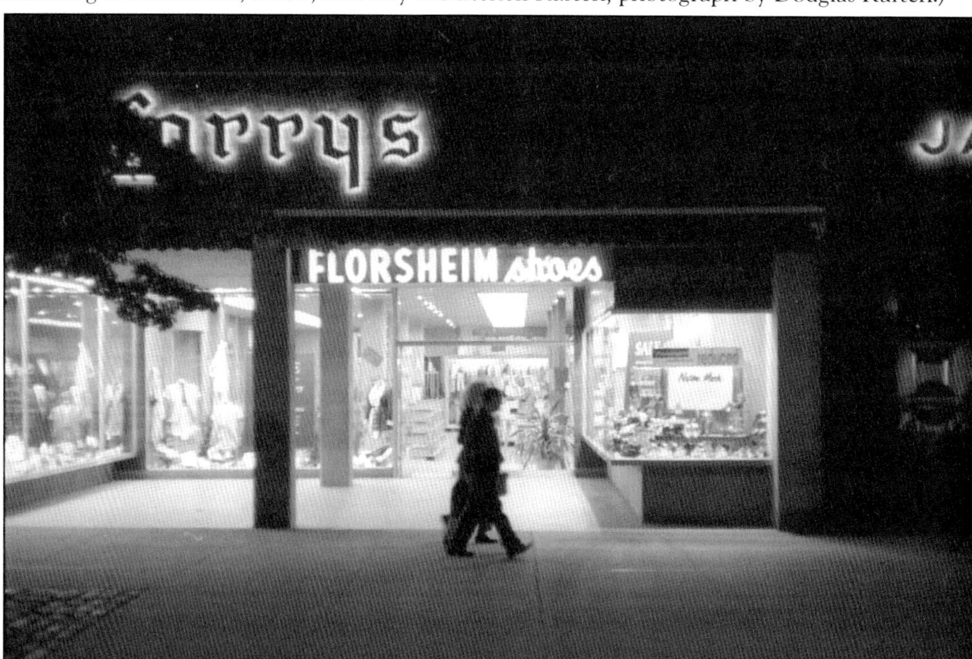

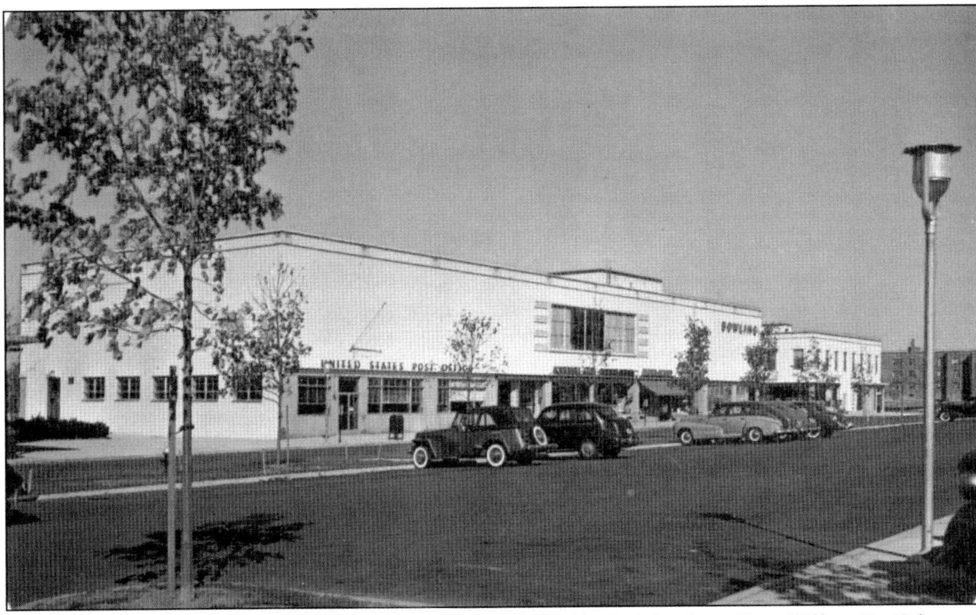

The postcard above shows the original location of the Fresh Meadows Post Office. In February 1949, the *New York Times* noted that mail now sent by area residents "will bear the Fresh Meadows postmark." The building in which the post office was originally located also was the site of the Bowling Center on the second floor. With respect to the commercial buildings such as the one depicted in the below photograph, *the New York Times* also reported, "No structure will be higher than two stories, to retain a 'feeling of openness' so desirable in suburban business areas, according to the architects, Voorhees, Walker, Foley & Smith." (Above, courtesy of Howard Mirsky; below, courtesy of New York Life Insurance Company Archives.)

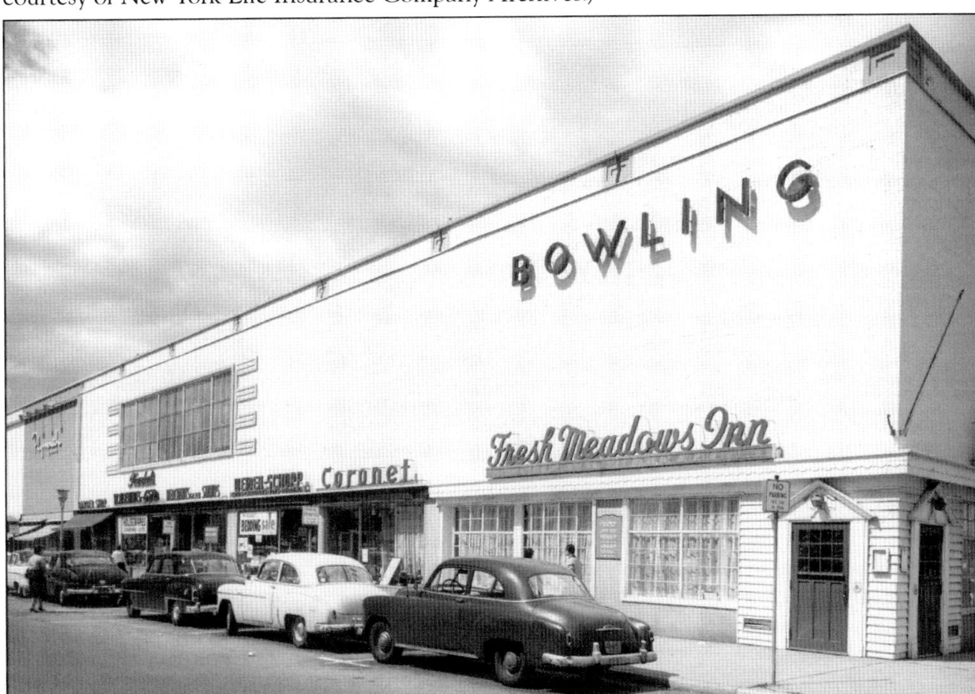

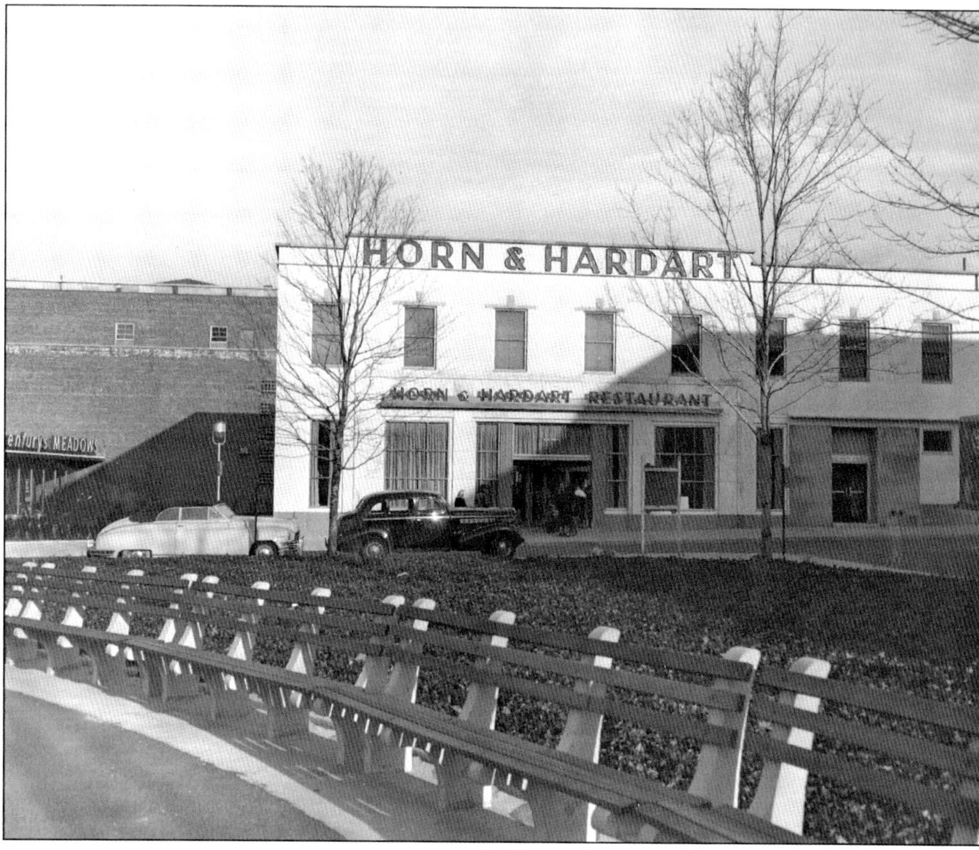

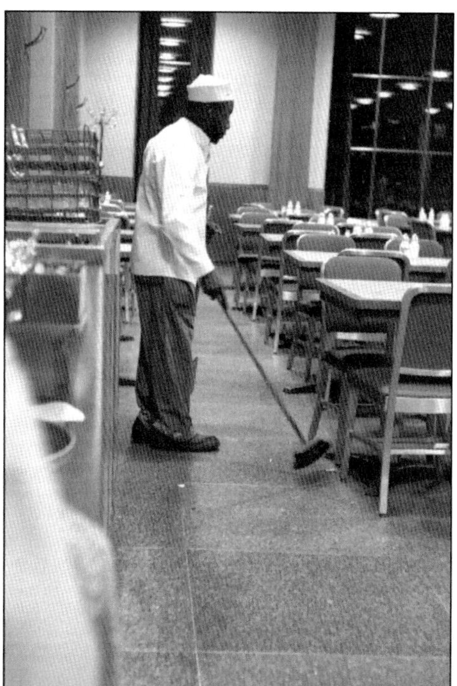

In December 1949, the New York Life Insurance Company announced that it had leased a large space in the shopping center to Horn & Hardart. When the restaurant opened in December 1950, it was Horn & Hardart's first expansion in the metropolitan area since the 1930s. It also was the first Horn & Hardart in the New York area to offer waitress service. The interior was described as having "Botticino marble and Circassian walnut." (Above, courtesy of Queens Fresh Meadows LLC, photograph by Jerry Saltsberg & Associates; left, courtesy of Mitchell Kaften, photograph by Douglas Kaften.)

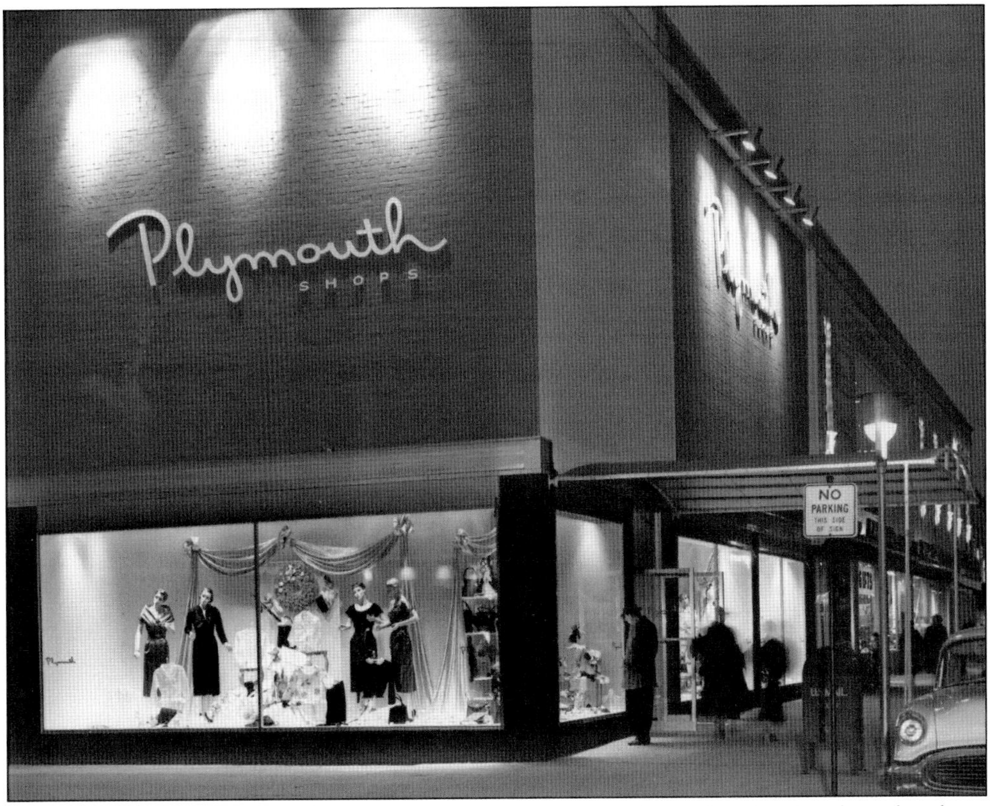

By the 1950s, the post office relocated to a nearby location on Horace Harding Boulevard and was replaced by the Plymouth Shop. The aerial view, taken from one of the 13-story buildings, also shows how the New York Life Insurance Company had planted a number of trees throughout the main Fresh Meadows shopping center by that time. (Both, courtesy of Queens Fresh Meadows LLC.)

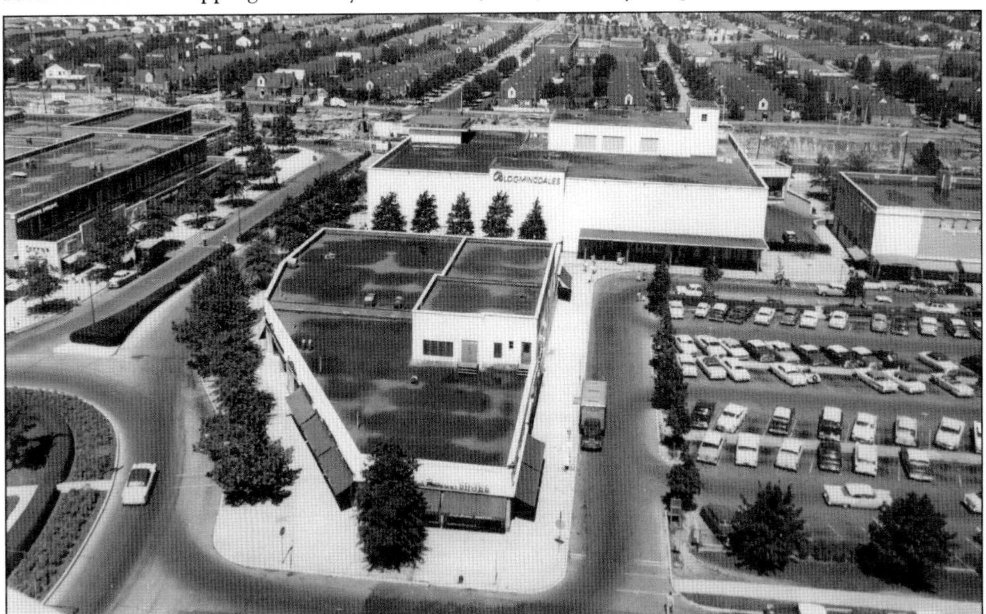

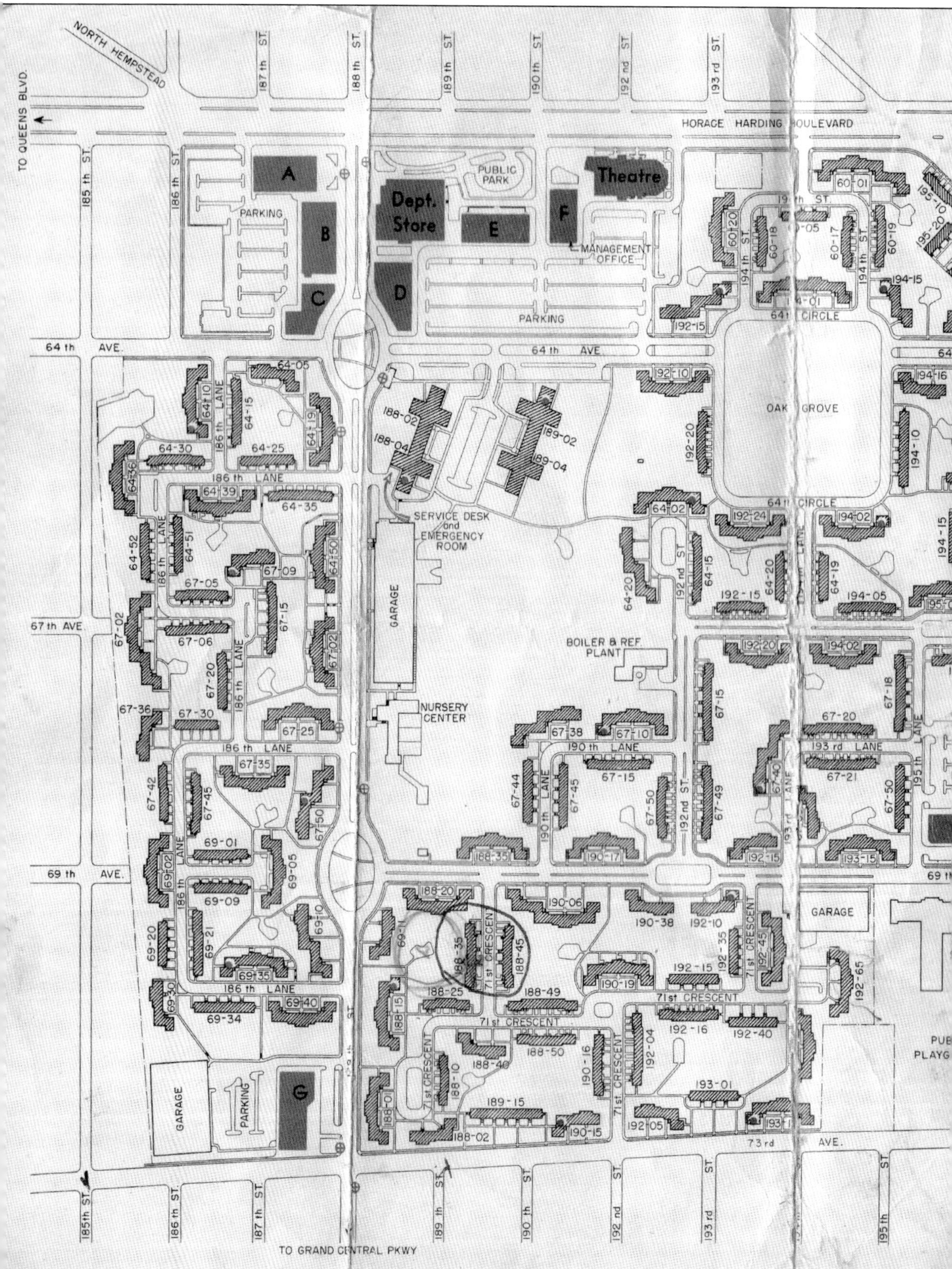
NORTH HEMPSTEAD
TO QUEENS BLVD.
HORACE HARDING BOULEVARD
185 th ST.
186 th ST.
187 th ST.
188 th ST.
189 th ST.
190 th ST.
192 nd ST.
193 rd ST.
A
B
C
D
E
F
G
PARKING
PUBLIC PARK
Dept. Store
Theatre
MANAGEMENT OFFICE
64 th AVE.
64th CIRCLE
OAK GROVE
SERVICE DESK and EMERGENCY ROOM
GARAGE
NURSERY CENTER
BOILER & REF. PLANT
186 th LANE
190 th LANE
193 rd LANE
67th AVE.
69 th AVE.
71st CRESCENT
73rd AVE.
TO GRAND CENTRAL PKWY
PUB
PLAYG

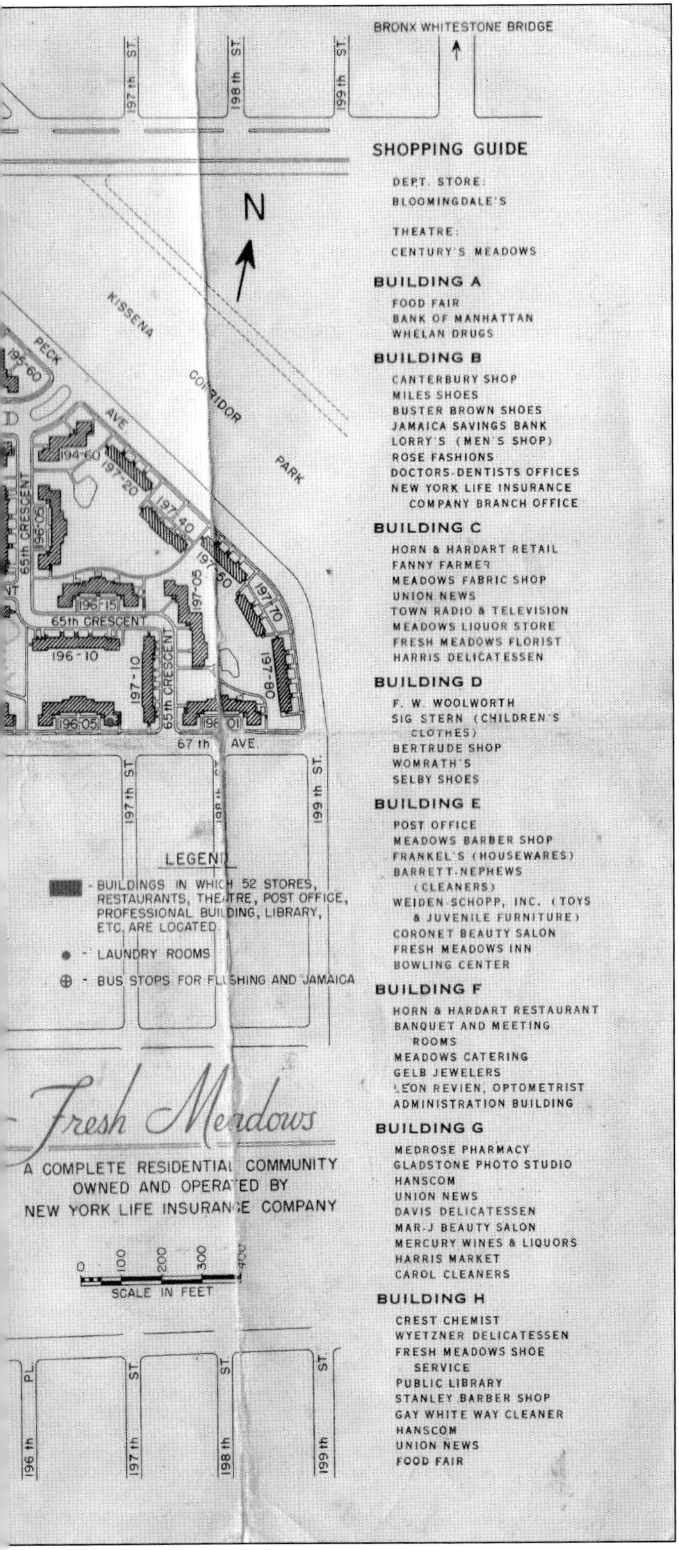

In December 1950, the New York Life Insurance Company announced that all of its commercial space had been rented. The final two leases were signed for a photography studio and a beauty salon. This map shows the entire layout of the Fresh Meadows development, including the eight commercial buildings and all of the commercial tenants. In the 1950s, the New York Life Insurance Company provided a map to all new tenants, along with a directory listing the phone numbers of area businesses, as well as information about the specialties of the doctors and dentists located in the Professional Building. (Courtesy of Louise Covitt.)

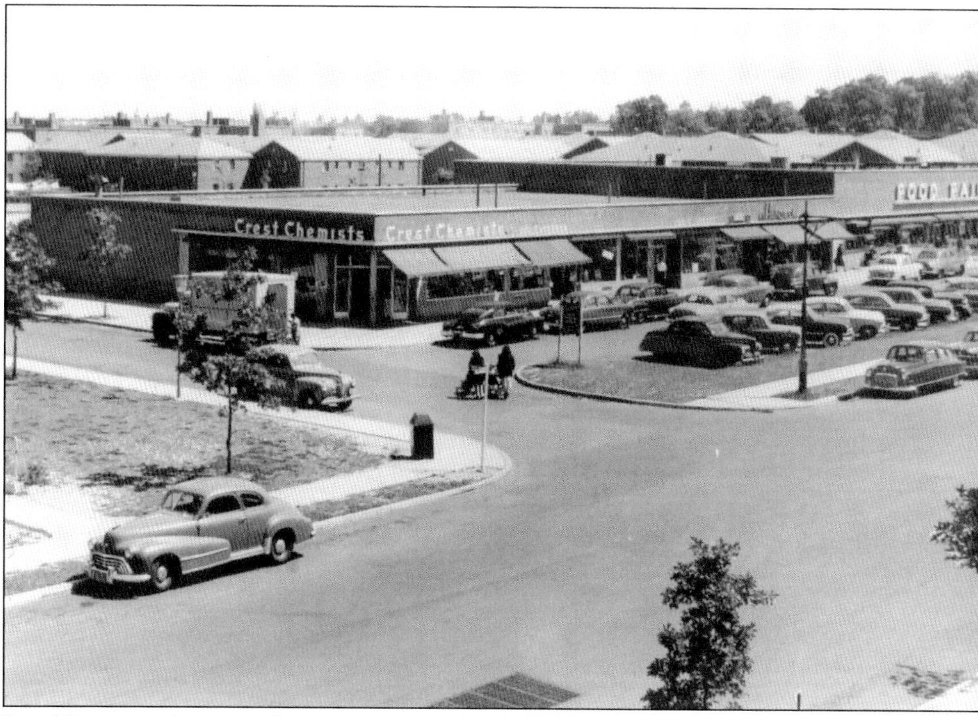

In addition to the main shopping center, the Fresh Meadows development had two smaller neighborhood shopping areas with nine stores in each area. One store group was located on 69th Avenue across the street from PS 26 and next to the Meadowlark Gardens housing complex. Food Fair was the major chain tenant at this location. (Above, courtesy of the Queens Historical Society; below, courtesy of New York Life Insurance Company Archives.)

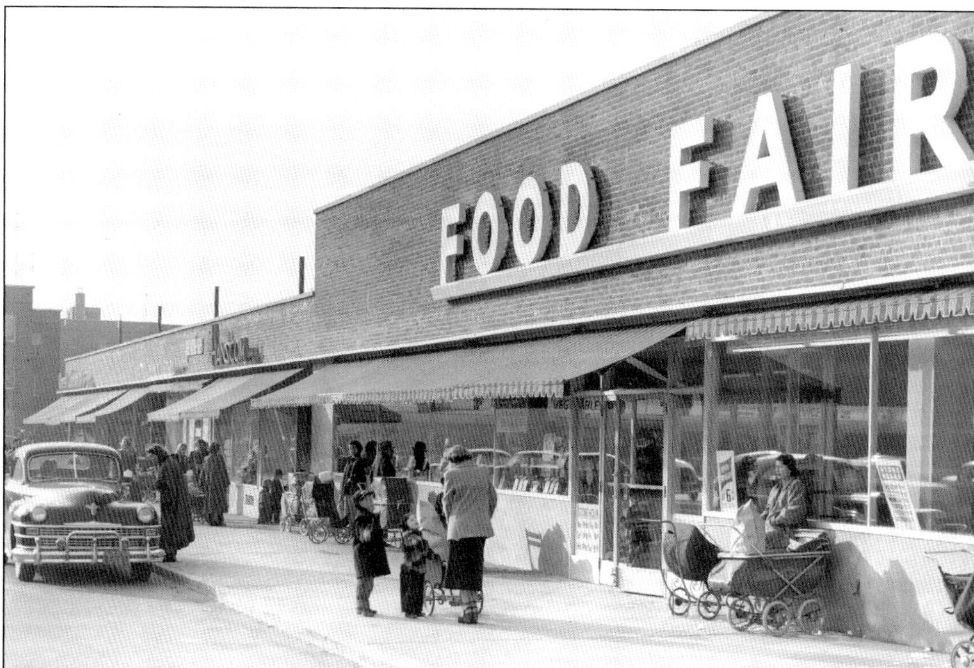

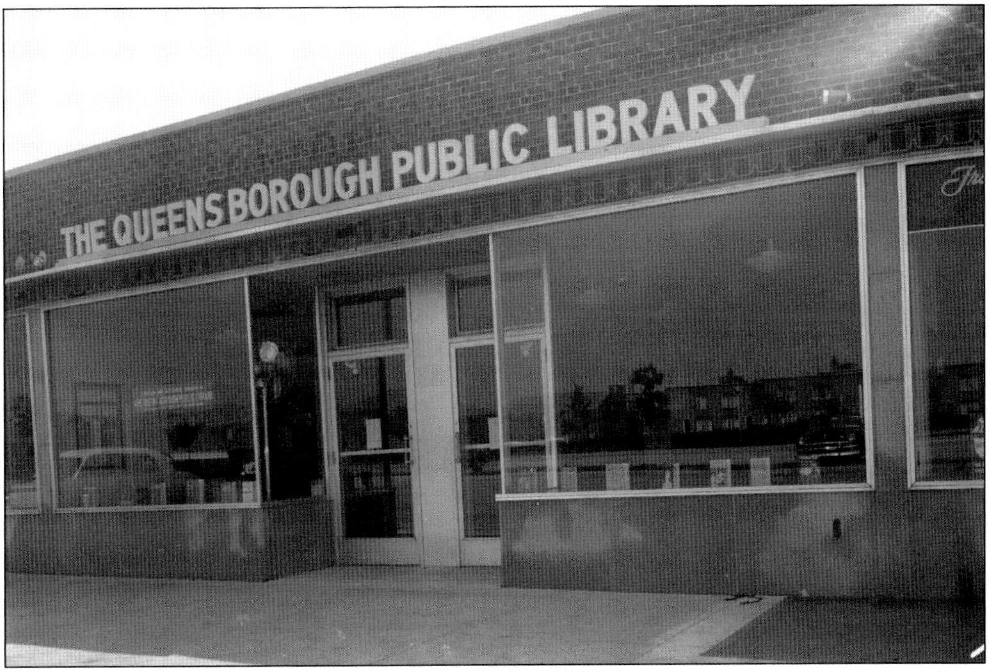

The Fresh Meadows branch of the Queens Borough Public Library originally occupied a storefront in the 69th Avenue group of shops. The specific address was 195-13 69th Avenue. The library recognized it needed more space and, in August 1957, announced that it would lease a new building to be constructed by the New York Life Insurance Company on Horace Harding Boulevard. (Above, courtesy of the Queens Borough Public Library, Long Island Division, Queens Borough Public Library Photographs; below, courtesy of Queens Fresh Meadows LLC, photograph by Jerry Saltsberg & Associates.)

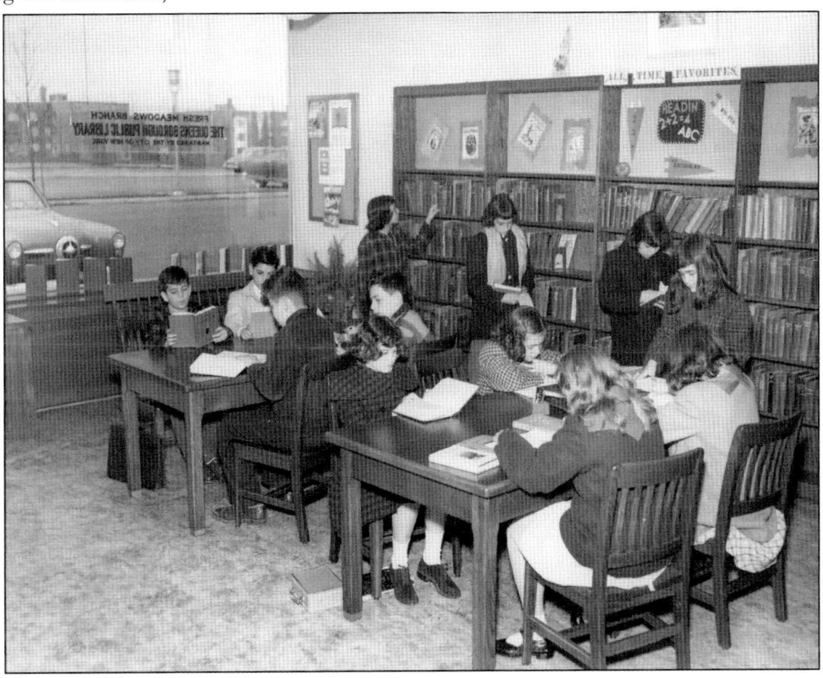

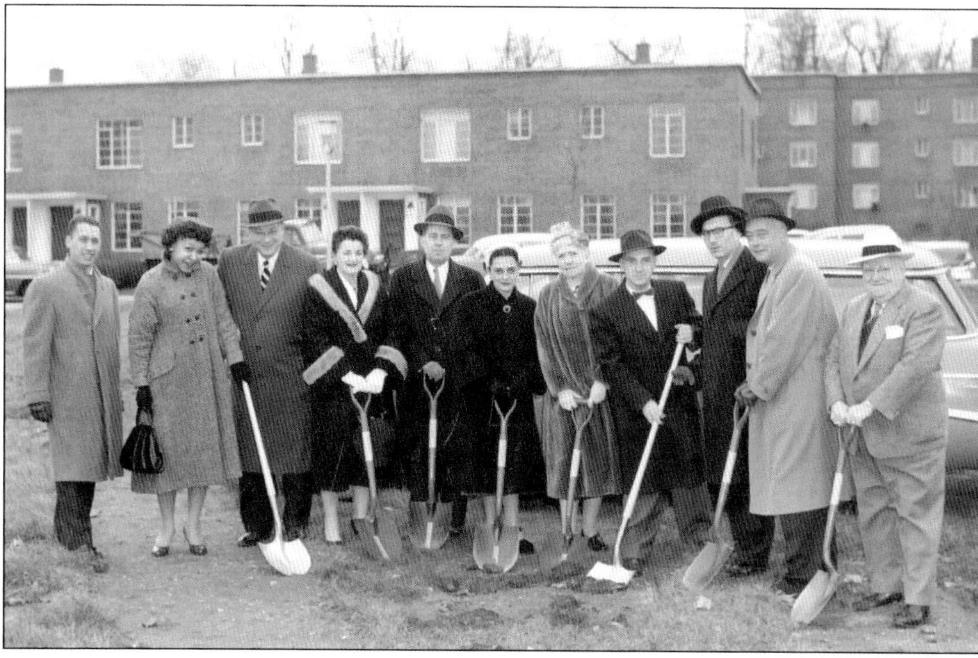

Ground-breaking ceremonies were held on November 25, 1957, for the new Fresh Meadows library branch located at 194th Street and Horace Harding Boulevard. The new building opened less than a year later on September 23, 1958. The young girl pictured below is getting her library card on opening day. (Both, courtesy of the Queens Borough Public Library, Long Island Division, Queens Borough Public Library Photographs.)

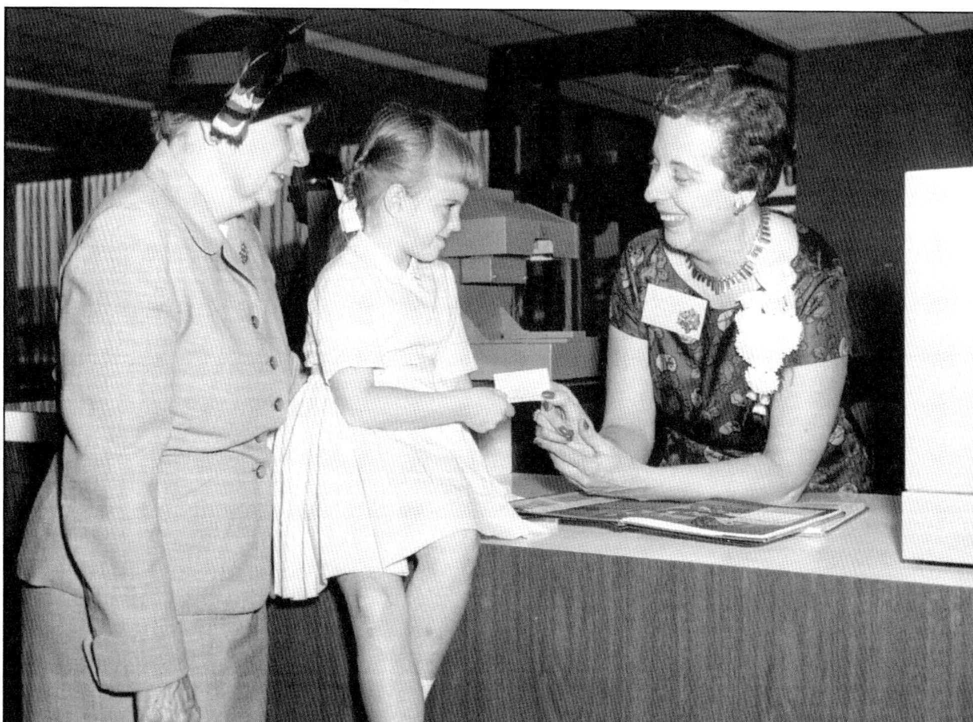

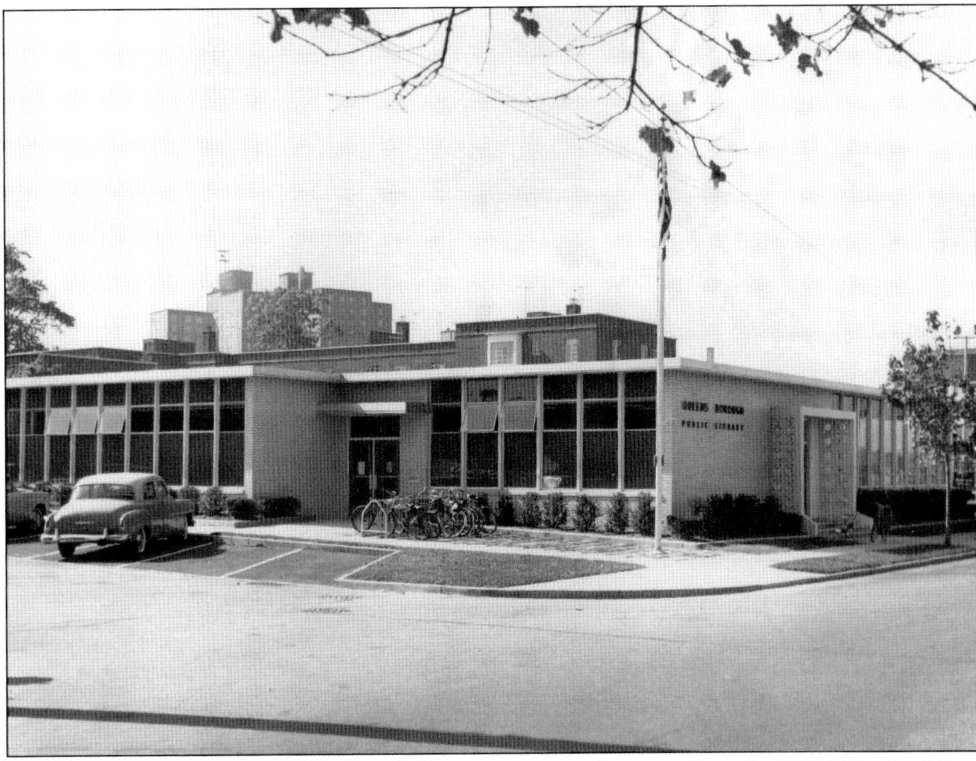

The new library was a white brick-and-glass structure with approximately 40,000 books. Many children bicycled to the library, as evidenced by the packed bicycle rack out front. The library was just down the street from the Century Meadows Theater, where many of these same children would years later attend Ryan Junior High School and Francis Lewis High School graduation ceremonies. The Century Meadows, which opened in November 1949, operated as a single-screen theater with a capacity of more than 2,000 for decades. (Above, courtesy of Queens Fresh Meadows LLC; below, courtesy of Fred Cantor.)

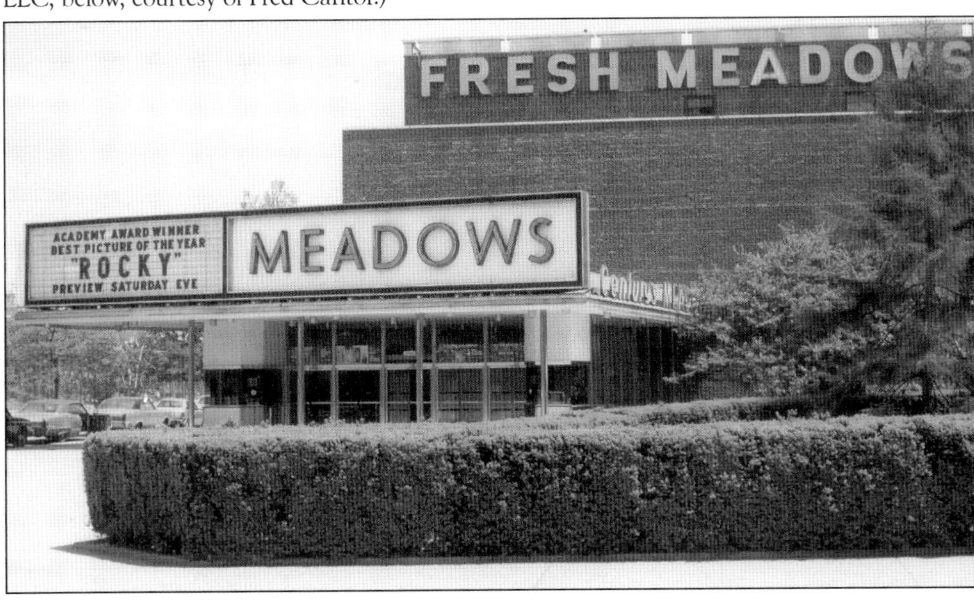

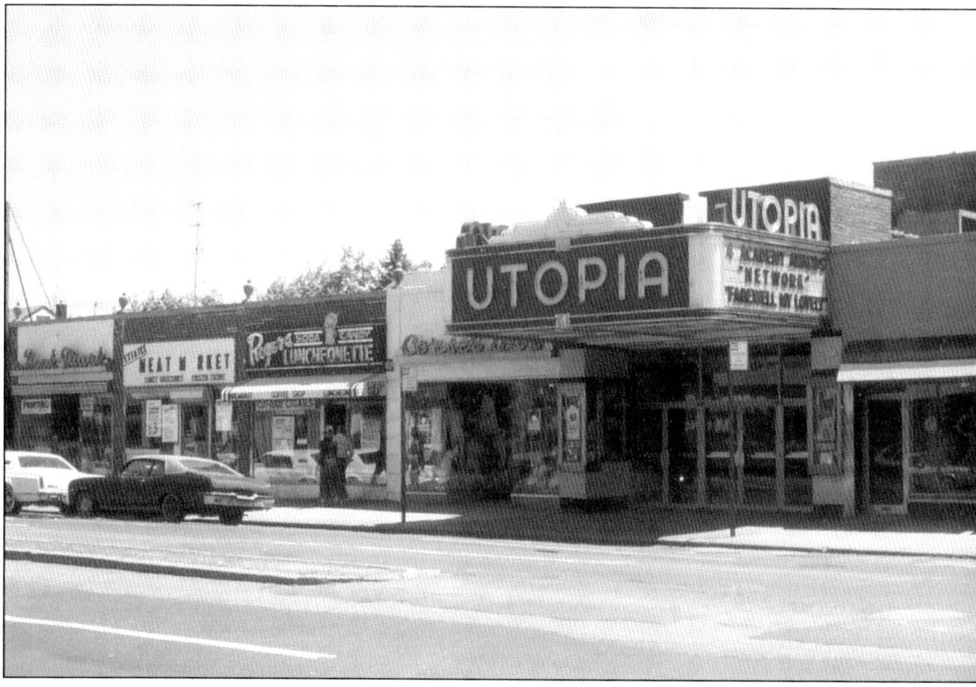

The Utopia Theater, featuring an Art Deco marquee, was another movie theater that served the Fresh Meadows community. It was a fixture on Union Turnpike for more than five decades. Rogers Luncheonette was just down the street from the Utopia Theater. It was a favorite destination for egg creams in the 1950s and 1960s (as well as for, apparently, "CUT-RATE CIGARS" when this photograph was taken in 1977). (Both, courtesy of Fred Cantor.)

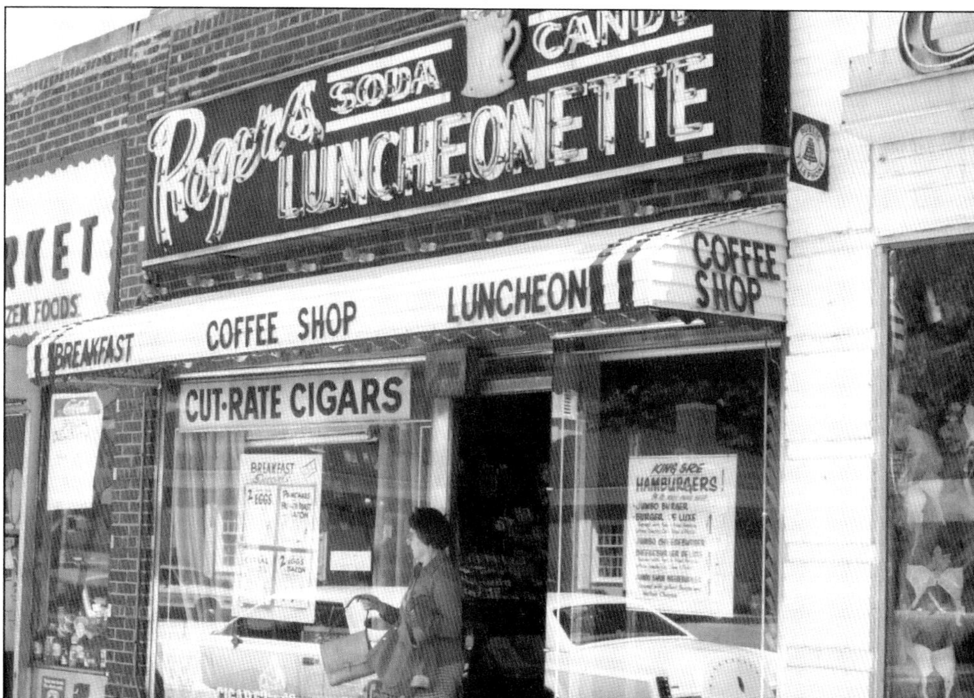

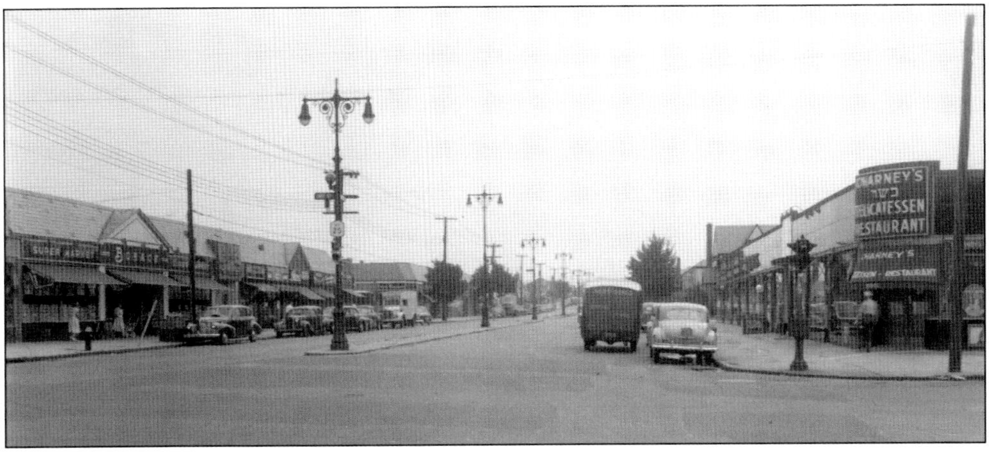

Union Turnpike is a commercial hub on the southern perimeter of the Fresh Meadows community that served as a center of commerce before the Fresh Meadows housing development was built. This photograph, taken in 1949, is of the intersection at 188th Street looking east. (Courtesy of the Queens Borough Public Library, Long Island Division, Borough President of Queens Collection.)

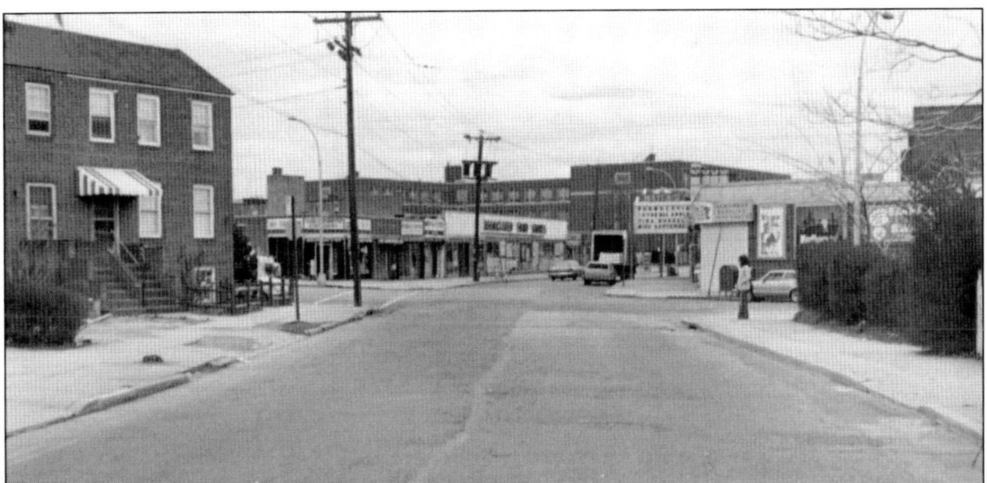

Fresh Meadow Lane, dating back to colonial times, was perhaps best known for the Mayfair Theater, which opened in 1941. Above is the intersection of Fresh Meadow Lane and 69th Avenue, looking north, with PS 173 in the background. This shopping area, designed primarily for pedestrian traffic, offered very limited parking. (Courtesy of the Queens Borough Public Library, Long Island Division, Long Island Daily Press Photo Morgue.)

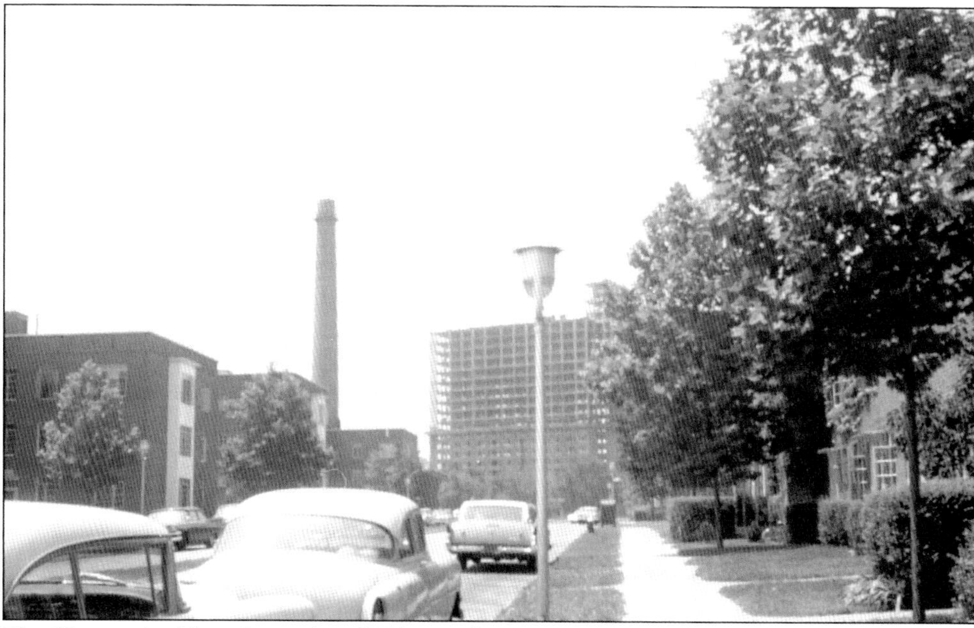

The 20-story building, located at 67-00 192nd Street, was completed in 1962. It was the 140th apartment building to be constructed in the Fresh Meadows development and added 279 apartments to the housing complex. Rents started at $133 a month for studio apartments, $175 for one-bedroom units, $220 for two-bedroom units, and $270 for three bedrooms. (Above, courtesy of Mitchell Kaften; below, courtesy of Queens Fresh Meadows LLC, photograph by Regency Pictorials.)

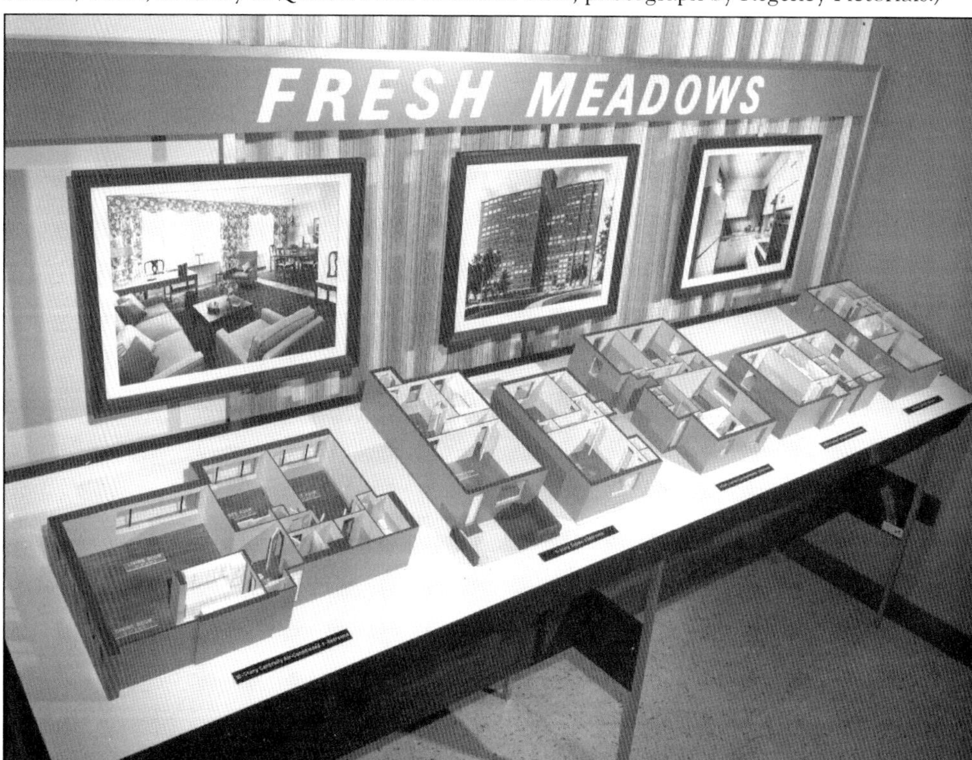

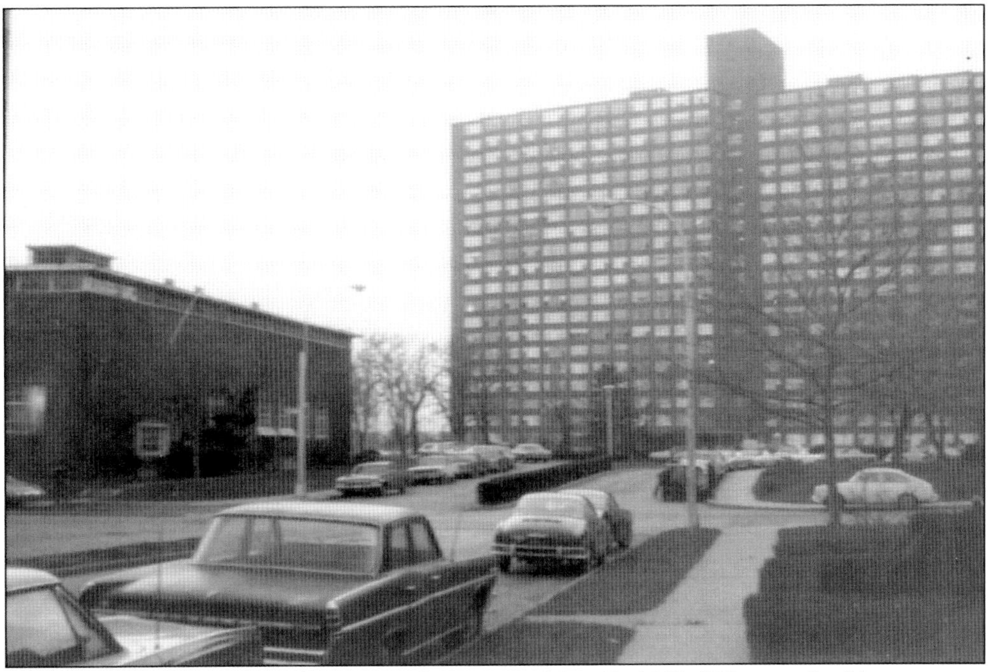

According to an article in *the New York Times* on May 13, 1962, "The new building is more of a luxury type than the others and has higher rentals. For the other buildings, the average rental is $34 a room a month, a 47 per cent increase over the 1947 rents that averaged $24 a month." The 6700 building, as it came to be known by local residents, had a doorman and a large upscale lobby. (Above, courtesy of Eddie Karp; below, courtesy of New York Life Insurance Company Archives.)

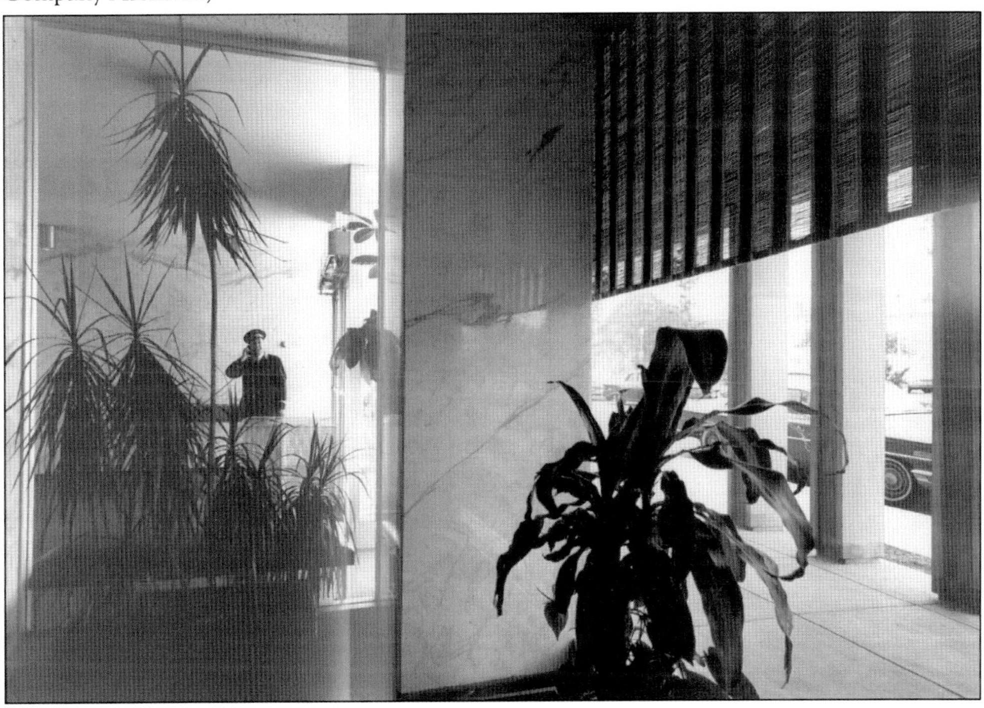

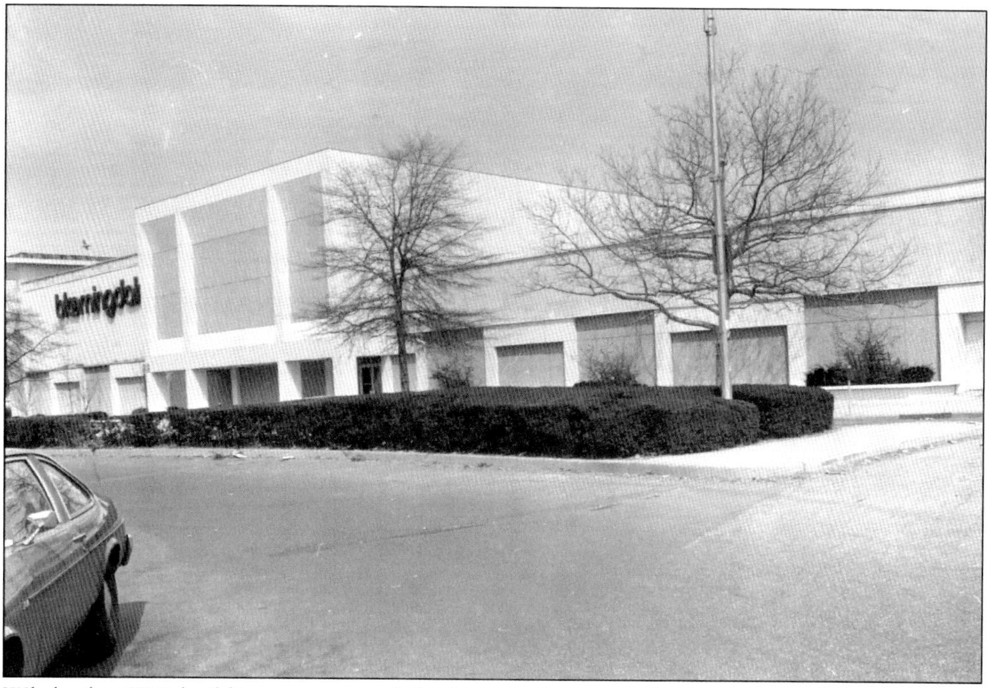

While the 6700 building represented the biggest change to the landscape after 1960 in the residential portion of the Fresh Meadows development, the most significant alteration to the main Fresh Meadows shopping center was probably the expansion of Bloomingdale's in 1973 (which later closed in 1991). The remodeling of the building resulted in the elimination of what had been a popular public square between Bloomingdale's and Woolworth's. Even though many businesses have come and gone over the years, there are some that have been operating for decades. Brother's Pizza has been a mainstay for many years on Horace Harding Expressway. (Above, courtesy of the *Queens Tribune* and the Queens Borough Public Library, Long Island Division, Joseph A. Ullman Photographs; below, courtesy of Dennis Koines.)

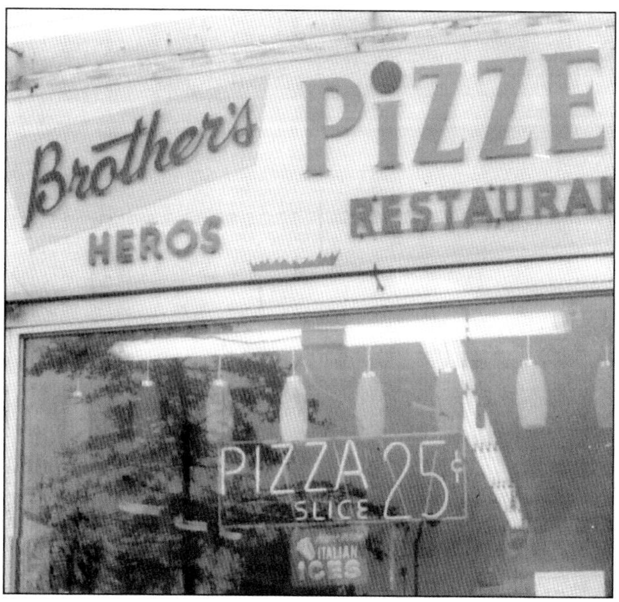

Two

Baby Boom

The end of World War II signaled the closing of one era for Americans and the beginning of another. The postwar years were defined by GIs returning to the lives they had left behind when they shipped out to serve their country. Many attended college (thanks to the GI Bill), married, and began having families in record numbers. Women, who had stepped up to take jobs vacated by men fighting the war, left the workforce, married, and began having babies—so many babies that the term "baby boomer" was coined to describe the approximately 76 million babies born between 1946 and 1964.

During the 1930s to early 1940s, new births in the United States averaged around 2.3 to 2.8 million each year. In 1946, the first year of the baby boom, new births in America skyrocketed to 3.5 million births and peaked at 4.3 million in 1957.

With virtually no building taking place during the war and little in the preceding years of the Great Depression, the United States faced an unprecedented housing shortage. Fresh Meadows was one of the many communities that sprung up in response to this unprecedented demand for housing for new families. The Fresh Meadows housing development was specifically designed to meet the needs of these returning veterans and their families.

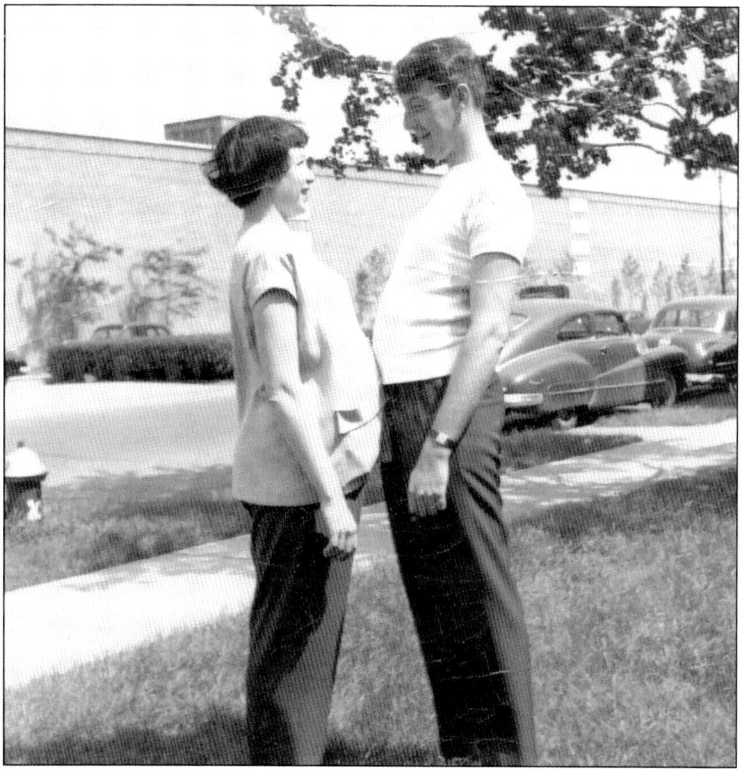

For Doris and Bill Weissler, their apartment on 188th Street was their first home after living with Doris's parents during the war when Bill was a lieutenant junior grade in the US Navy based in Panama. Doris, pregnant here with their first child in 1950, recalls that in the spring, when coats were shed, it seemed as if every woman was pregnant, sparking the nickname "Fertile Meadows." (Courtesy of Doris Weissler.)

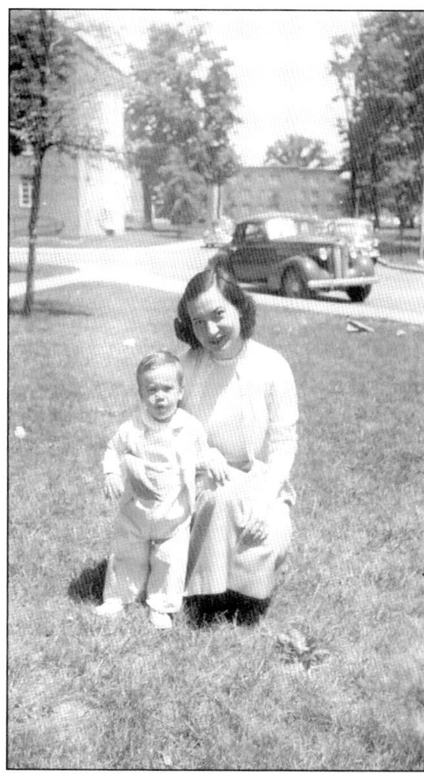

Reggie Richmond poses with her toddler Steve in front of their home at 192-15B 64th Circle in 1953. The Oak Grove is to the right. Steve's father, Mel Richmond, served in the US Army Infantry and landed on Utah Beach a few days after D-day. (Courtesy of Steve Richmond.)

Sybil Sheinberg, pictured in 1954 holding her first child, Donna, and her husband, Paul Sheinberg, were among the earliest residents of the 13-story buildings, moving from the Upper East Side of Manhattan on December 1, 1947. (Courtesy of Donna Sheinberg Gulotta.)

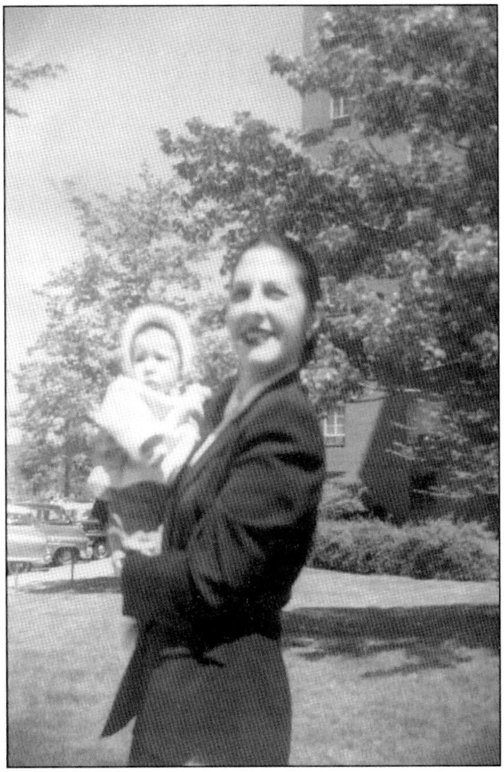

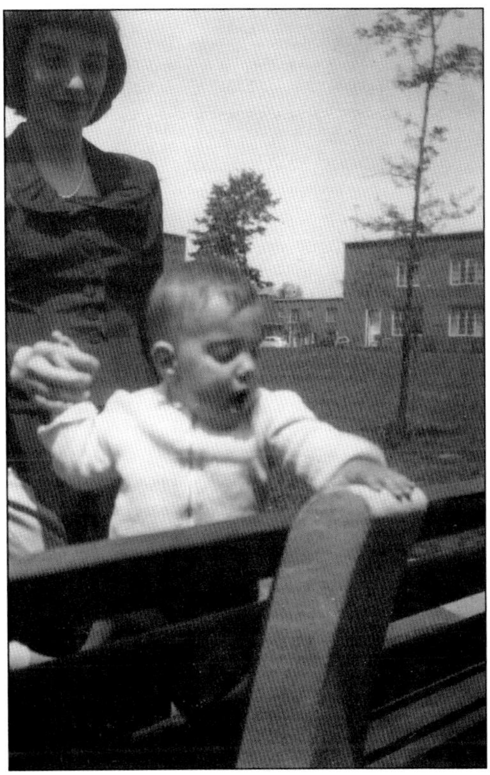

New mothers like Pearl Cantor, pictured with her son Marc in 1950, had to walk no further than their own backyard to find paths to stroll with their infants. Benches lined the paths, providing areas in which to relax and socialize with other young mothers and their children. Sidney Cantor, Pearl's husband, served in the US Army in the Pacific theater. (Courtesy of Fred Cantor.)

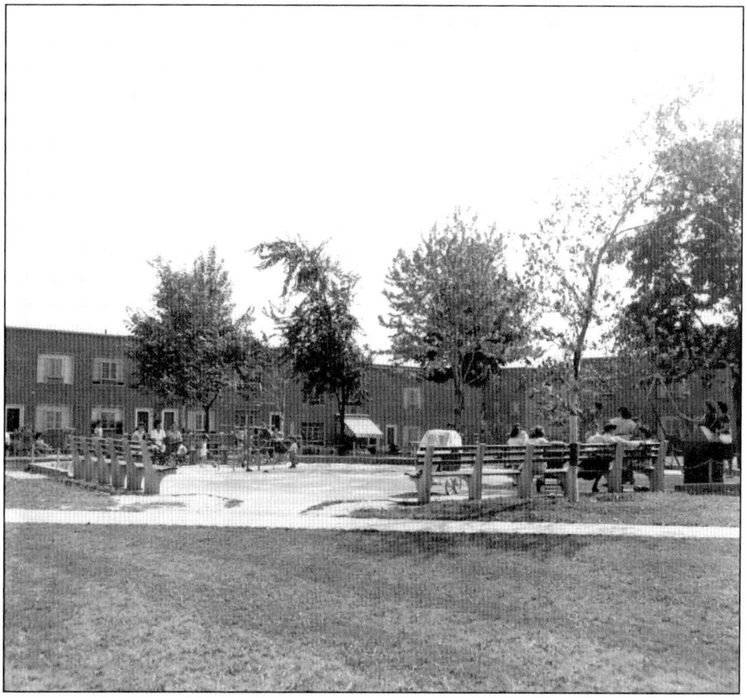

There were ultimately 30 playgrounds for preschool children located throughout the Fresh Meadows development. Each playground had benches for parents to sit on while supervising their children and socializing with friends and neighbors. To ensure the safety of the youngest residents, baseball and football were not permitted on these tot lots. (Courtesy of Queens Fresh Meadows LLC.)

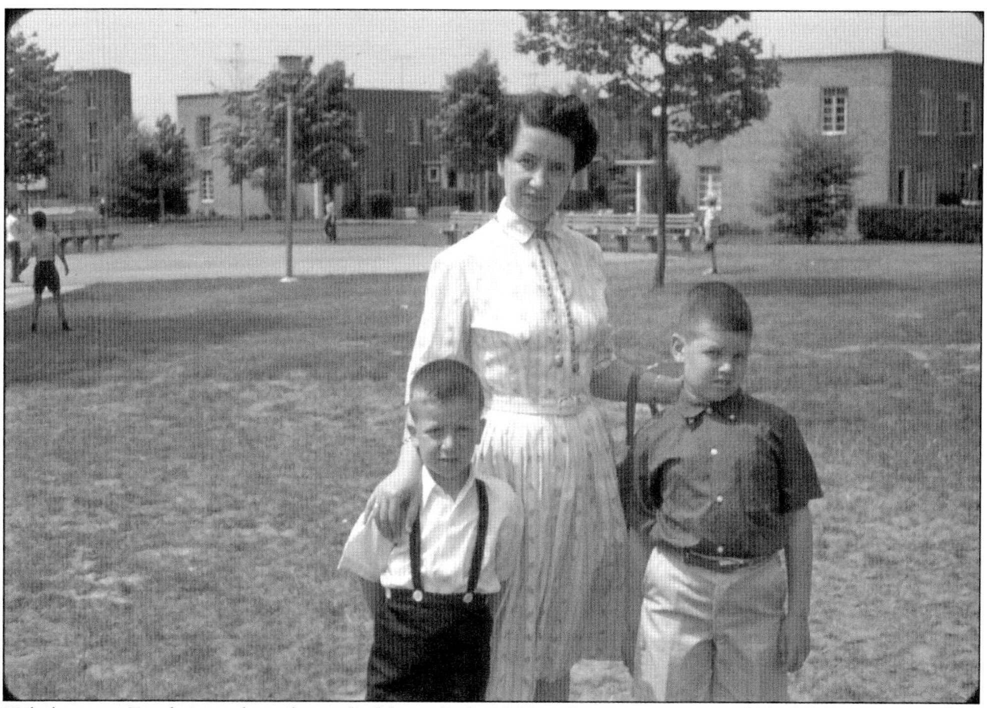

While most Fresh Meadows households included US military veterans of World War II, one that did not was the family of Pearl and Yehudi Fichman. Pearl Fichman is pictured above with her sons Eytan (left) and Mark around 1957. The Fichmans were Holocaust survivors from Romania, and Pearl Fichman later told the story of her Holocaust experiences in a memoir entitled *Before Memories Fade*. (Courtesy of Eytan and Mark Fichman.)

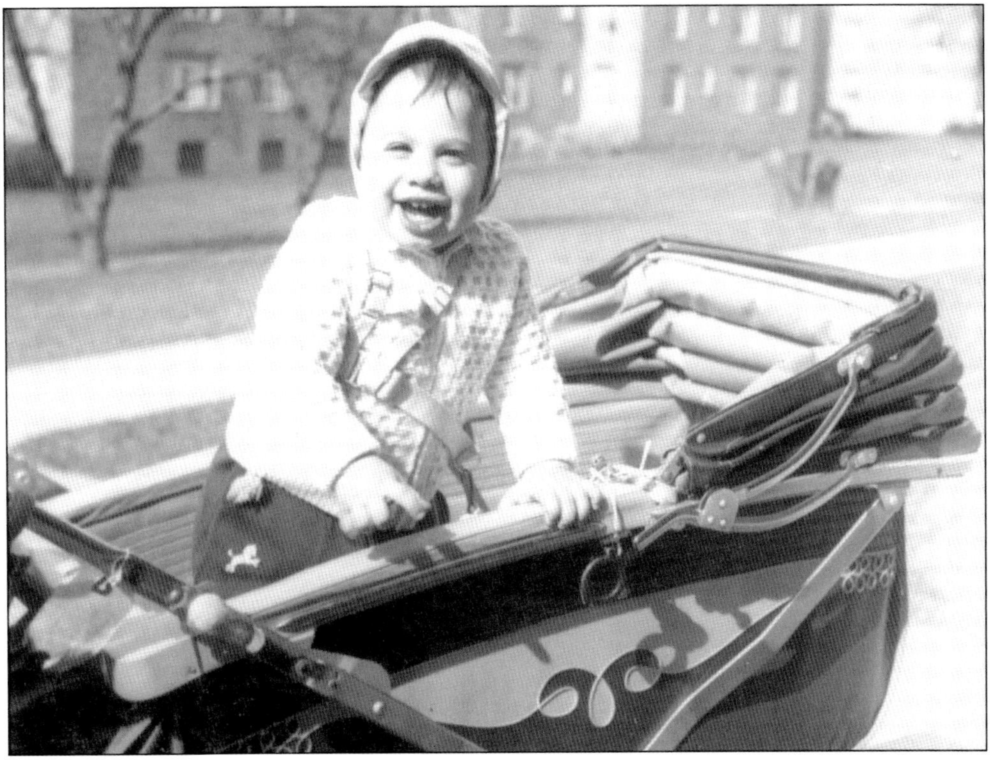

Baby carriages were everywhere in the early years of Fresh Meadows. By the mid-1950s, Little League had become so popular that entire families would show up for games. The *New York Times* reported that "baby carriage brigades get too close to base lines and time must be called to clear the field." Fred Lager, pictured above in 1955, seems to be thoroughly enjoying his carriage ride. Babies were just as ubiquitous in Meadowlark Gardens, a garden-apartment complex located just south of the Fresh Meadows development. Scott Marticke, pictured below, is standing in front of his grandparents' apartment at 197th Street and 67th Avenue in 1956. (Above, courtesy of Anita Toby Lager; below, courtesy of Scott Marticke.)

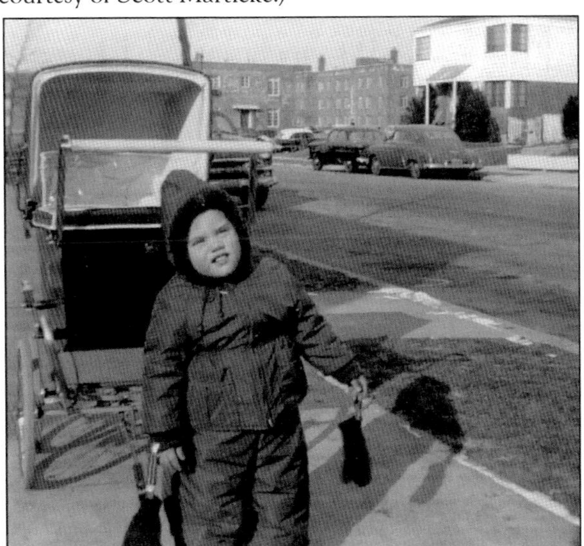

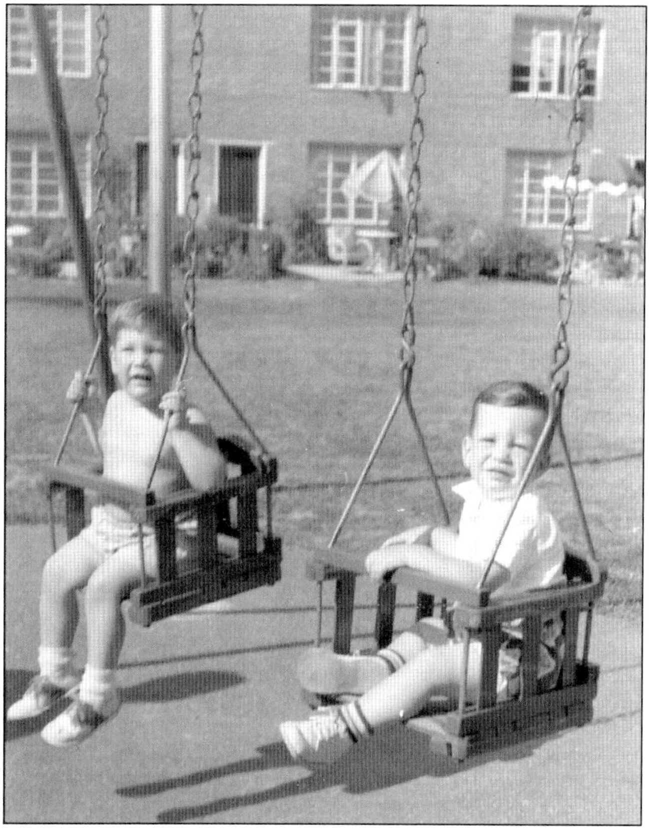

The fact that no apartment was more than a few steps from a playground meant that boomer babies spent many days swinging and playing in the playgrounds located throughout the Fresh Meadows development. Mark Weissler (right) is pictured at left in 1952 swinging alongside his cousin Teddy Tesser in a playground located near his family's duplex on 194th Street. Below, Robert Sternbach shares a slide with a panda bear in 1951. (Left, courtesy of Doris Weissler; below, courtesy of Stephen Sternbach.)

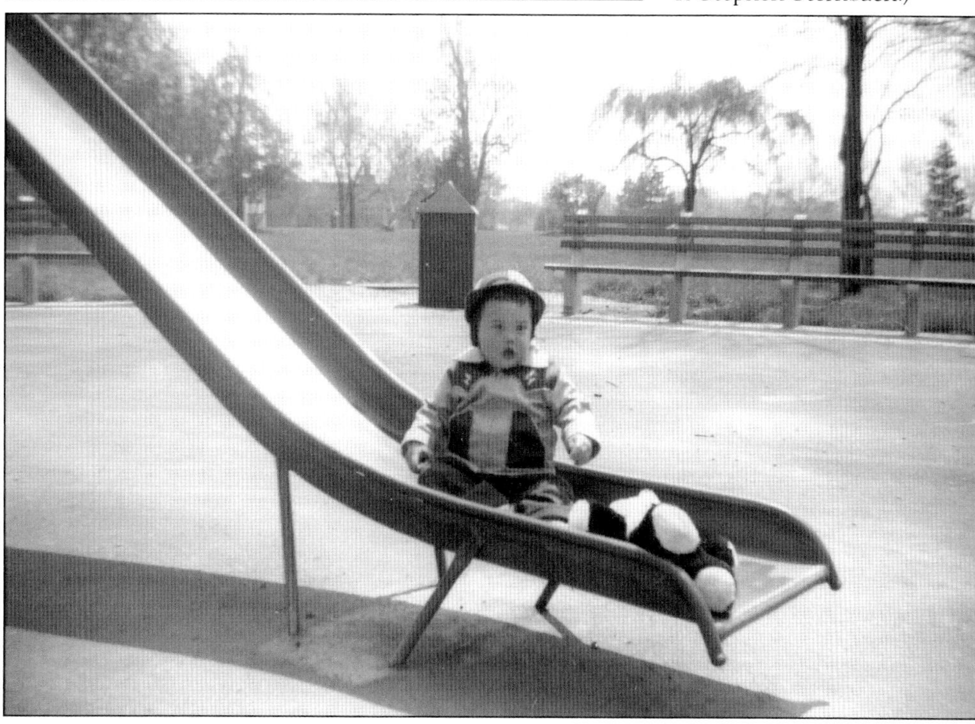

The grassy areas surrounding the playgrounds provided ideal places for toddlers to explore and play. Louise Covitt appears ready for a game of catch in 1955. Louise's father, Lee Covitt, a master sergeant in the US Air Corps, served as a weather forecaster in Europe. (Courtesy of Louise Covitt.)

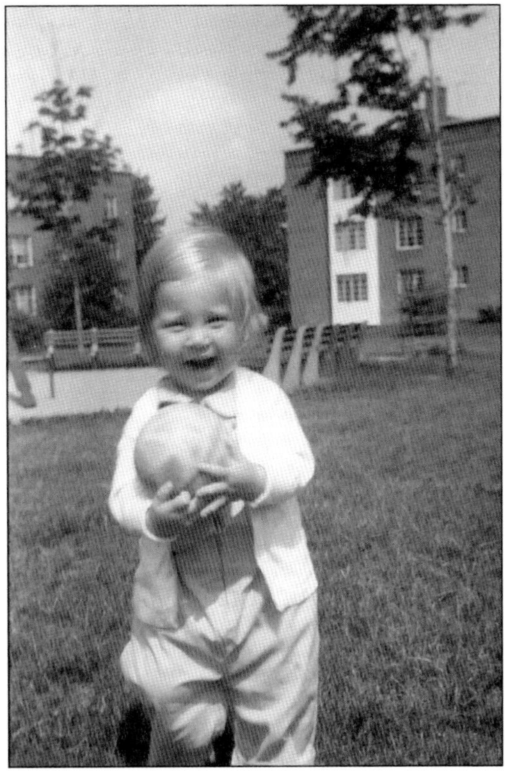

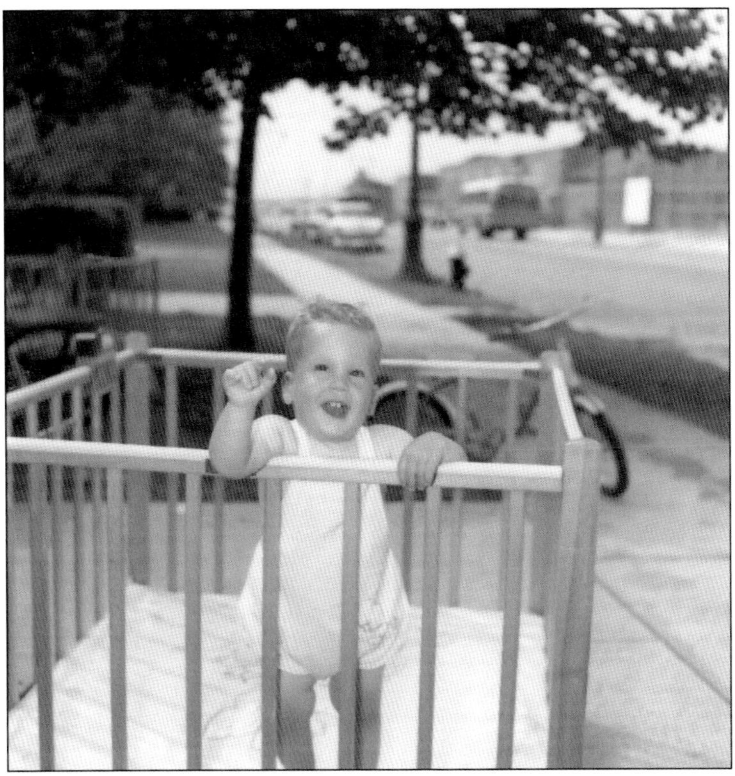

Front lawns of duplex apartments also served as play areas. In 1956, Robert Simon enjoys the fresh air from his playpen in front of the Simon family's home on Peck Avenue. PS 179, the school Robert would attend a few years later, can be seen in the background. (Courtesy of Robert Simon.)

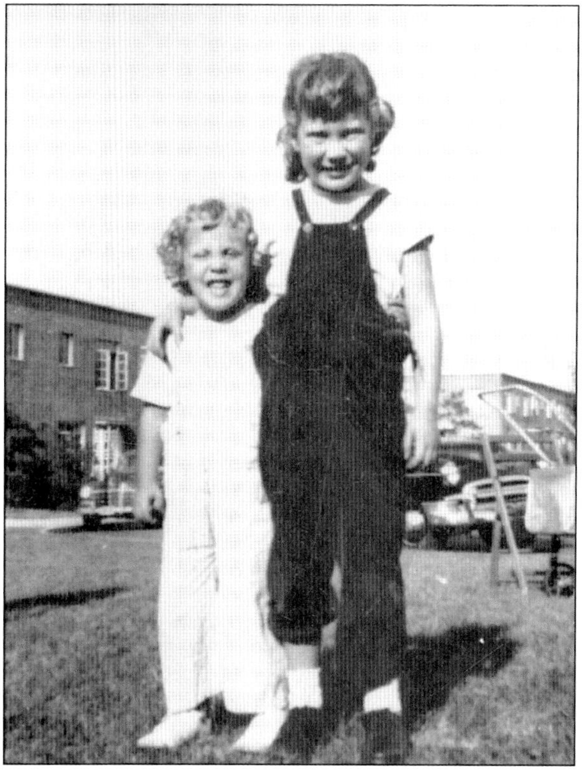

While it was easy to step outside to find neighborhood playmates, it was just as much fun to play with your little sister at times. At left, Deborah Newmark (left) and her sister Helene share a moment. Below, Marla Roberts (left) holds hands with her sister Abby in front of their Cape Cod–style home at 69-22 185th Street. While the blocks of private homes did not have the same density of children as the Fresh Meadows development, there was never a problem finding friends close by. (Left, courtesy of Deborah Newmark Frost; below; courtesy of Marla Roberts Leader.)

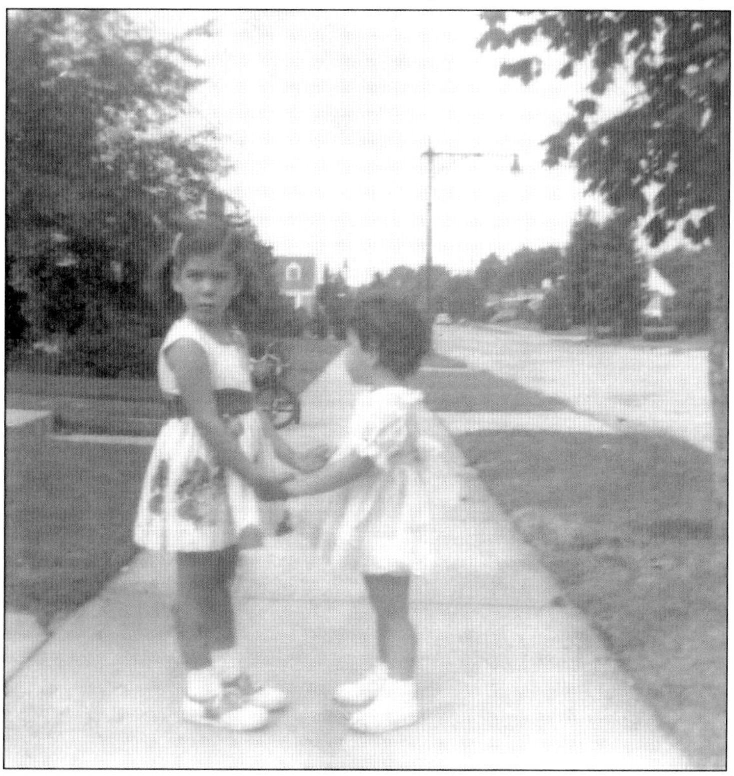

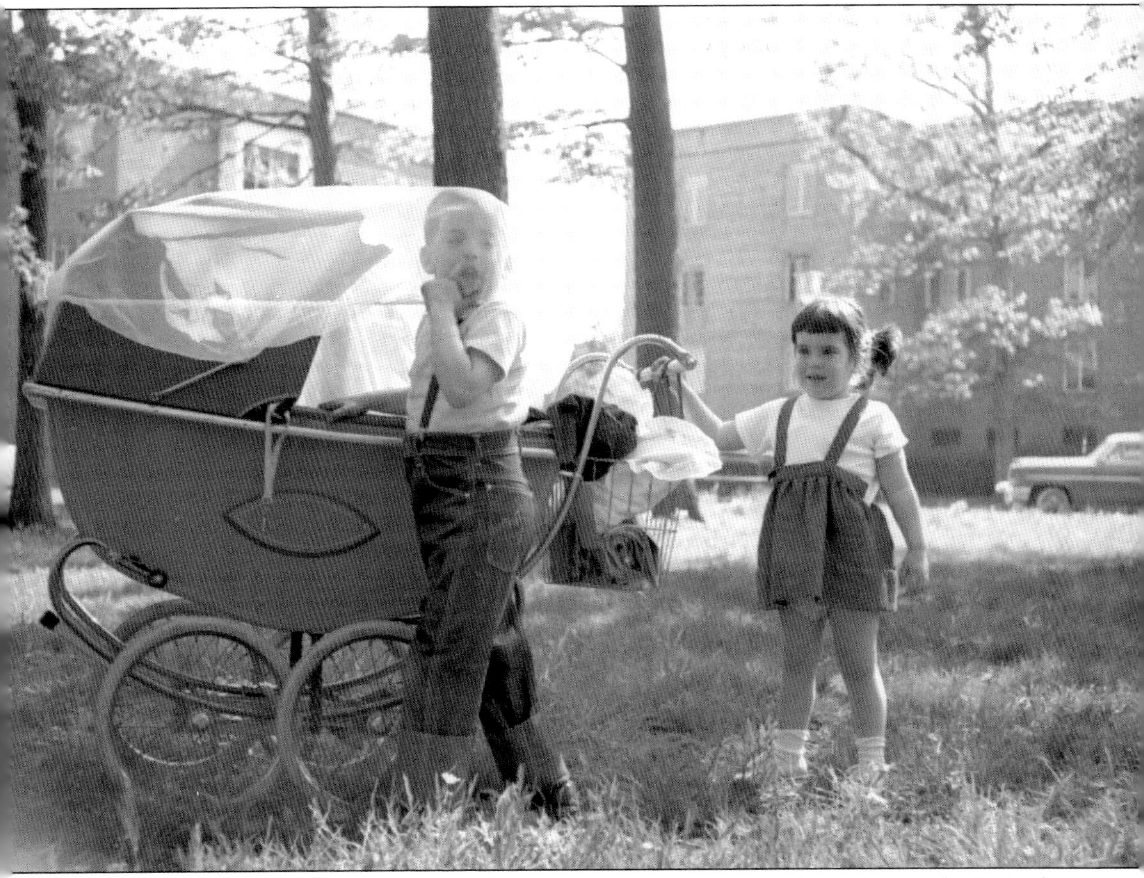

Family size in the United States increased sharply in the postwar years. According to the United States Census Bureau, during the Great Depression, fertility rates averaged 2.2 births per woman. That rate rose steadily to a postwar peak of 3.7 births per woman in 1957. Growing families resulted in some residents moving several times within the Fresh Meadows housing complex, often from one-bedroom apartments to two bedrooms and then again to an even larger three-bedroom unit. Pictured above in 1954 are the children of Pearl and Douglas Kaften, Mitchell, Jane, and their infant sister Sandy in the carriage. (Courtesy of Mitchell Kaften; photograph by Douglas Kaften.)

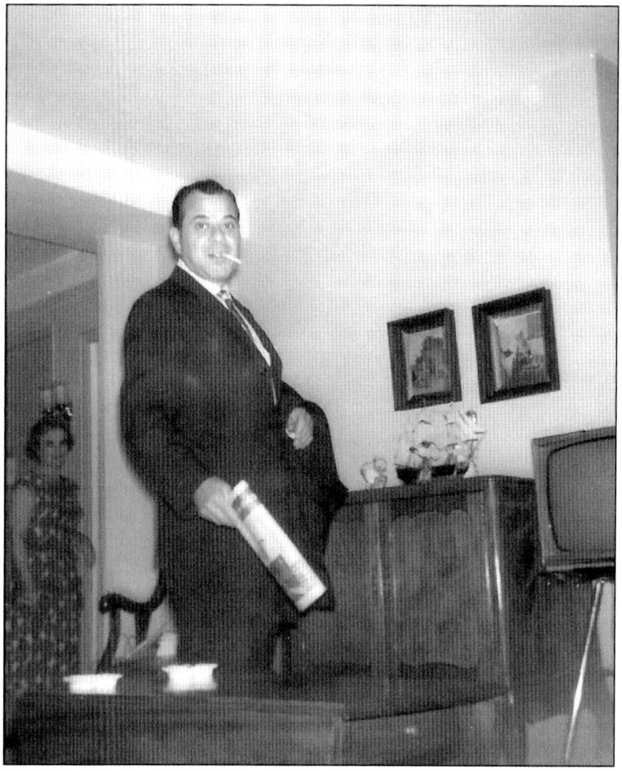

Many men commuted daily into Manhattan. Bernard "Butch" Mirsky is pictured at left in 1963 arriving home after a day of work. Twenty years earlier, Butch was fighting with the Army in North Africa when Germany's Afrika Korps were defeated. Twenty years later, he was just another Fresh Meadows dad coming home. Other men had much shorter commutes. Bill Weissler, pictured in 1954 with his sons Eric (left) and Mark in their duplex apartment, owned Corday Cleaners on Horace Harding Boulevard at 182nd Street. Other local businesses owned by residents included the toy store Playpen (owned by Paul Greenstein), the Florsheim shoe concession in B & B Lorry's, and the Weiden-Schopp. (Left, courtesy of Howard Mirsky; below, courtesy of Doris Weissler.)

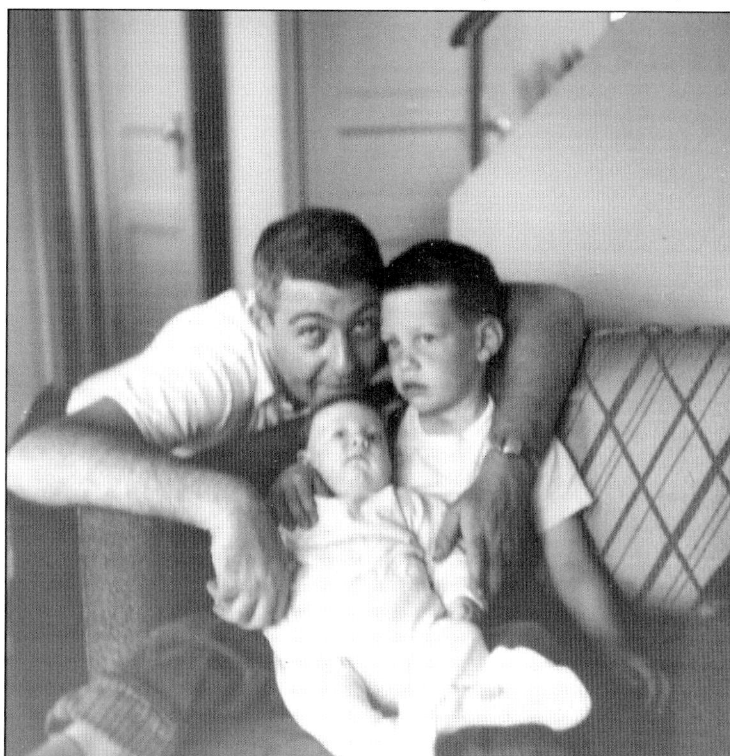

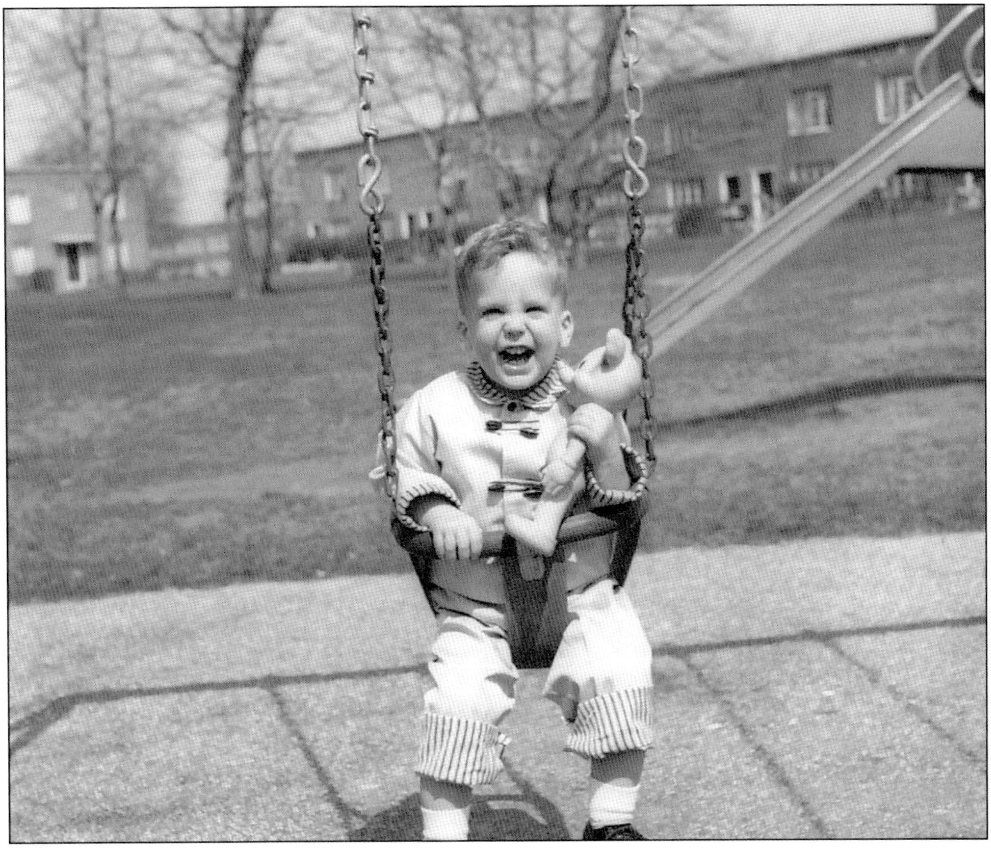

Baby boomers were the first generation to grow up with television in their homes, and its influence was visible at the youngest ages. Above, in 1956, Robert Simon shares a swing with Mickey Mouse behind his family's duplex apartment on Peck Avenue. In the photograph at right, Fred Cantor is with his Farfel the Dog puppet. Farfel, a ventriloquist's hound dog dummy, who was named for the Jewish pasta dish, was best known for appearing in Nestlé's Quik television commercials airing from 1955 to 1965. (Above, courtesy of Robert Simon; right, courtesy of Fred Cantor.)

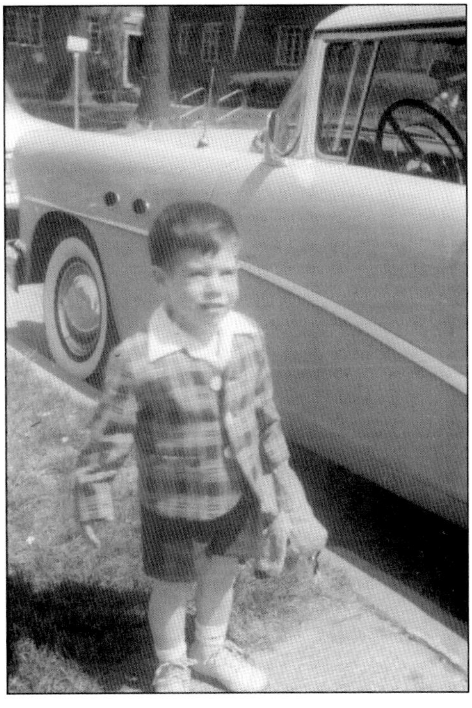

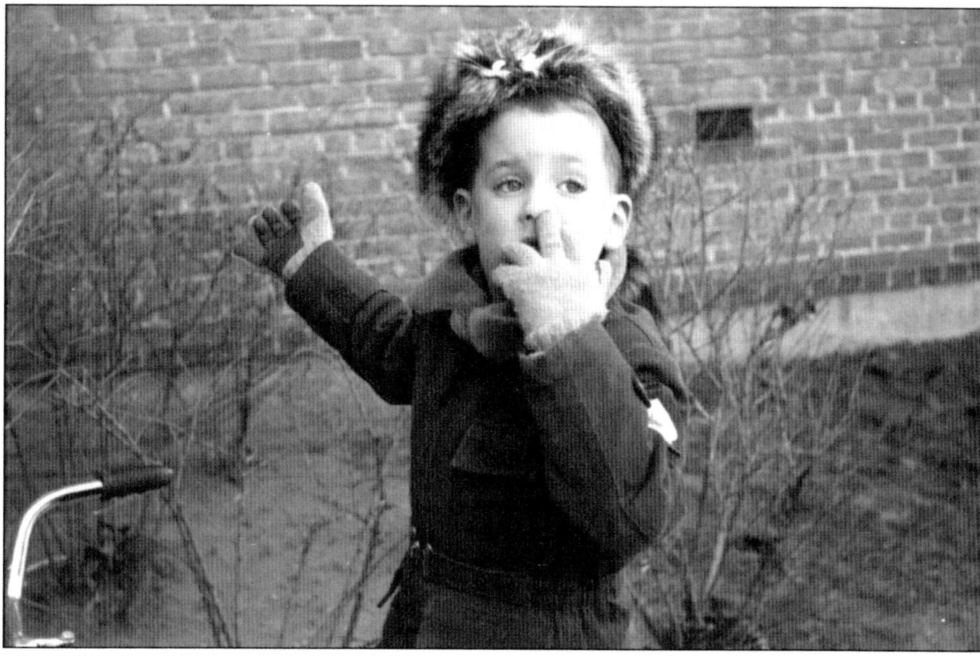

The influence of television upon the boomer kids of Fresh Meadows is also apparent in this photograph of Mitchell Kaften wearing a coonskin cap, similar to the one worn by the actor Fess Parker on the Disneyland *Davy Crockett* television series of the 1950s. (Courtesy of Mitchell Kaften; photograph by Douglas Kaften.)

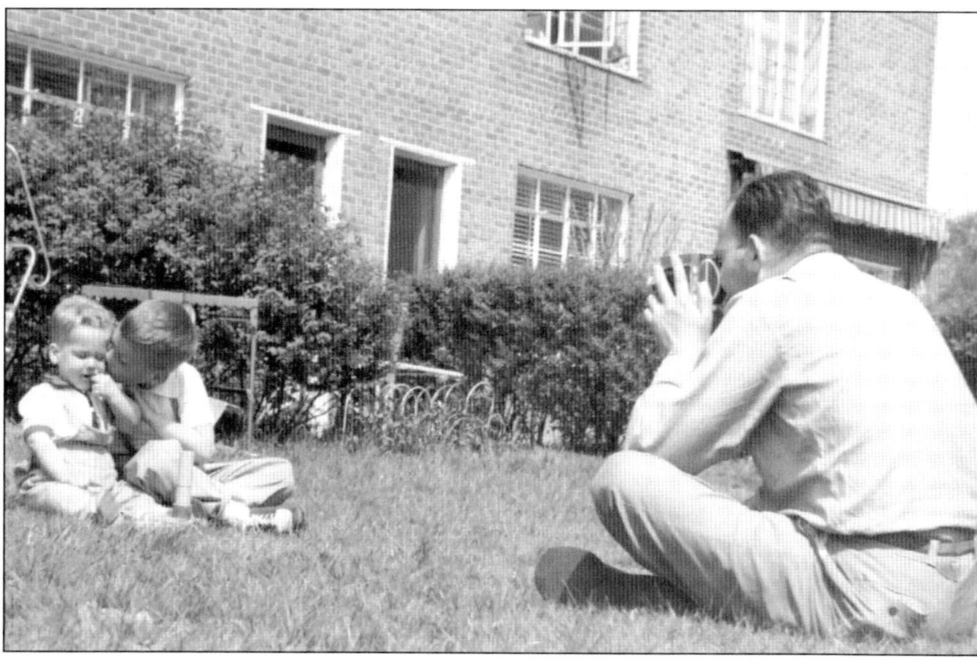

It has been said that the baby boom generation is the most studied and documented generation of all time. For many boomers, the documentation of their lives began when their parents took 8-mm home movies. Above, Seymour Simon films his sons Robert (left) and Neil in the backyard of their duplex in 1956. (Courtesy of Robert Simon.)

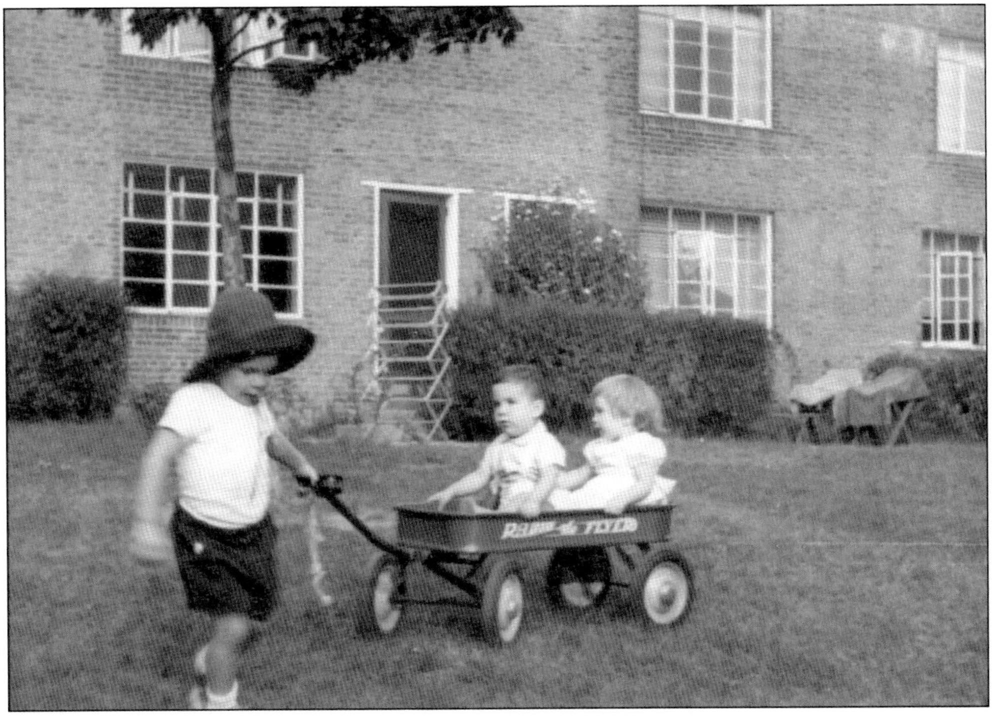

The little red wagon, another classic 1950s icon for children, was a common sight in Fresh Meadows. Above, Steven Abrams pulls his sister Linda (right) and friend Stephen Sternbach in a Radio Flyer wagon behind a duplex apartment. Duplex apartments afforded residents some of the benefits of living in a private home, such as the opportunity to use portable clothes dryers, like the one in the background, to dry their laundry in the open air. At right, Fred Lager (left) and Anita Toby Lager share their Greyhound wagon. (Above, courtesy of Stephen Sternbach; right, courtesy of Anita Toby Lager.).

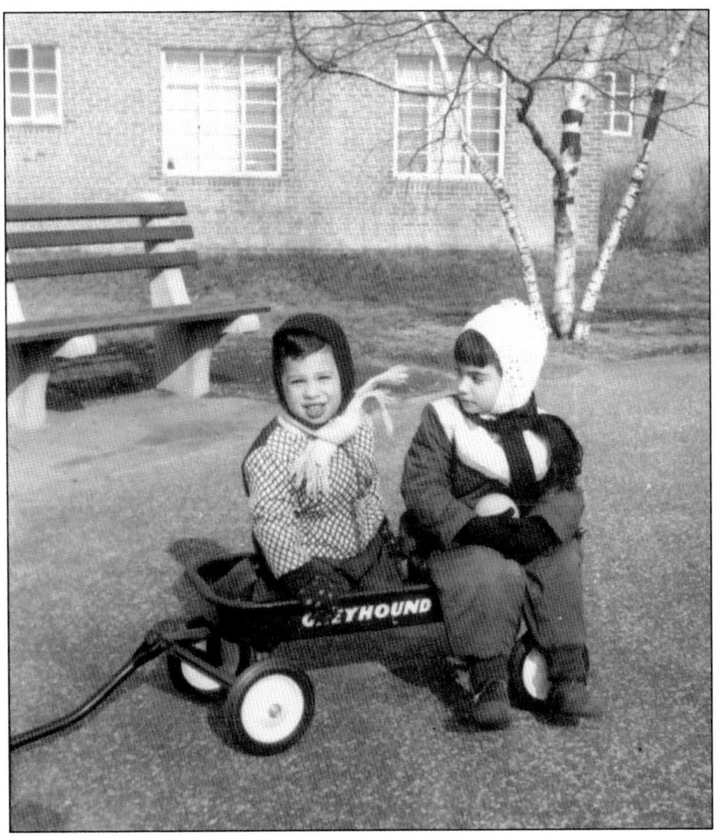

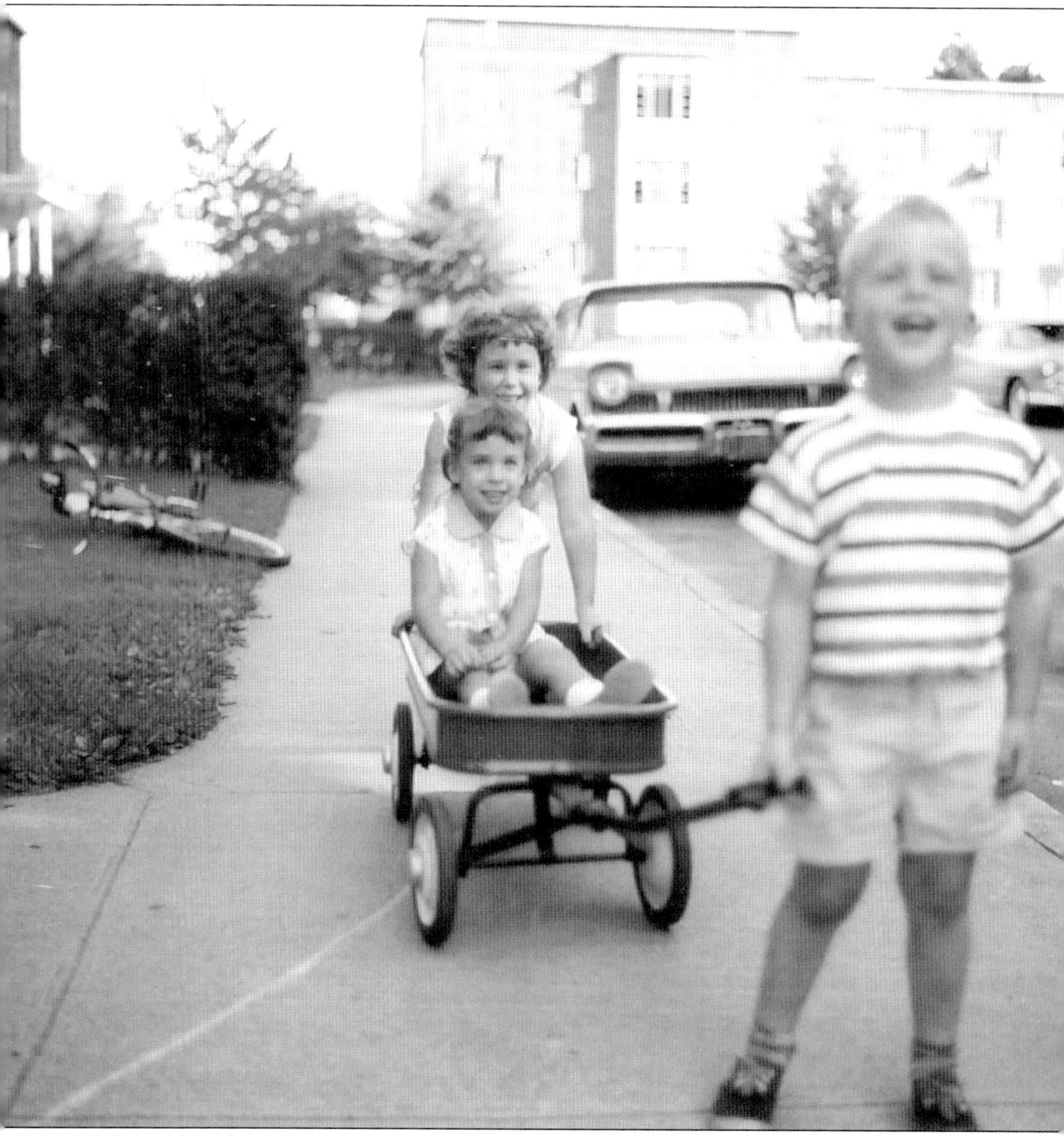

Michael Weithorn happily gives a ride to Celeste Gerowin as his sister Lois assists. Celeste's father, Carl Gerowin, who served as a captain in the US Army Air Corps Criminal Investigation Division, took this photograph in 1961. Michael and Lois Weithorn's father, Stanley Weithorn, served in the 84th Infantry and was wounded in the Battle of the Bulge. According to Michael Weithorn, who went on to create the television series *The King of Queens*, "There was an idyllic quality to growing up in Fresh Meadows that could never exist today. No one thought twice about children walking around the community by themselves, even as young as six or seven years old. And of course, there was such easy proximity to other children. Just step outside your back door and there was always something going on; a game of Red Light/Green Light, a snowball fight, tree climbing. Play dates did not exist, as there was no need for them. Every afternoon turned into a spontaneous group play date." (Courtesy of Celeste Gerowin and Michael Weithorn.)

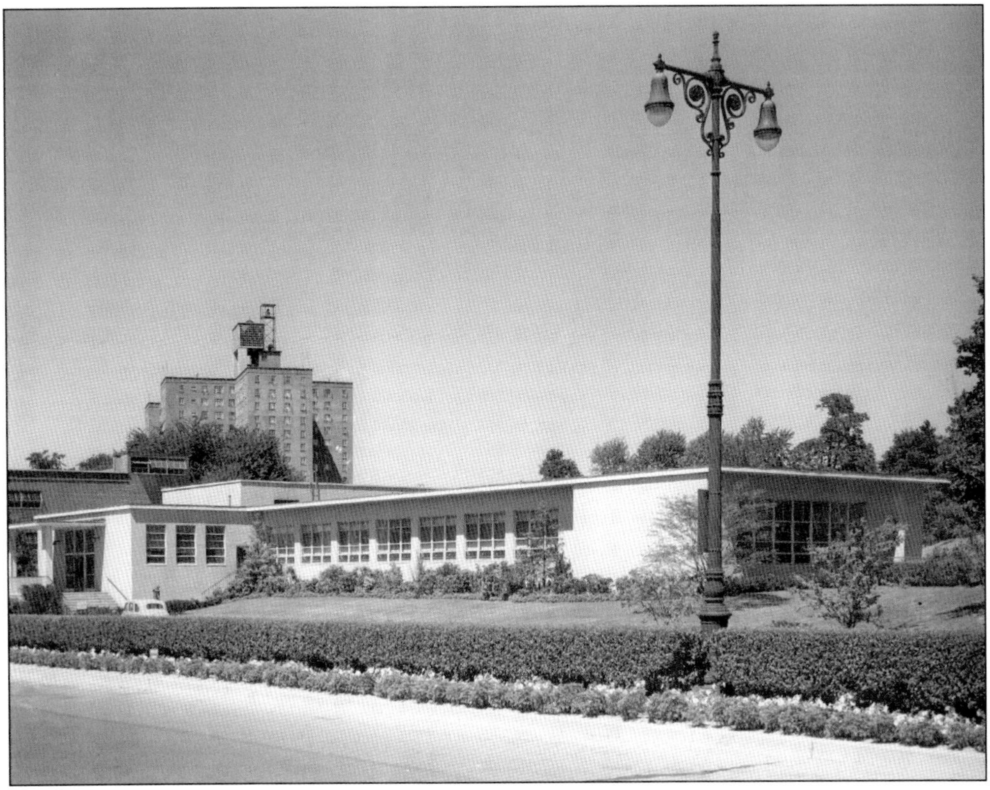

Some Fresh Meadows children attended preschool at the Fresh Meadows Nursery School on 188th Street, later the Creative Nursery School and Day Camp. Catering exclusively to three- and four-year olds, the building was equipped with miniature bathroom fixtures that allowed young children to be more independent. Here, Sandy Kaften (right) and Lucy Jaffa freshen up at Sandy's sister's birthday party held at the school in the late 1950s. At various times, the building also housed extracurricular activities such as a ballet school. In 1961, the Fresh Meadows Civic Association organized elementary school students to protest New York Life's plan to convert the building into an office building. That plan did not come to fruition. (Above, courtesy of Queens Fresh Meadows LLC; right, courtesy of Mitchell Kaften, photograph by Douglas Kaften.)

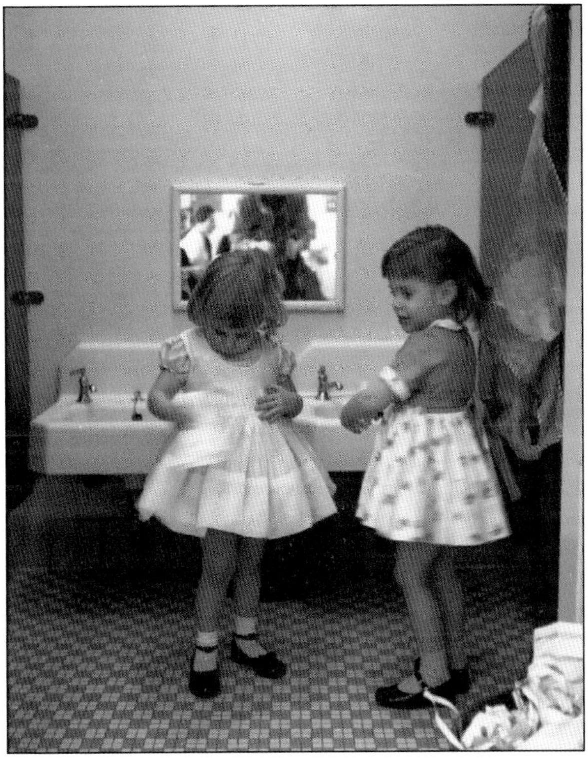

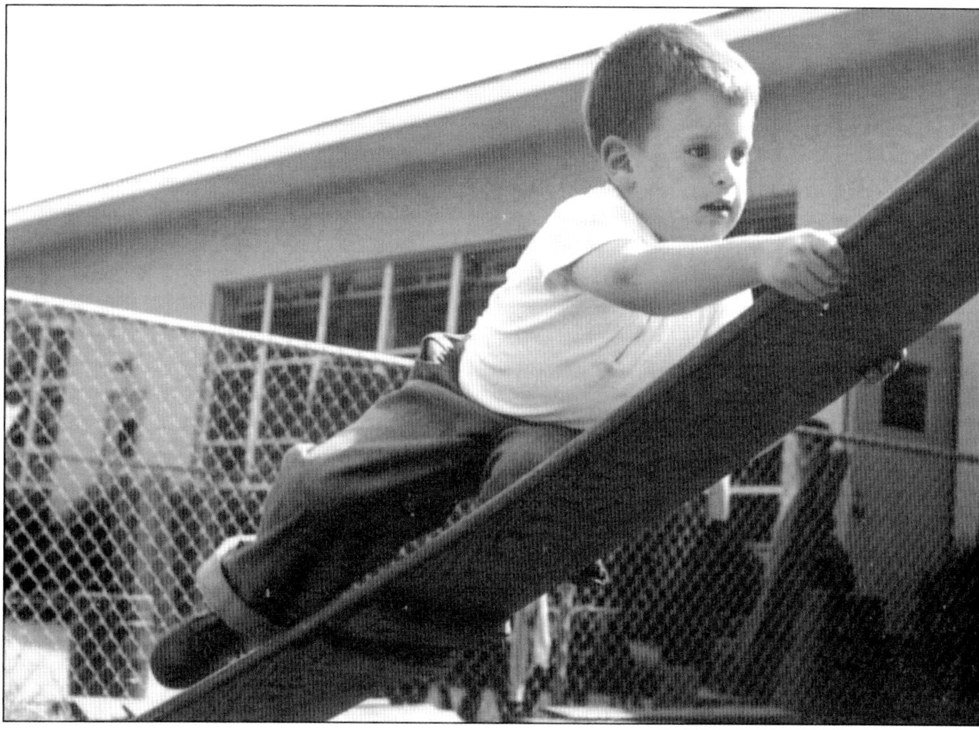

The nursery school program included both indoor and outdoor activities for preschoolers. Above, Mitchell Kaften tries a delicate balancing act on a seesaw in the play area in the rear of the building. Below, children use their imagination as well as their hands to create all matter of things in the oversized sandbox. Many who attended in the 1950s and 1960s have fond memories of Eddie Spaghetti and the theme song lyrics, "On the line, on the line, on the side of the line, we cheer for Creative in the rain or the shine." (Above, courtesy of Mitchell Kaften, photograph by Douglas Kaften; below, courtesy of Queens Fresh Meadows LLC, photograph by Jerry Saltsberg.)

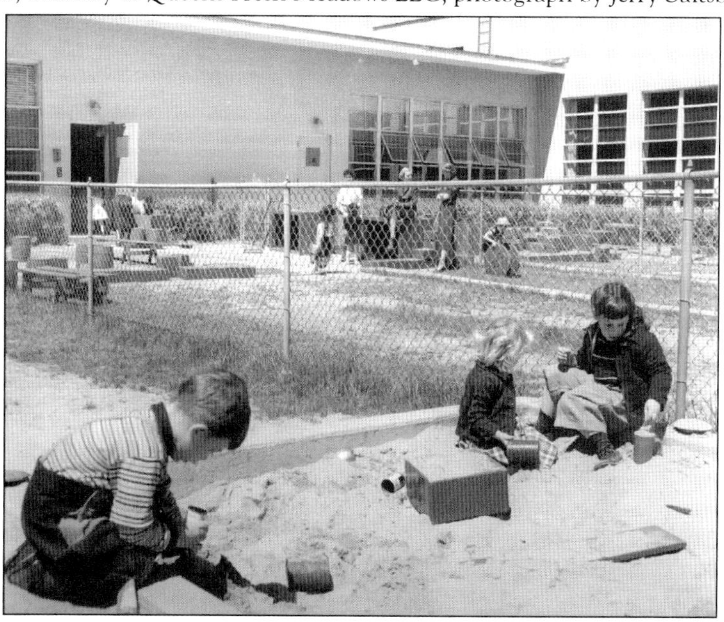

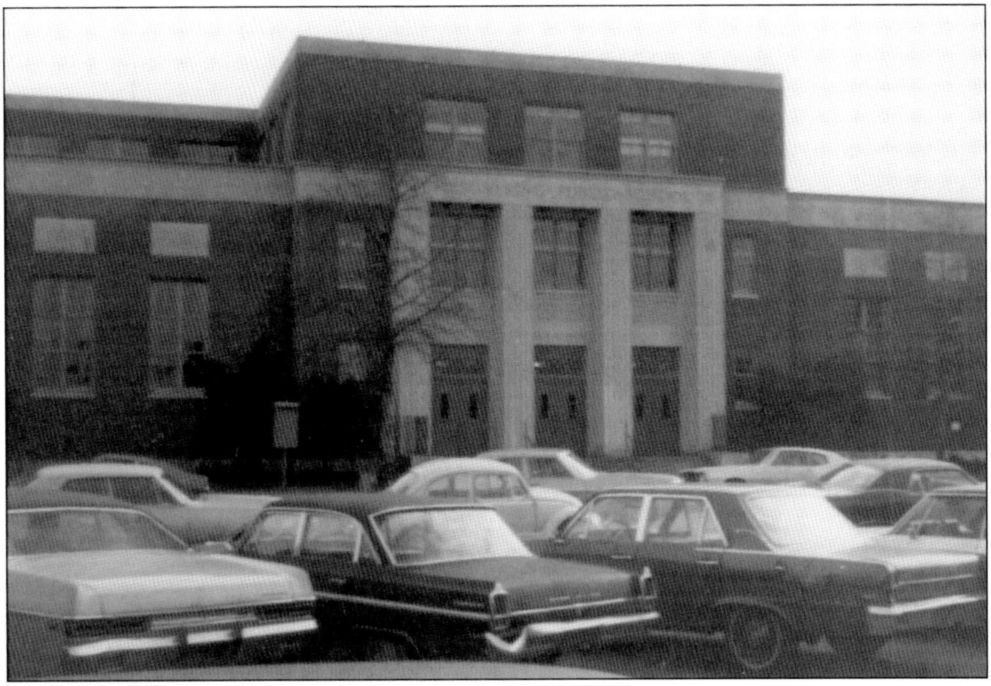

The New York Life Insurance Company deeded six acres for the Rufus King School, PS 26, near the southern border of the Fresh Meadows housing development. Opened in February 1949, the school served children from kindergarten through the eighth grade. The opening of George J. Ryan Junior High School, JHS 216, in 1954 relieved some of the overcrowding at PS 26 by serving seventh and eighth graders. PS 26 then became a K-6 school accommodating 1,480 students. This 1954 kindergarten class at PS 26 had 37 children, reflecting the first wave of children born in the Fresh Meadows housing development. When it became apparent that the opening of JHS 216 would not do enough to ease the overcrowding at PS 26, residents petitioned the New York City Board of Education for another elementary school. (Above, courtesy of Eddie Karp; below, courtesy of Sandra Furstman.)

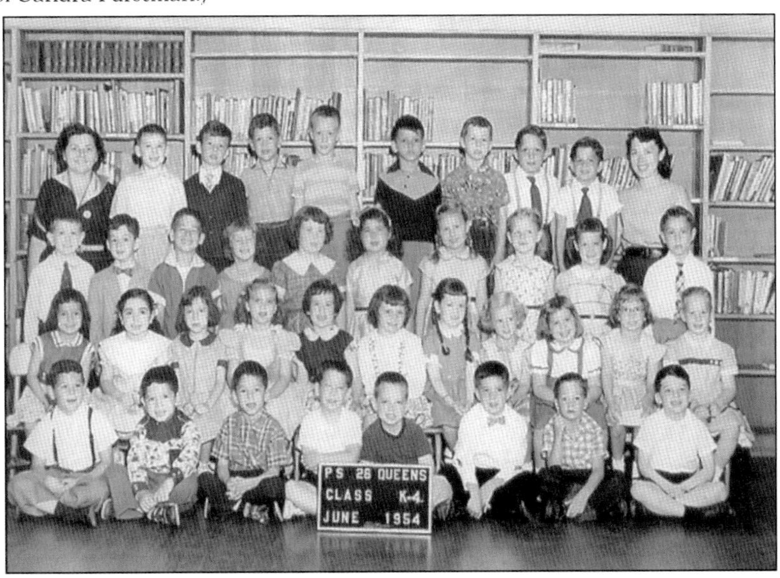

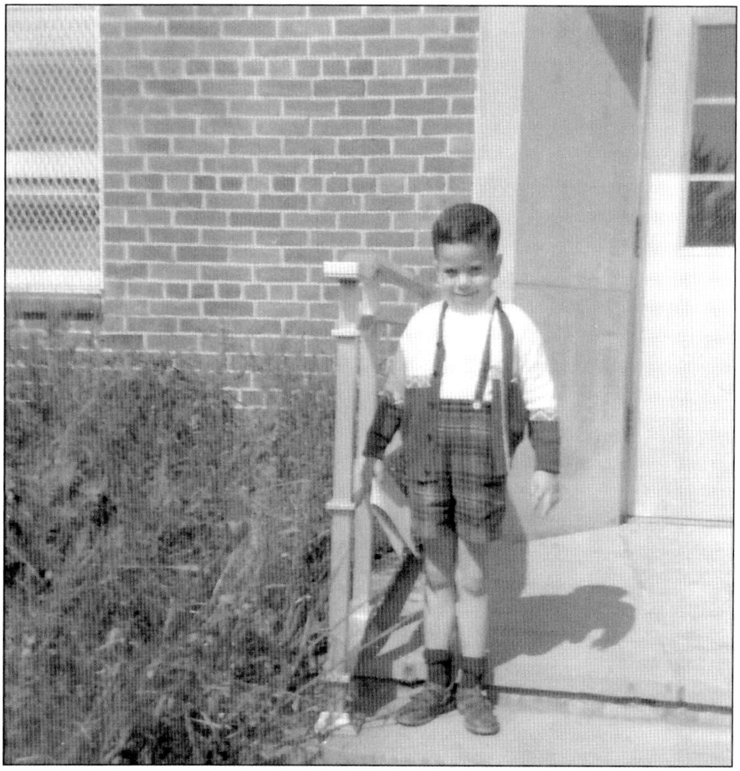

In the 1950s, there was a distinct difference between school clothes and play clothes. The first day of kindergarten was a momentous occasion, especially since many children of that era did not attend preschool, making this their first school experience. It was a time to look your very best. At left is Howard Mirsky on his first day at PS 179 in 1956, and below is Scott Marticke on his first day at PS 26 in 1959. (Left, courtesy of Howard Mirsky; below, courtesy of Scott Marticke.)

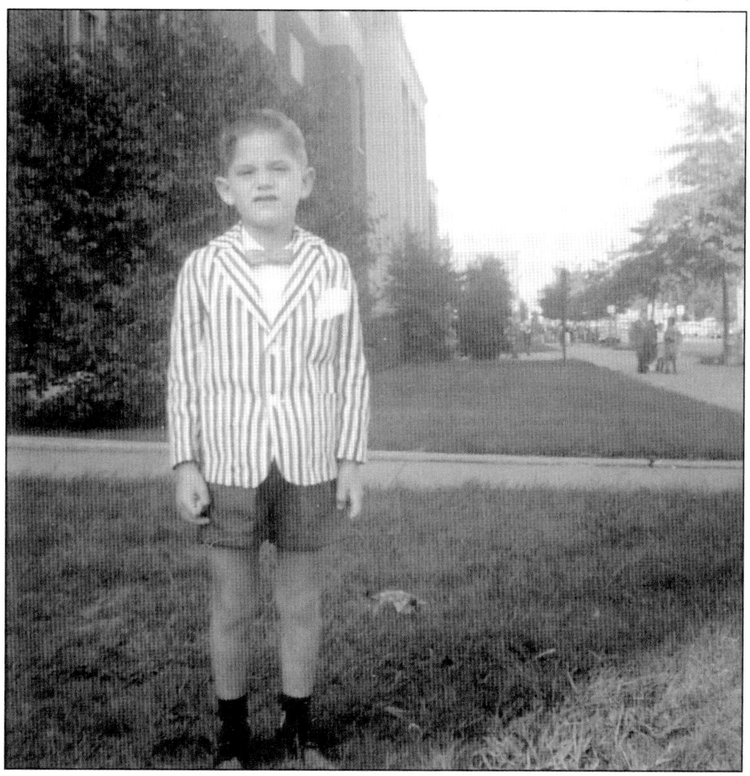

These pairs of siblings in front of PS 179 in the early 1960s illustrate the concept of school clothes. At right, Neil Simon (left) and his brother Robert are wearing bolo ties. Below, Erica Goldberg (left) and her sister Audrey are wearing coordinated dresses and cardigans. (Right, courtesy of Robert Simon; below, courtesy of Erica Goldberg Blau.)

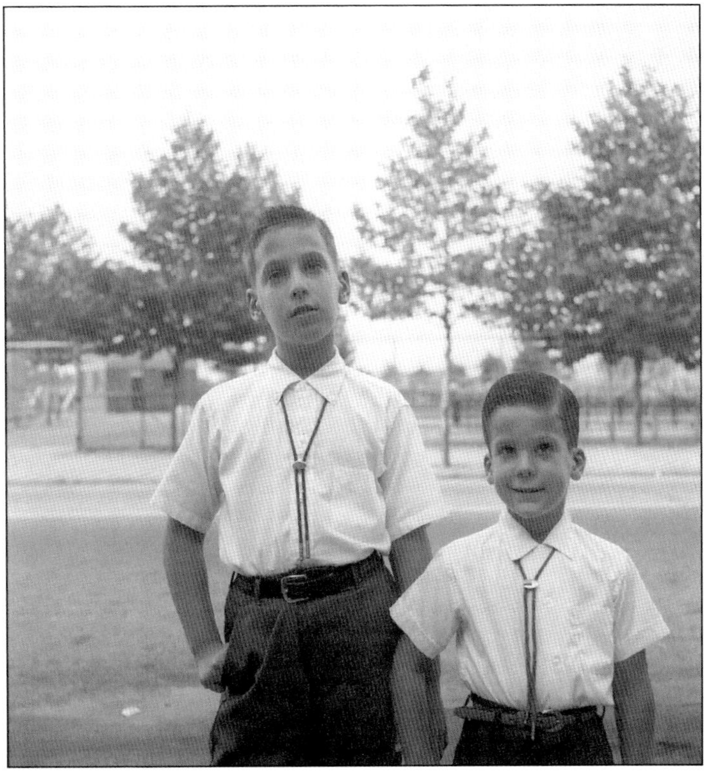

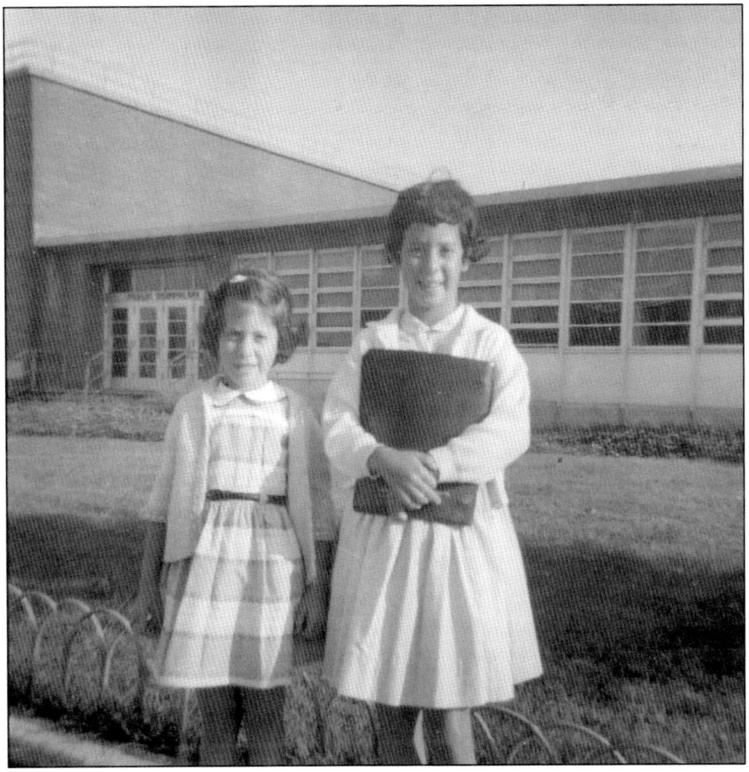

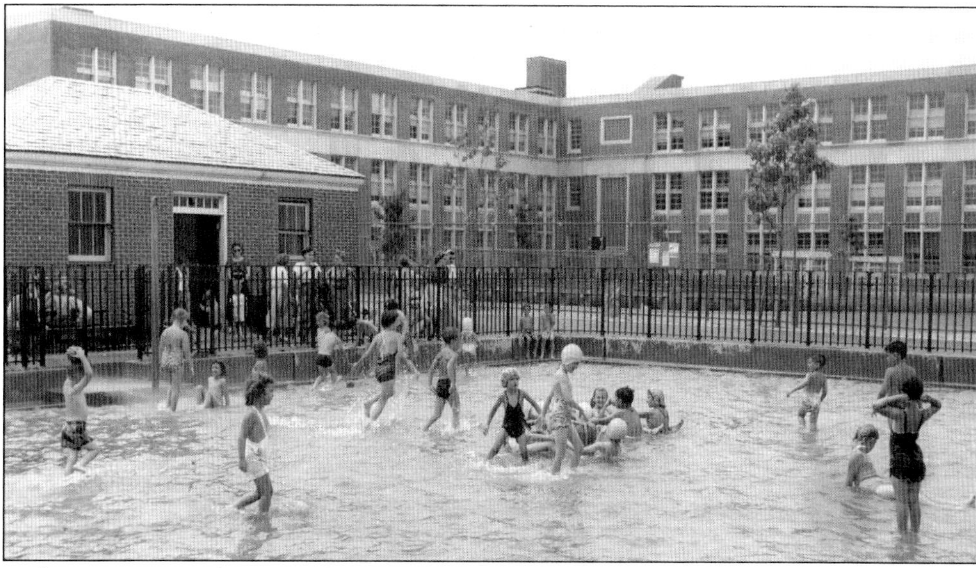

In the summertime, the PS 26 playground transformed into a spray pool, delighting neighborhood children as well as parents who appreciated the convenience of having a safe place for their children to cool off at during long, hot summers. The PS 26 schoolyard was also where students enjoyed recess. The close proximity to Shea Stadium bred many New York Mets fans, such as Robert Berger, below, in the Mets jacket and cap. It was also true, however, that some kids, like Peter Diskint (left), favored the Los Angeles Dodgers, the team that many of their parents had grown up rooting for when they were the Brooklyn Dodgers. To the right of Peter Diskint is Tony Luttman, and on the far right is Michael Levy. (Above, courtesy of New York Life Insurance Company Archives; below, courtesy of Robert Berger.)

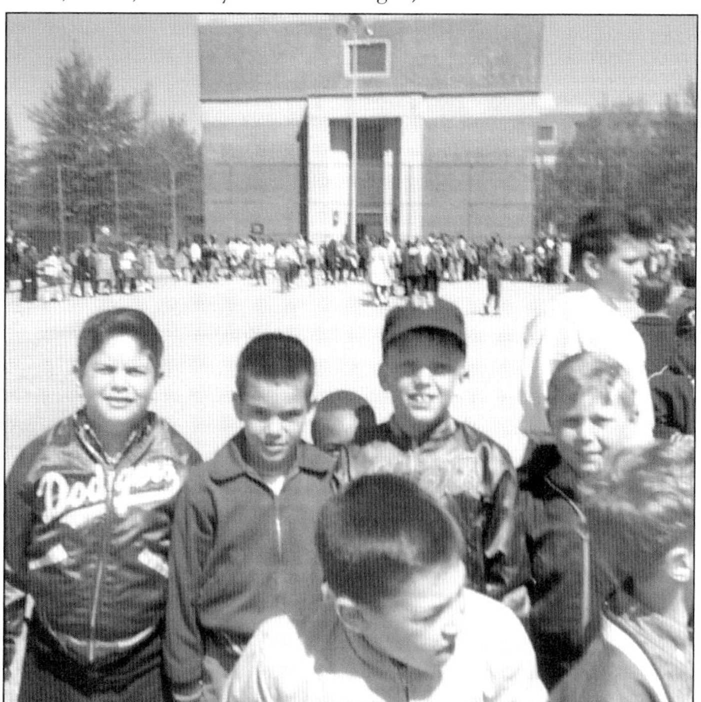

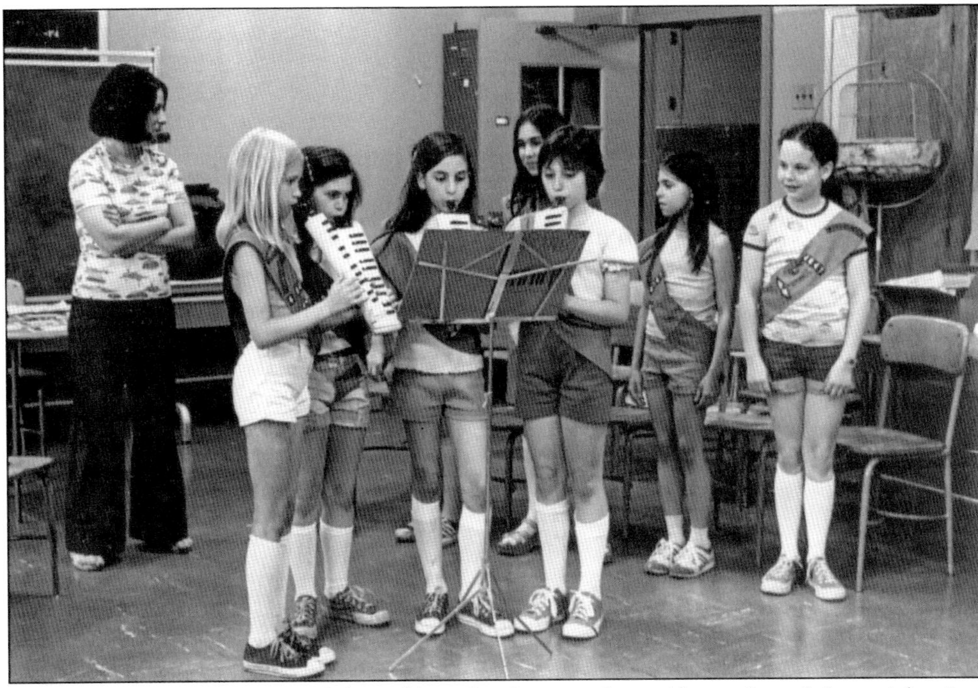

Music was an integral part of the public school curriculum. Above, from left to right, Inta Balgalvis, Samantha Rockower, Elizabeth Russo, and Kathy Silverstein practice the pianica at PS 26 in 1975 as classmates look on. By the 1970–1971 school year, class size at PS 26 was greatly reduced, as evident in this photograph of a kindergarten class. Kneeling in front from left to right are (first row) Peter Ackerman, three unidentified children, John Chuang, Andrew Klein, Vasuo Toyota, Bryan Moore, and Lori Ives; (second row) unidentified, Michelle Elgart, Inta Balgalvis, Kathy Silverstein, Jaclyn Zion, unidentified, Deborah Kaplan, Mark Levine, Stephanie Deragon, and Todd Braverman; (back row) teacher Mrs. Aarak, unidentified, and Judy Silverstein. (Both, courtesy of Aina Balgalvis.)

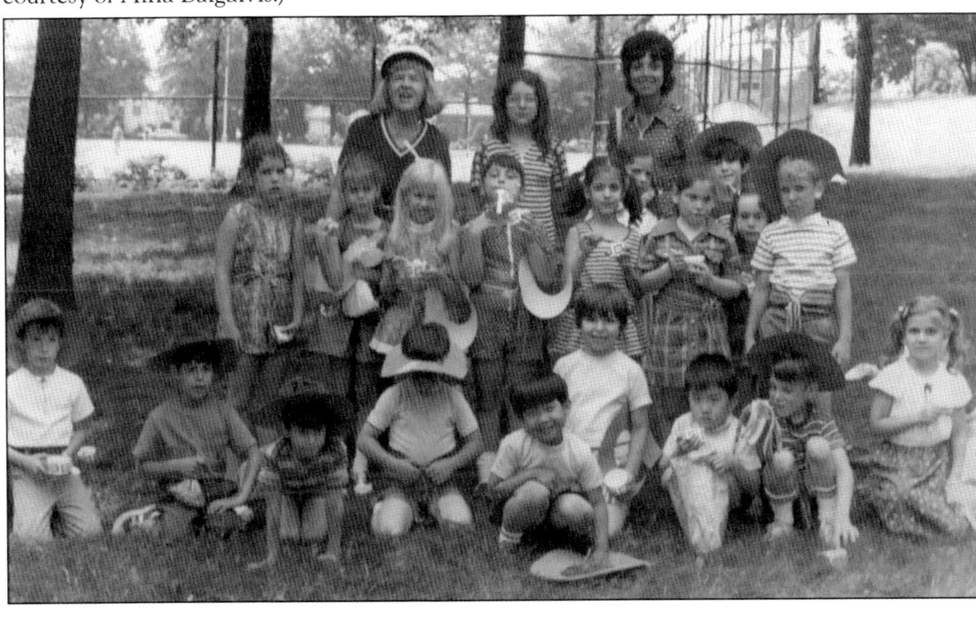

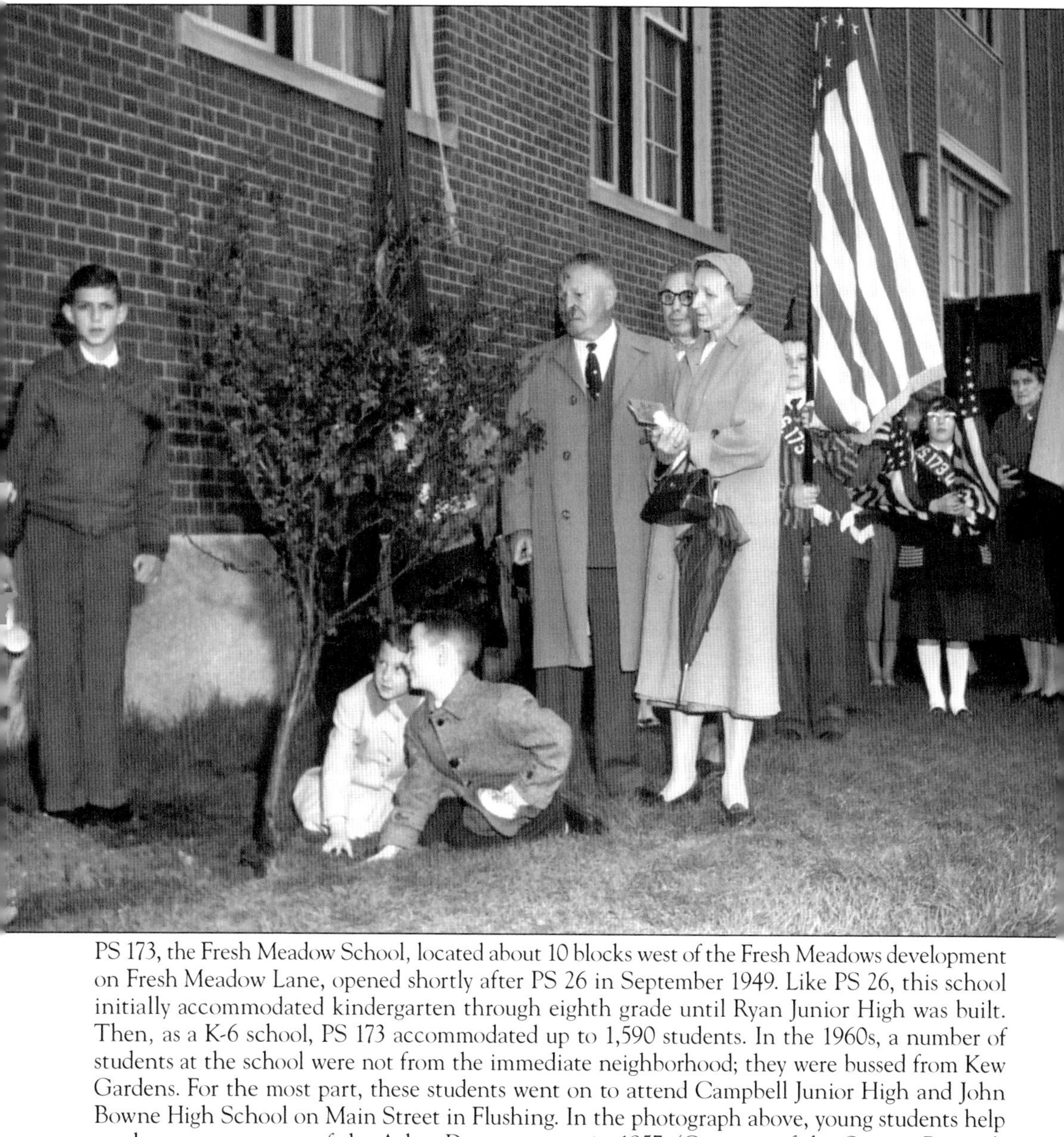

PS 173, the Fresh Meadow School, located about 10 blocks west of the Fresh Meadows development on Fresh Meadow Lane, opened shortly after PS 26 in September 1949. Like PS 26, this school initially accommodated kindergarten through eighth grade until Ryan Junior High was built. Then, as a K-6 school, PS 173 accommodated up to 1,590 students. In the 1960s, a number of students at the school were not from the immediate neighborhood; they were bussed from Kew Gardens. For the most part, these students went on to attend Campbell Junior High and John Bowne High School on Main Street in Flushing. In the photograph above, young students help to plant a tree as part of the Arbor Day ceremony in 1957. (Courtesy of the Queens Borough Public Library, Long Island Division, Illustrations Collection–Fresh Meadows.)

Students at PS 173, with their parents' permission, were allowed to go out for lunch to one of the restaurants located just one block south of the school on Fresh Meadow Lane. Among the favorite choices were two luncheonettes, Manny's and Jean & Sol's (which were then called candy stores); Ye Olde Pizza Shoppe (later Angelo's and Al's); and Sid's Kosher Delicatessen. Sid, as he was known to all of the kids, served in the US Army in Europe during World War II and is seen at right with his wife, Edna, in 1964. At the time, a kid could get a Hebrew National hot dog, French fries, and a Dr. Brown's soda for less than a dollar. Below is the sixth-grade graduation photograph of Edna Goldschlager's class in 1966. (Above, courtesy of Debra Davidson; below, courtesy of Louise Covitt.)

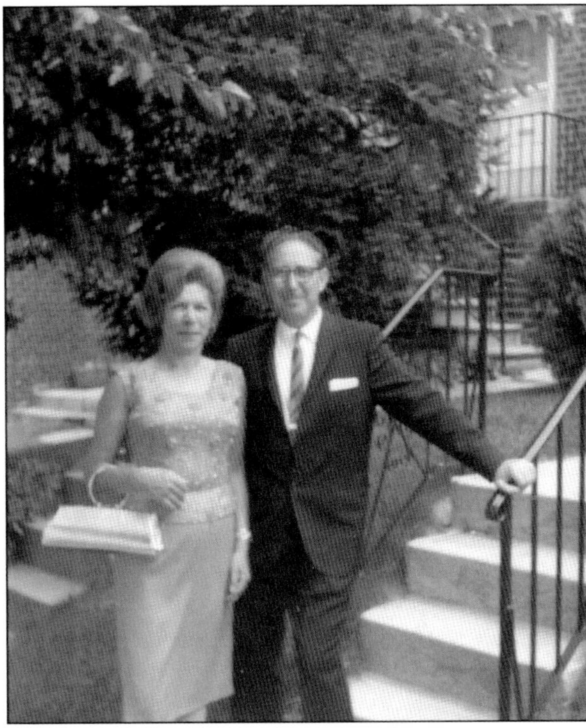

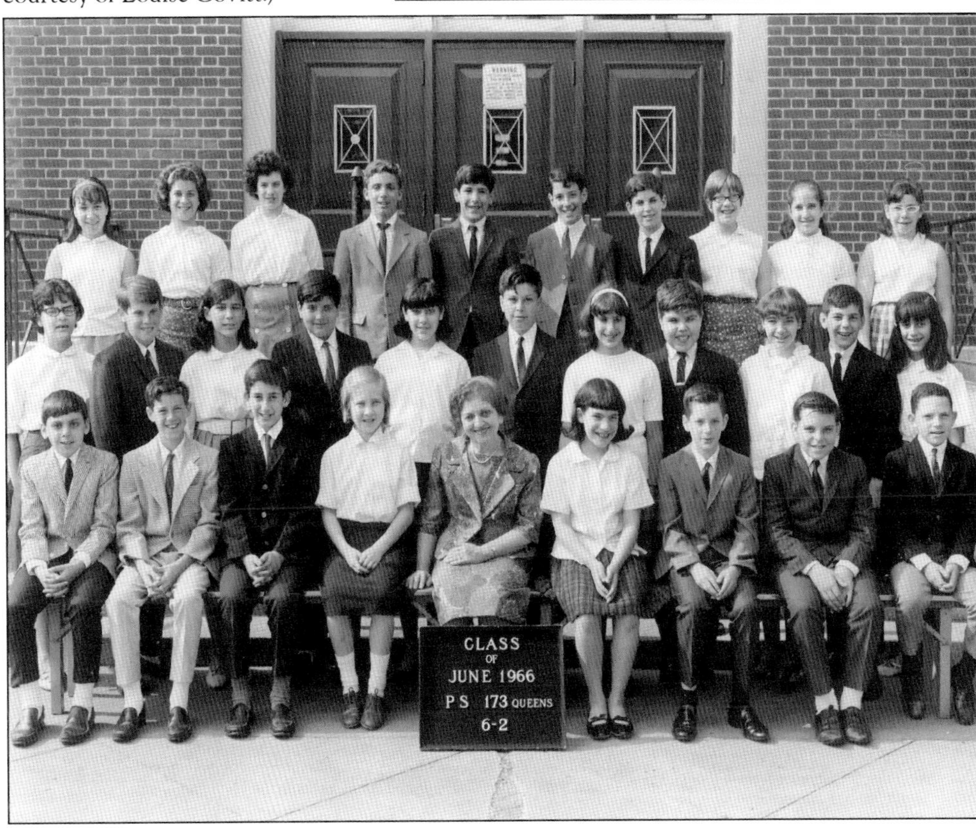

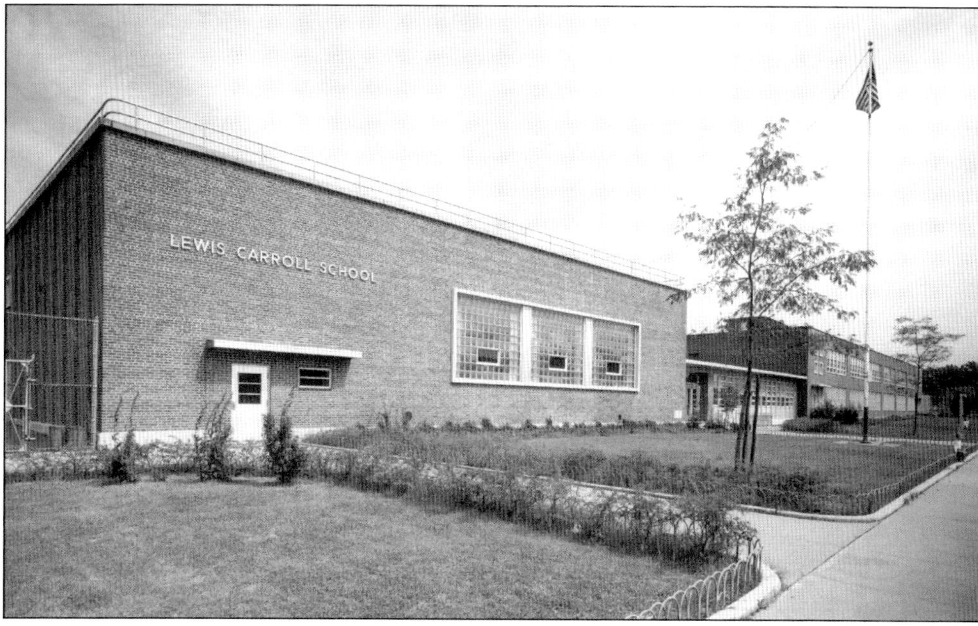

To alleviate the overcrowding at PS 26, the NYC Board of Education established a new school, the Lewis Carroll School, PS 179. Initial plans were to locate the school on 185th Street between Horace Harding Boulevard and 64th Avenue, but the school was ultimately constructed in early 1955 at the intersection of Horace Harding Boulevard and Peck Avenue. (Courtesy of New York Life Insurance Company Archives.)

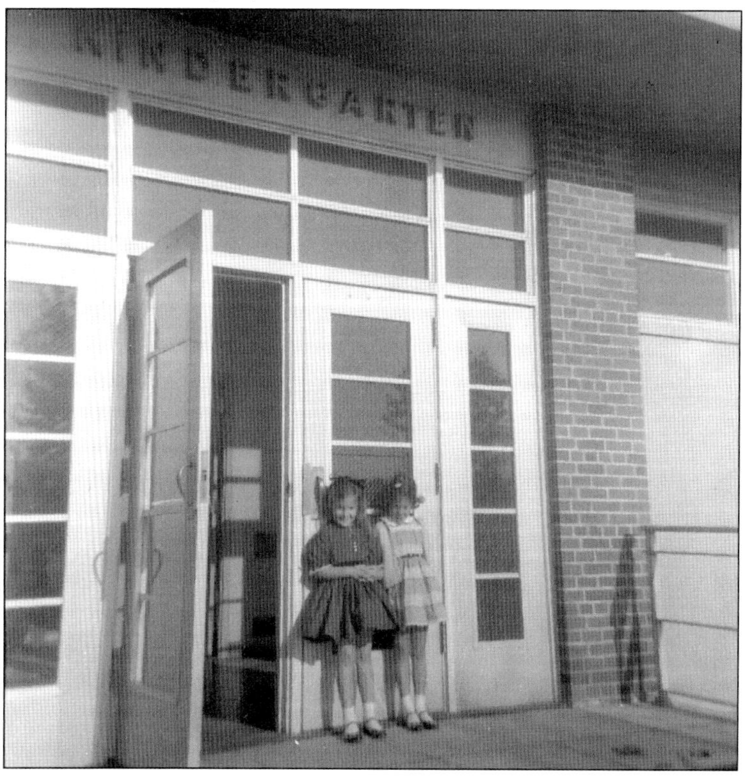

PS 179 was a much smaller school than either PS 26 or PS 173, having a capacity of only 727 students. The school featured a separate entrance for the youngest students. At left are Cynthia Kahn (left) and Erica Goldberg on their first day of kindergarten in 1960. (Courtesy of Erica Goldberg Blau.)

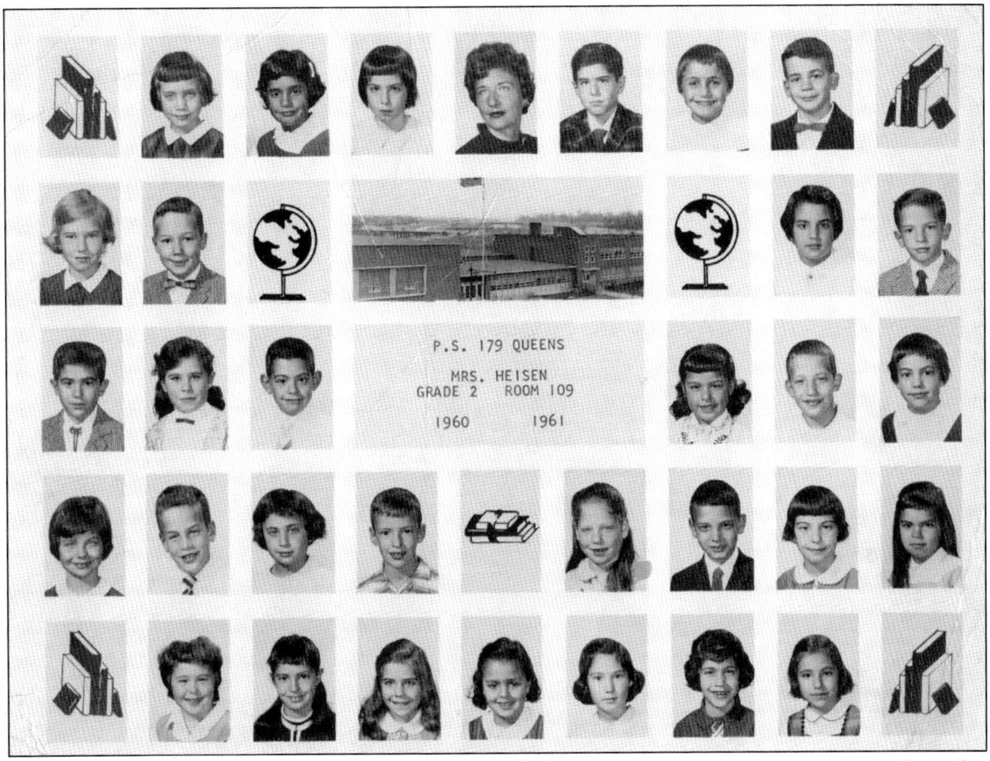

The smaller size of the Lewis Carroll School made for a more intimate environment than the other neighborhood schools. With half the number of students of both PS 26 and PS 173, it was possible for a student to know virtually every child in his or her grade. Two members of the custodial staff, Pedro and Georgina Rodriguez, were beloved by many students in the 1950s and 1960s. Above is Mrs. Heisen's second grade class in 1961. Below is Mrs. Donow's first-grade class in 1956. (Above, courtesy of Fred Cantor; below, courtesy of Steve Dorff.)

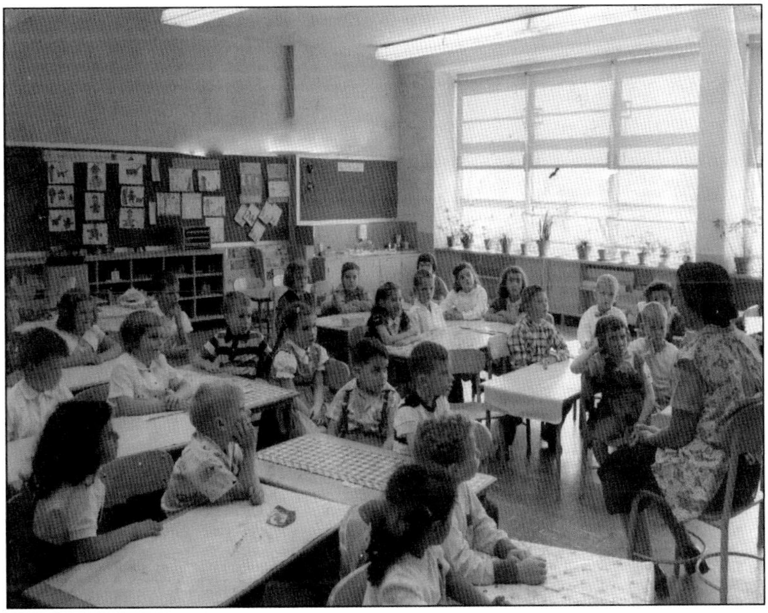

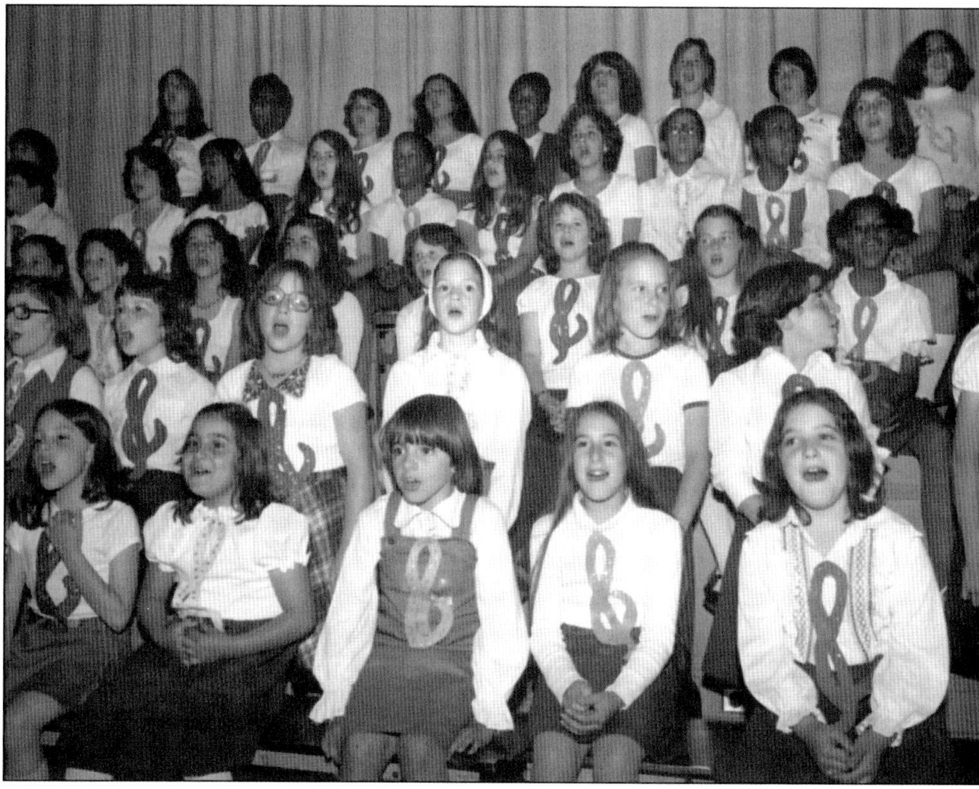

There were many highlights of the school year, including dance festivals, talent shows, spelling bees, science fairs, and class plays. One very memorable incident involved a class performance at PS 179 in the late 1950s in which one of the parents attending was actor Paul Newman. Legend has it that Newman stood in the rear of the auditorium to avoid causing a distraction. The unintended result was many mothers missing much of the performance as they craned their necks to get a glimpse of the handsome actor. Above is a performance of the PS 173 glee club in 1978, and below is the PS 179 rhythm band rehearsing in the late 1950s. (Above, courtesy of the *Queens Tribune* and the Queens Borough Public Library, Long Island Division, Joseph A. Ullman Photographs; below, courtesy of Fred Cantor.)

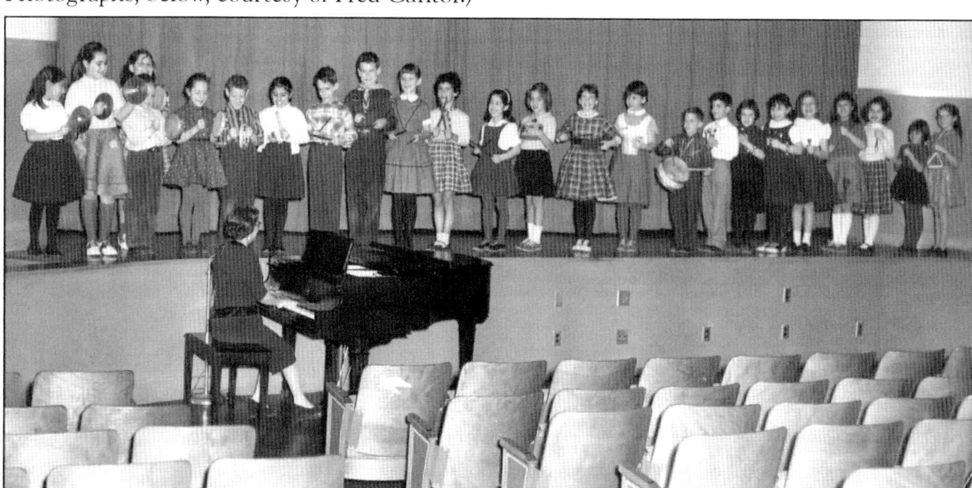

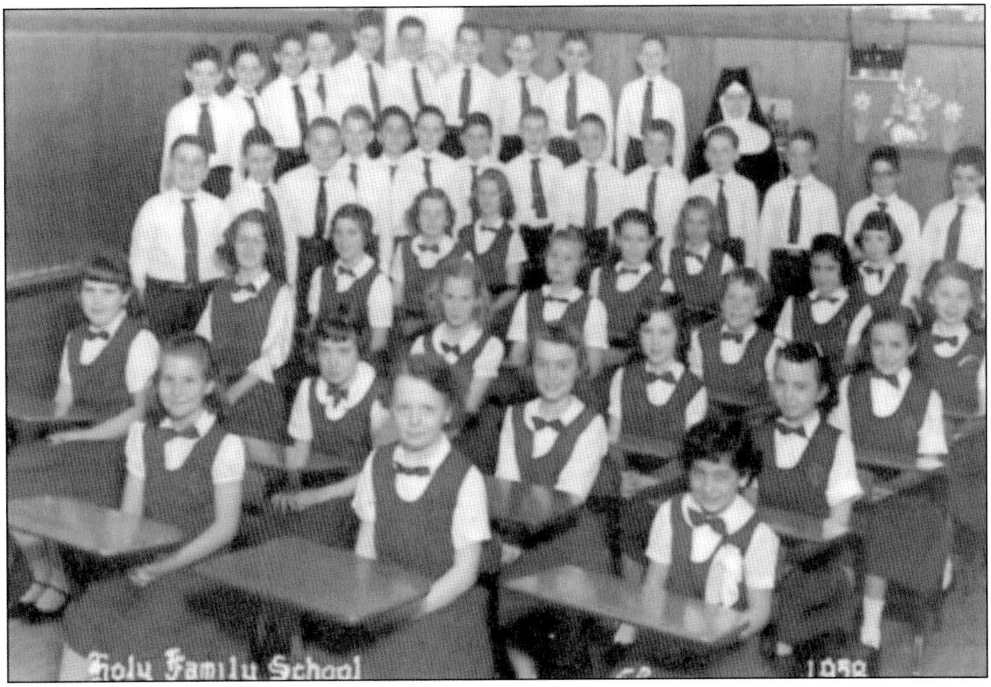

In addition to the public schools, two Catholic schools served the area. The Holy Family School, which students attended for kindergarten through the eighth grade, was located just west of Utopia Parkway at 74th Avenue. Bishop Edmund J. Reilly High School was adjacent to PS 179 at the corner of Francis Lewis and Horace Harding Boulevards. Some public school students were dismissed early one afternoon a week so they could attend religious instruction at Holy Family. Above is a fifth-grade class at Holy Family School in 1958, and below is Bishop Reilly High School. (Above, courtesy of Carol Kolinger; below, courtesy of New York Life Insurance Company Archives.)

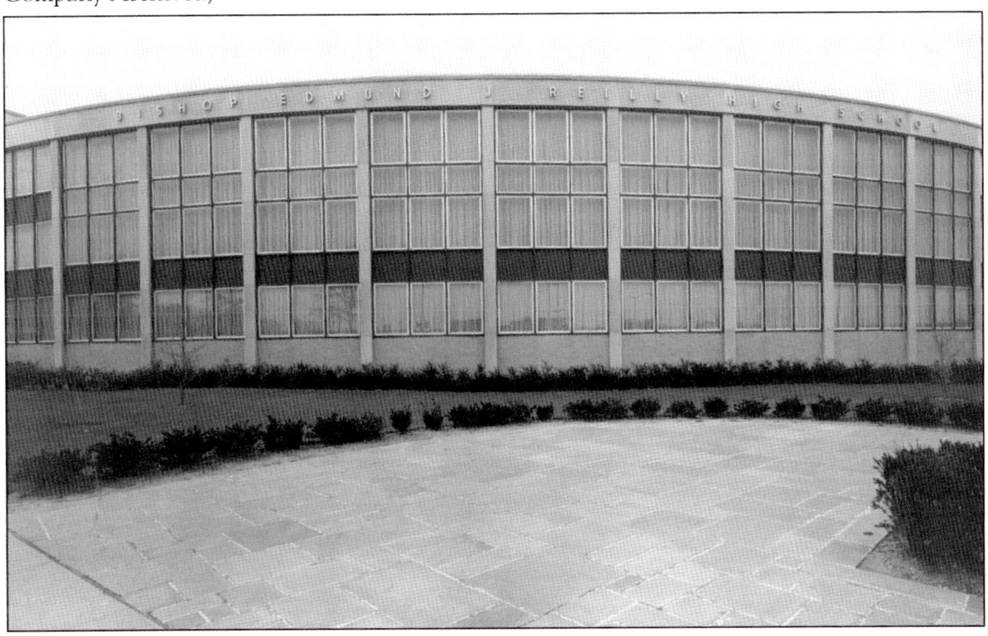

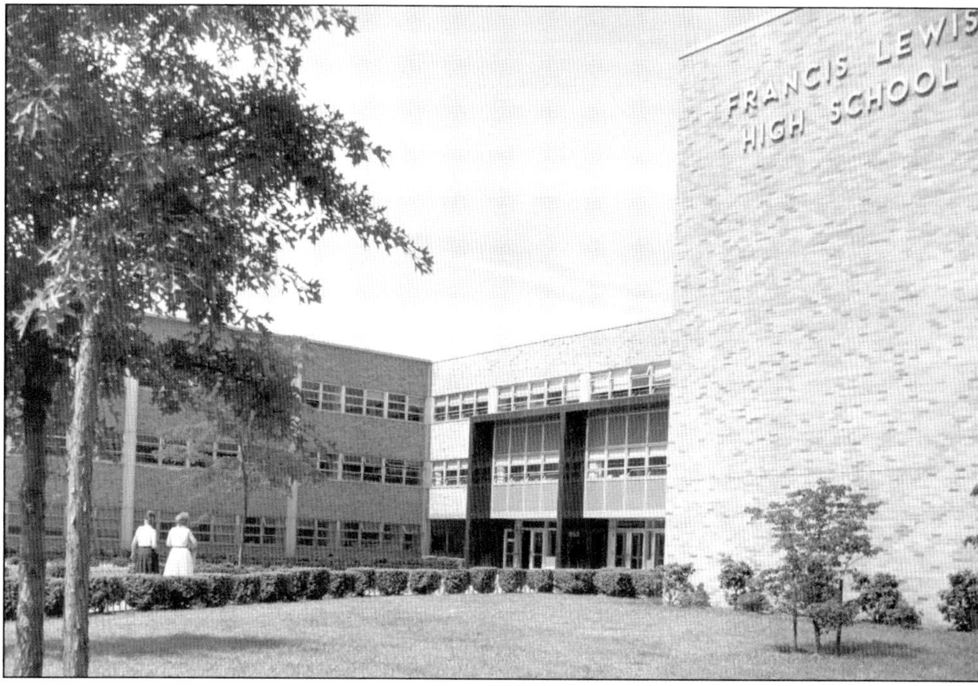

Francis Lewis High School opened in 1960, just as the oldest baby boomers were ready for high school, and graduated its first class in 1963. Almost immediately, the school was filled beyond capacity, necessitating double and triple sessions to accommodate the excess student population. The overcrowding ended with the opening of Benjamin N. Cardozo High School in Bayside in 1967. A favorite hangout of Francis Lewis students was the Island Diner located at the intersection of Utopia Parkway and Horace Harding Boulevard. Below, Laurie Meckler and Leo Baumohl are crossing Utopia Parkway on their way to the diner in the early 1970s. (Above, courtesy of New York Life Insurance Company Archives; below, courtesy of Steven Quat.)

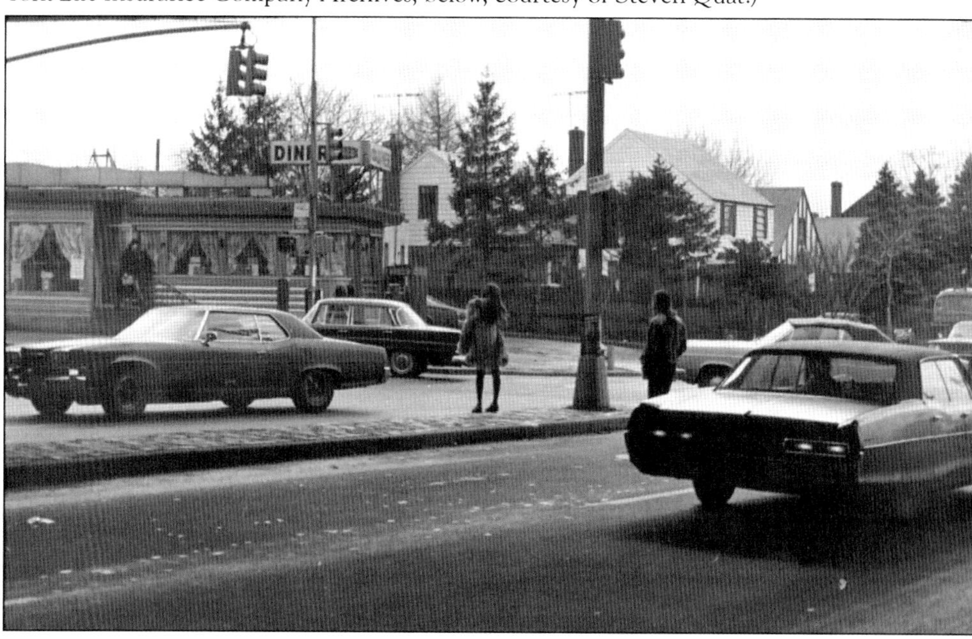

Three

Events and Special Occasions

Life in Fresh Meadows during the postwar years was a unique blend of urban and suburban living. With Manhattan just a bus and subway ride away, residents of Fresh Meadows could easily access the museums, theaters, and other cultural institutions of New York City. Unlike their suburban counterparts, teenagers were not dependent upon automobiles to have a social life, and younger children could walk to a nearby store to purchase baseball cards, comic books, and bubble gum.

Yet, one of the things that made Fresh Meadows special was that it often seemed like a small town with its local events and traditions. Each major holiday brought its own set of traditions to Fresh Meadows, from Christmas carolers in a horse-drawn carriage to the annual Little League parades. In many ways, Mayberry, the town made famous on *The Andy Griffith Show*, had nothing on Fresh Meadows.

Of course, not every event was a positive one. For many New Yorkers who were not familiar with the borough of Queens, their first introduction to Fresh Meadows was when Fresh Meadows made headlines as the "poster child" for the areas of Queens woefully neglected in the aftermath of the blizzard of 1969. Mayor John V. Lindsay's reception when he visited to inspect the situation is often cited as a catalyst in the demise of his political career. It was not until 40 years later when St. Francis Prep was ground zero for the swine flu epidemic that Fresh Meadows would be so prominently in the news again.

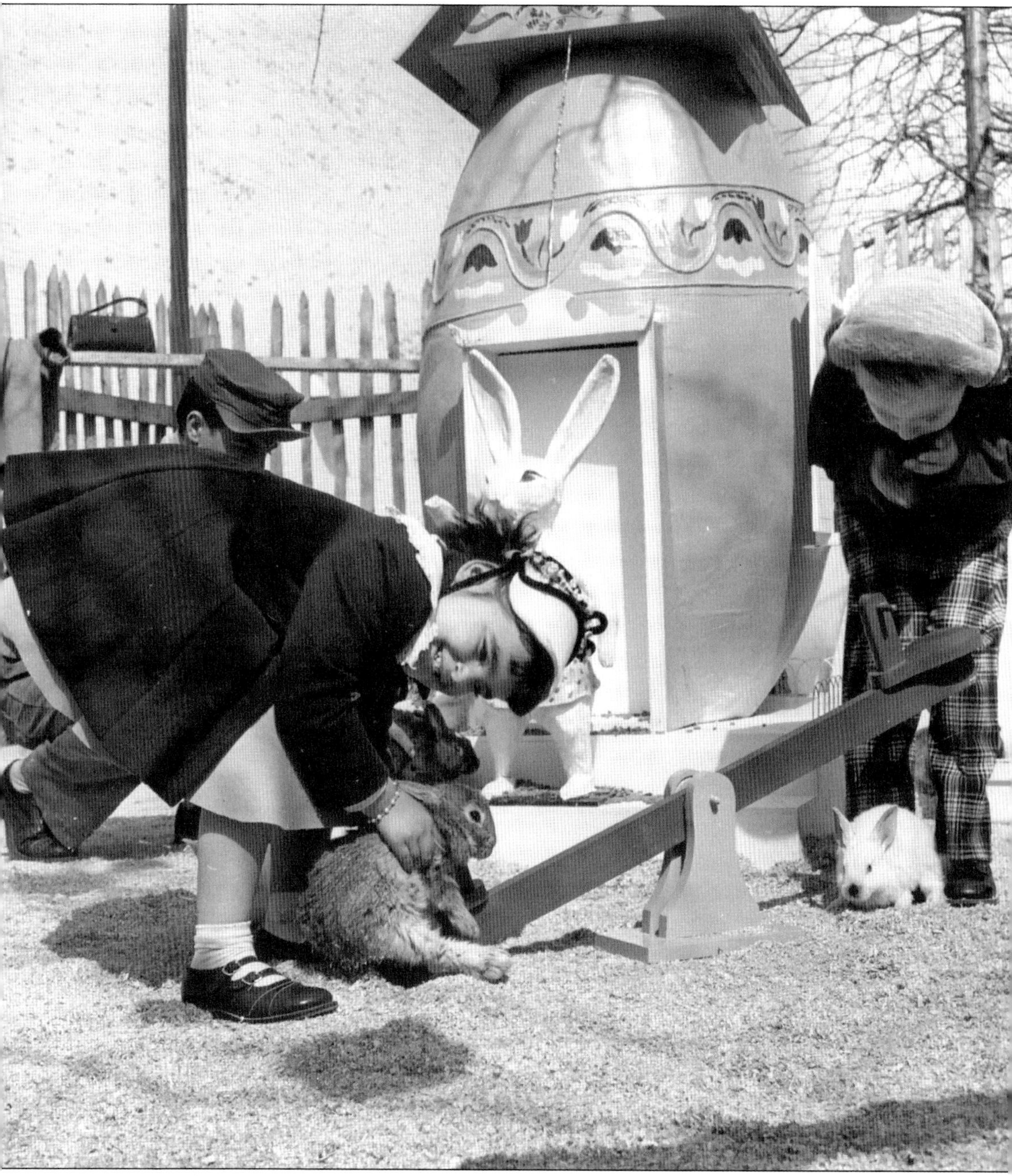

For two weeks in 1955, the Fresh Meadows Merchants Association and the New York Life Insurance Company delighted the children of Fresh Meadows by hosting a pre-Easter event. Children were able to feed carrots to 24 baby rabbits in an outdoor enclosure called Easter Bunny Town. The *New York Times* noted "Trees in the enclosure bore strange fruit—pink, yellow, and blue plastic eggs." Above, little girls help the rabbits negotiate the seesaw. In the background is a four-foot-high lavender egg-shaped rabbit house. (Courtesy of New York Life Insurance Company Archives; photograph by Jerry Saltsberg & Associates.)

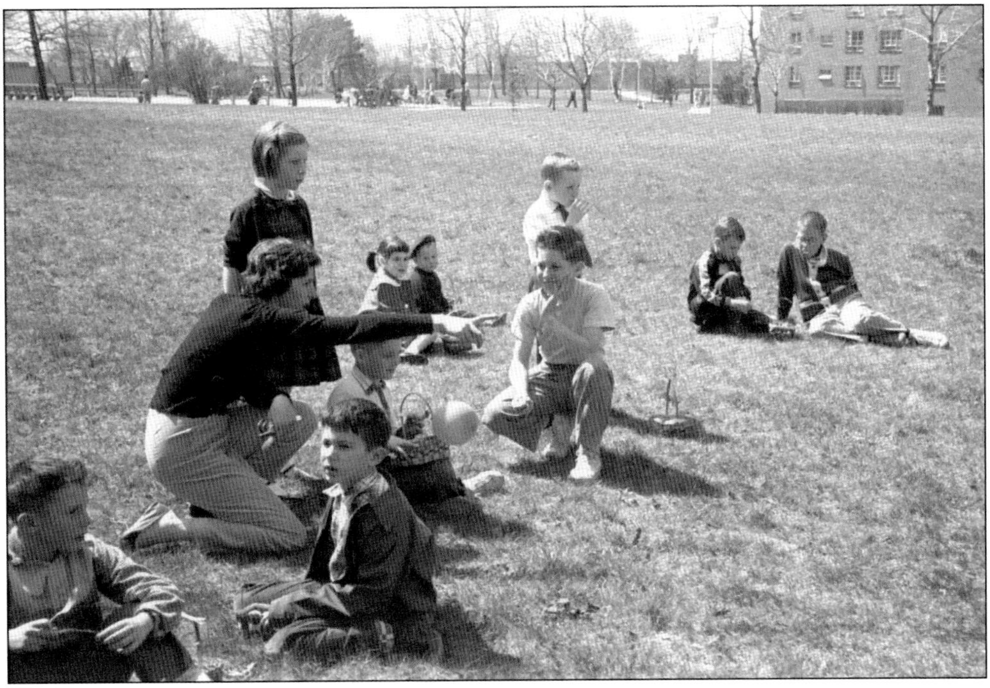

Easter egg hunts were a natural in the vast grassy areas. Above, Bea Pollock helps neighborhood children strategize for optimal egg collection in the mid-1950s. Below, Mitchell Kaften (white shirt) and a group of kids begin the dash to find eggs in the shadow of one of the 13-story buildings. (Both, courtesy of Mitchell Kaften; photographs by Douglas Kaften.)

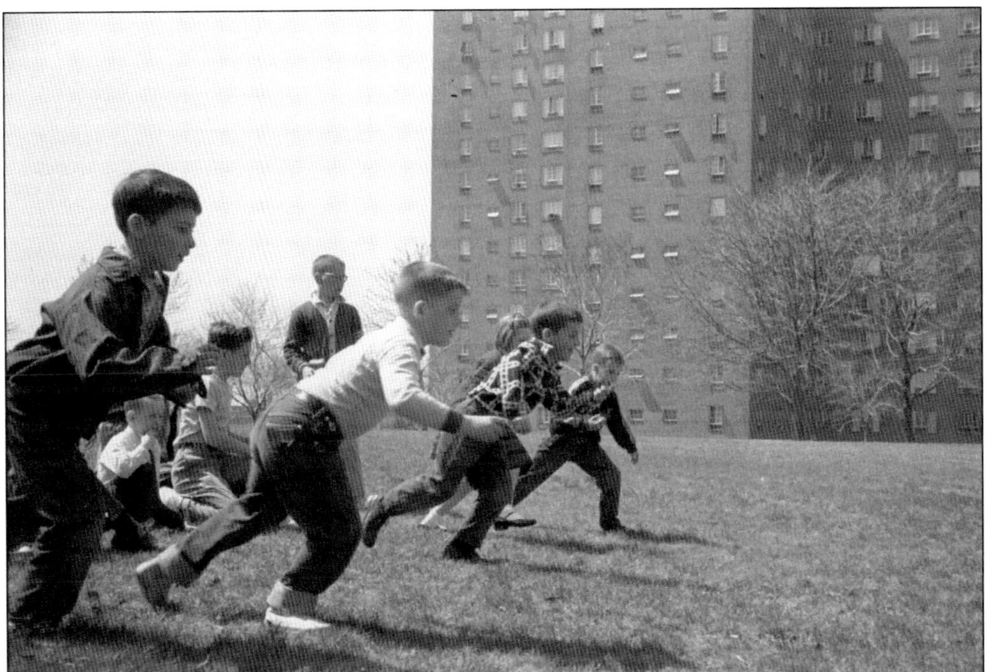

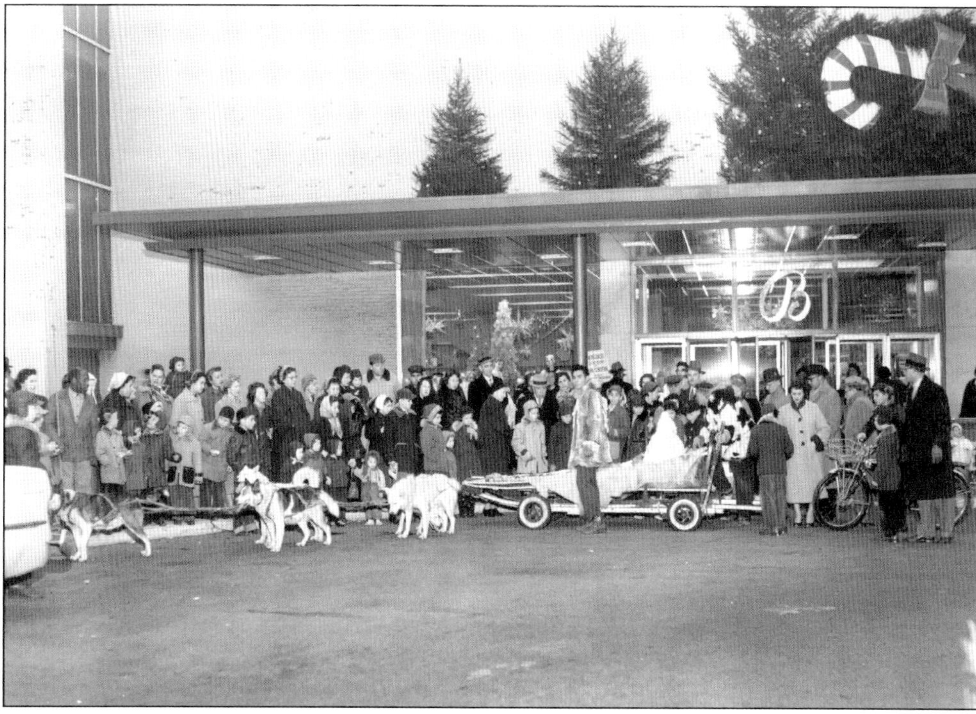

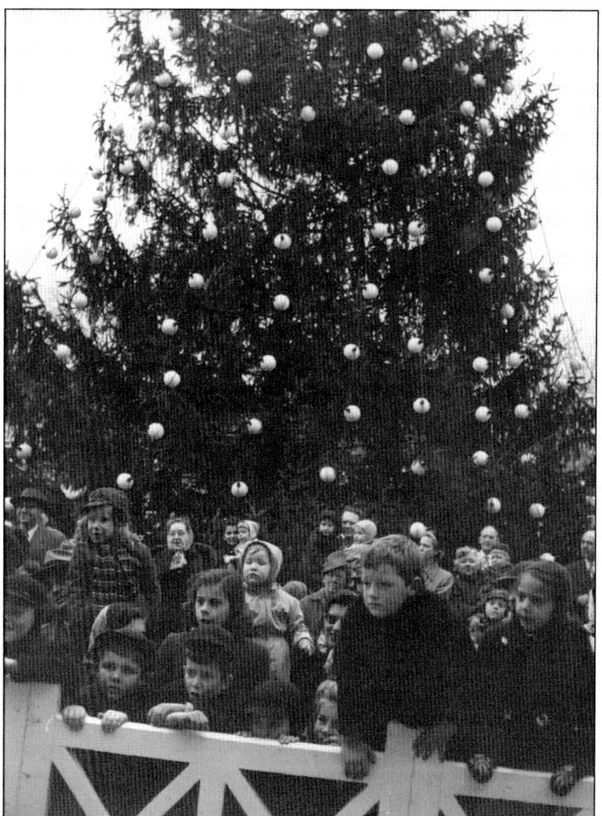

During the Christmas holidays the Fresh Meadows Merchants Association organized many special events. The day after Thanksgiving, Santa would arrive at Bloomingdale's. Ceremonies that evening would include the switching on of the lights in the store windows as well as the lighting of the Christmas tree. An advertisement by the merchants association from 1950 described a presentation of *The Night Before Christmas* as well as the promise of celebrities joining the festivities. Before the Long Island Expressway (LIE) was built, the tree lighting took place in the park on the north side of Bloomingdale's. Once construction of the LIE began, the tree lighting moved to the circle on 188th Street at 64th Avenue. (Above, courtesy of New York Life Insurance Company Archives; left, courtesy of Queens Fresh Meadows LLC. Both photographs by Jerry Saltsberg & Associates.)

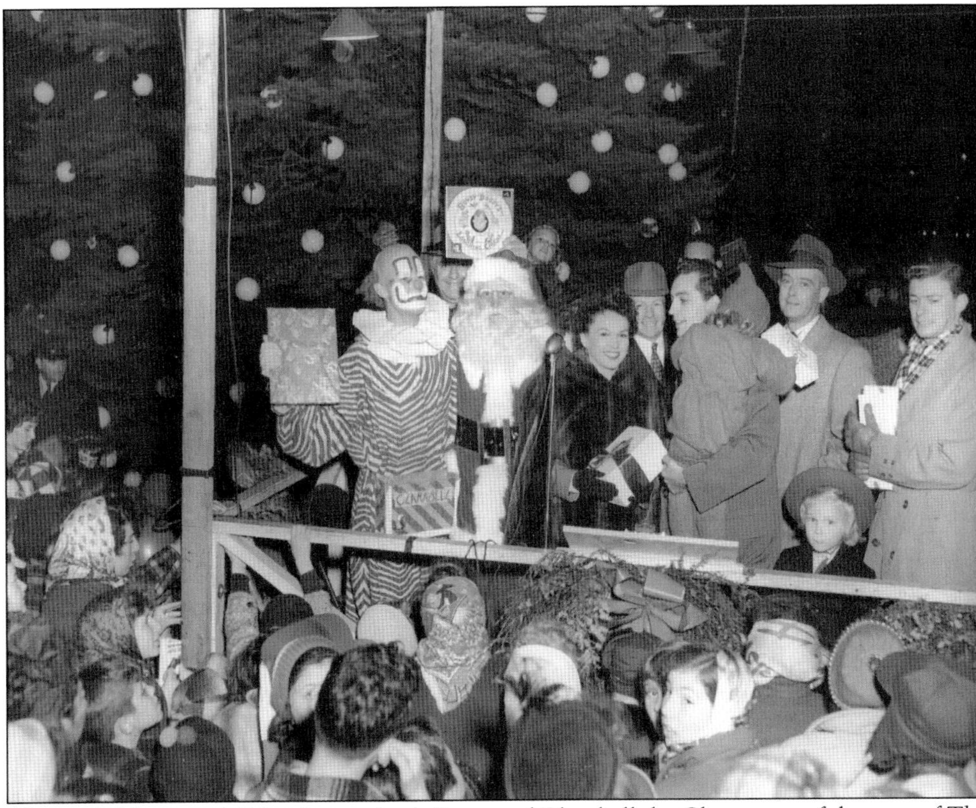

Above, children are delighted to see both Santa and Clarabell the Clown, one of the stars of *The Howdy Doody Show,* at the tree-lighting ceremony. Beginning in 1948, a horse-drawn quartet of Dickens carolers made its rounds through Fresh Meadows each holiday season. (Both, courtesy of Queens Fresh Meadows LLC; photographs by Jerry Saltsberg & Associates.)

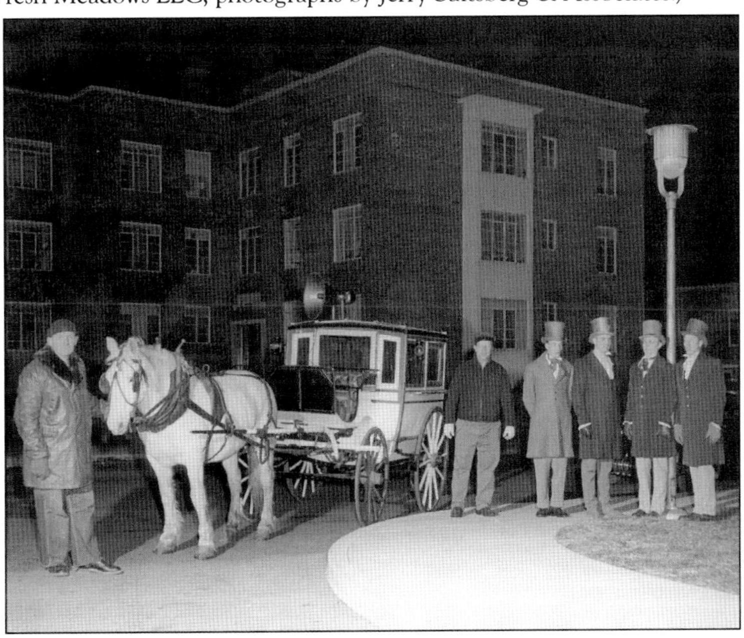

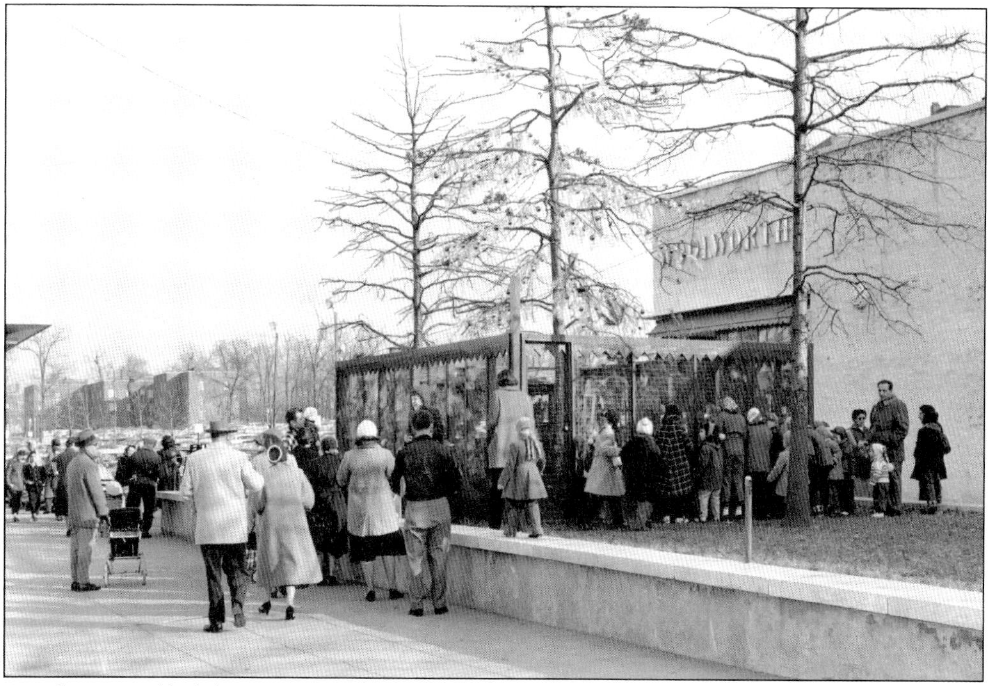

Another annual holiday event was a petting zoo situated in the public square between Bloomingdale's and Woolworth's. Children enjoyed interacting with deer, sheep, llamas, and donkeys. (Both, courtesy of Queens Fresh Meadows LLC; photographs by Jerry Saltsberg & Associates.)

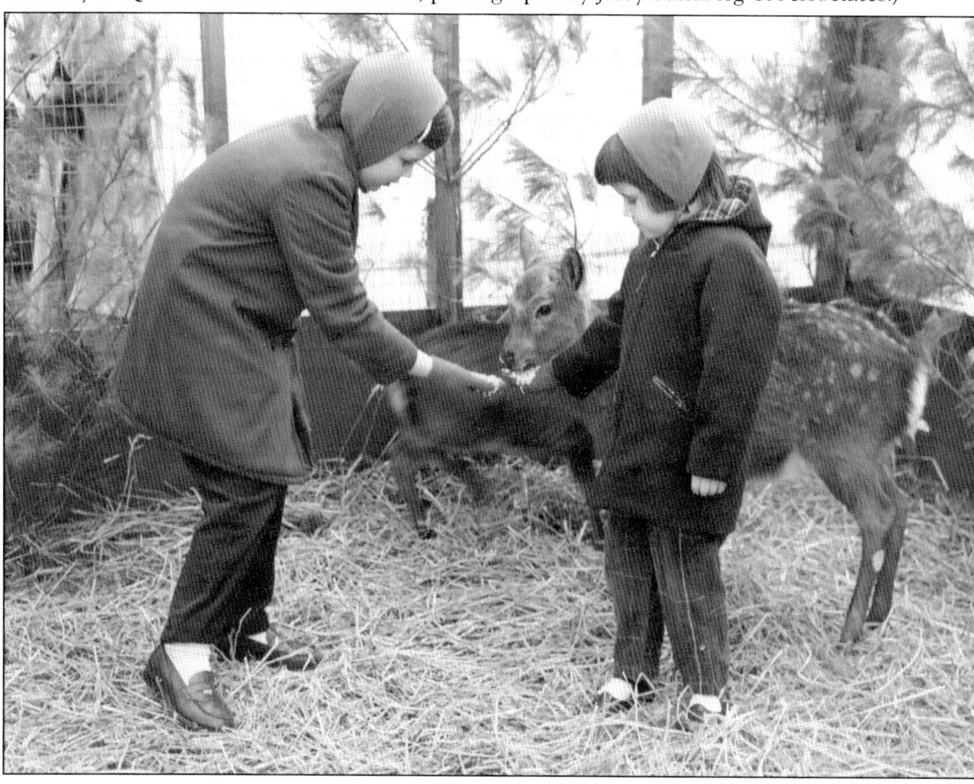

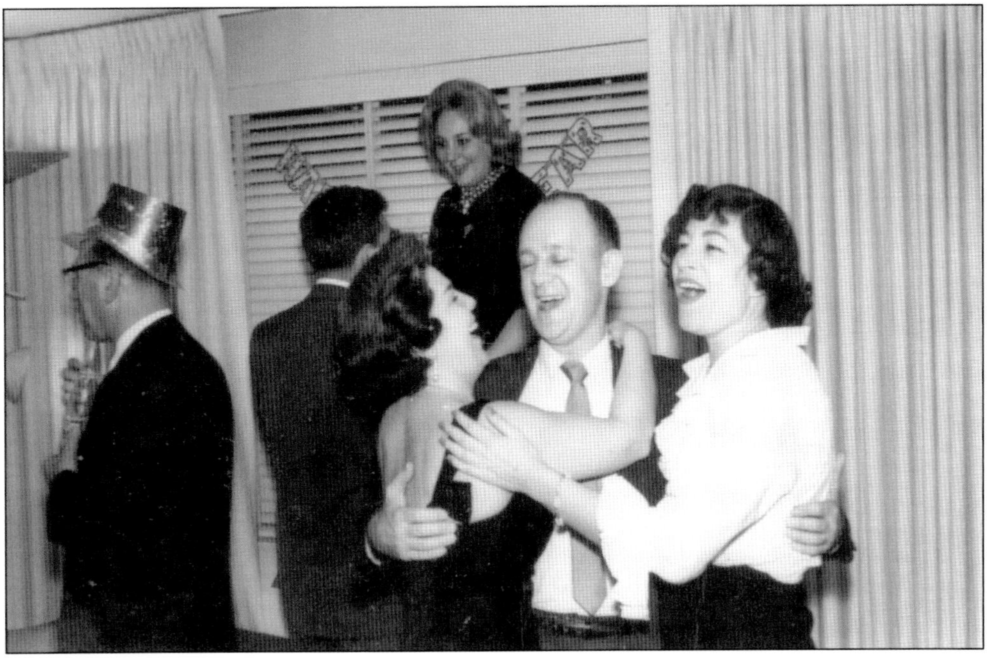

The end of the holiday season brought New Year's Eve celebrations, such as this party in the home of Doris and Bill Weissler. Celebrating in the foreground from left to right are Nancy and Nate Kelne with Doris Weissler. In the background are two unidentified men and Jane Merson. (Courtesy of Doris Weissler.)

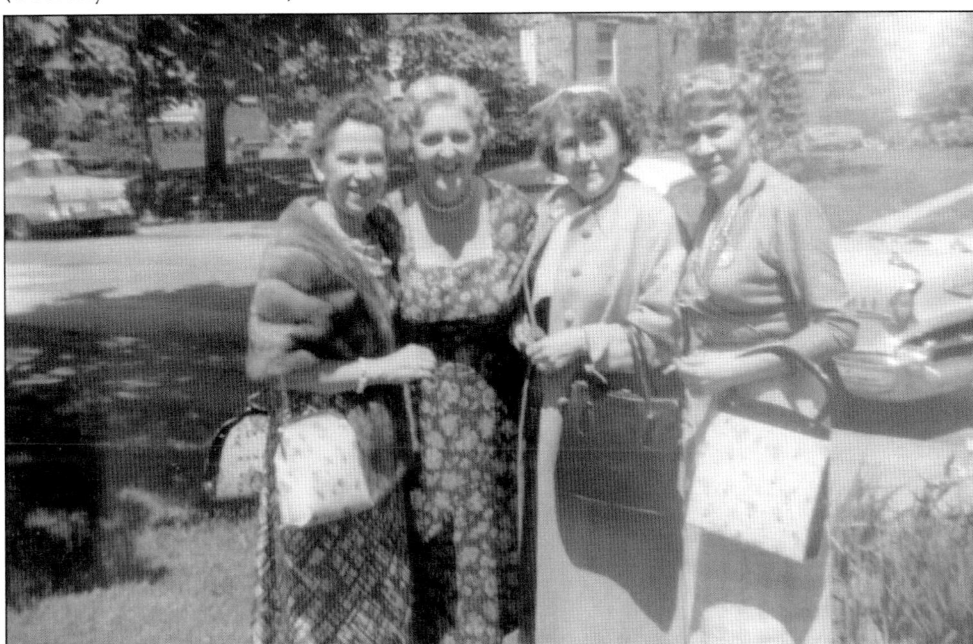

Springtime brought confirmations and graduations. On 179th Street just north of Union Turnpike, sisters Jo Lehan (left) and Mae Callahan (right), along with friends Ruth McGregor (second from left) and Connie Galeski, gather to attend the confirmation of Jo and Mae's daughters at Holy Family Roman Catholic Church in 1958. (Courtesy of Carol Kolinger.)

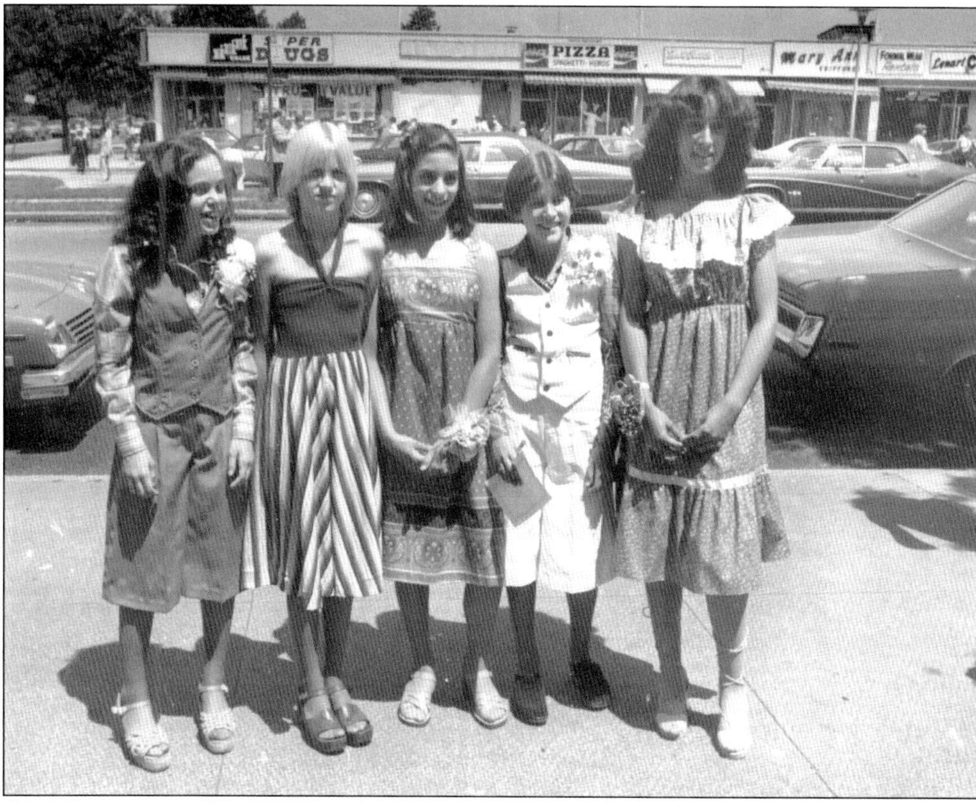

Graduations were always a time of celebration. Here, from left to right, are Pamela Dein, Inta Balgalvis, Elizabeth Russo, Jill Bloom, and Sandy Packer at their graduation from PS 26 in 1977. In the background, one can see the evolution of the 69th Avenue Shopping Center with Tru Value Drugs and the Fresh Meadows Pizzeria where Crest Chemists and Wyetzner's Deli had once been. (Courtesy of Aina Balgalvis.)

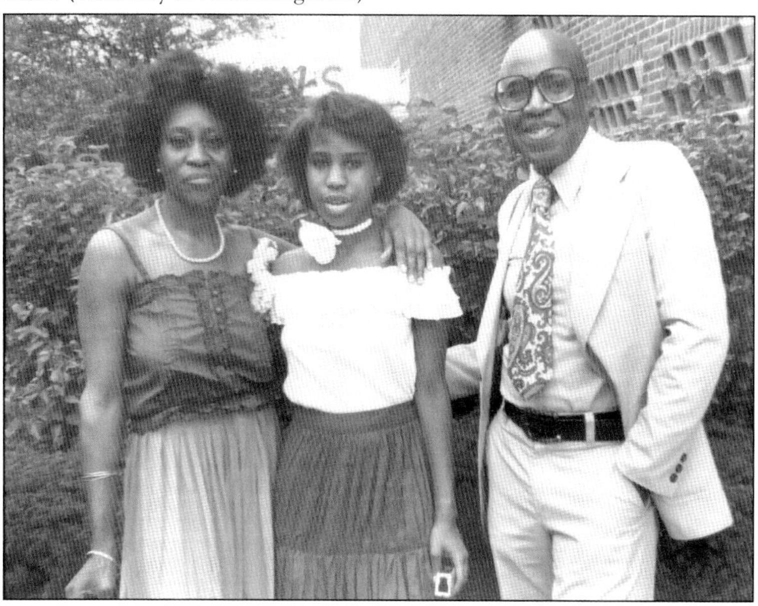

George J. Ryan Junior High School held graduation ceremonies at the Century Meadows Theater for many years. At left, Kim Huey celebrates with her parents, Charlotte Huey and Dr. Charles Huey, in 1978. Charlotte was a popular teacher at Francis Lewis High School in the 1970s. (Courtesy of Aina Balgalvis.)

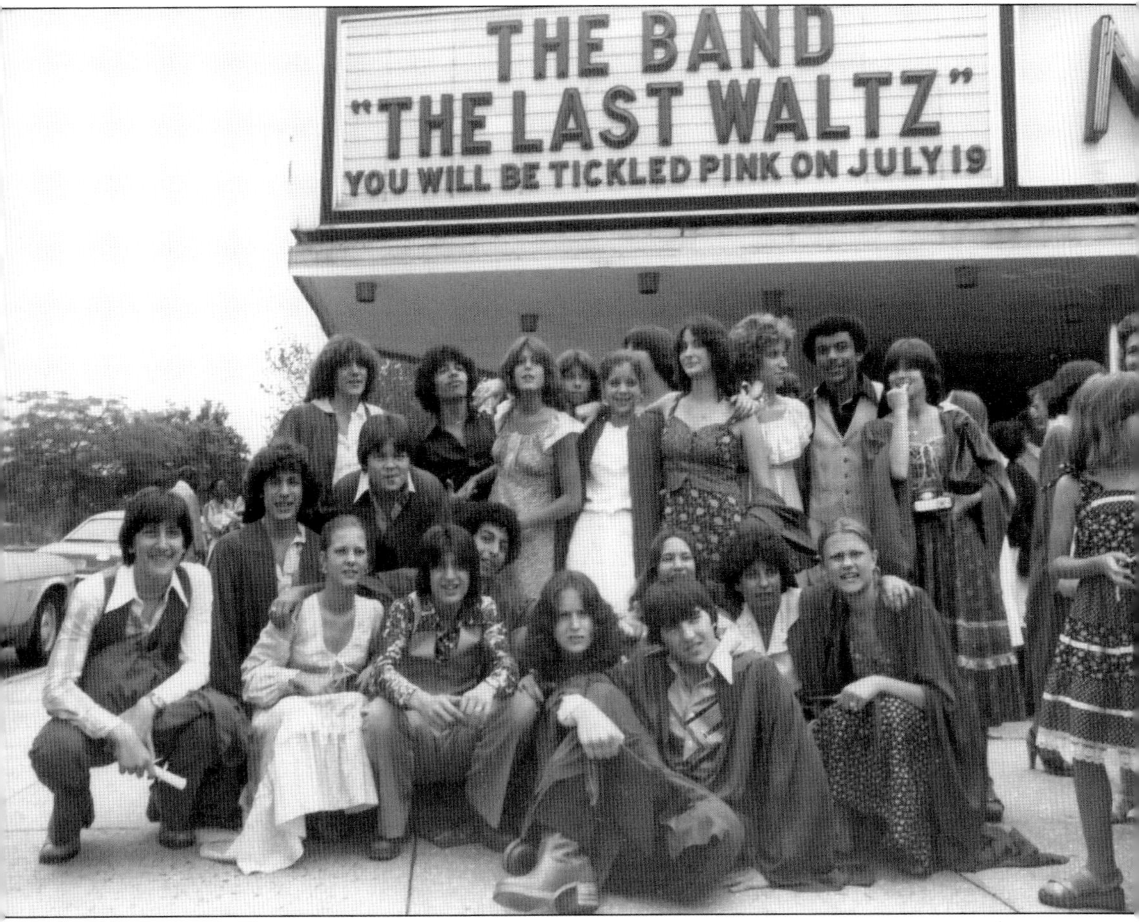

Members of the George J. Ryan class of 1978 posed under the marquee of the Century Meadows Theater, which was featuring the film *The Last Waltz* at the time. That title was very apropos as this would be the last time some of these students would be together. Graduates went on to several different schools, primarily Francis Lewis and Jamaica high schools. It would also be the last time Ryan would hold a graduation at the theater. In the following months, the large theater was divided in half to become a twin theater whose auditoriums were no longer large enough to accommodate Ryan graduates. From left to right are (kneeling) Steven Gugick, Jeff Haber, Chris Weiss, Harold Jannen, Kenny Beers, Michael Antar, Amie Fishman, Sal Echel, Laura Gewurz, Sondra Seiden, and Ieva Balgalvis; (standing) Denise Teller, Francis Agostini, Chriss Fuchs, Dianne Blancato, Lynne Bloom, Debbie Siskind, Gale Gelayder, Susan Levine, Raul Valentin, and Laurie Lazarus. (Courtesy of Aina Balgalvis.)

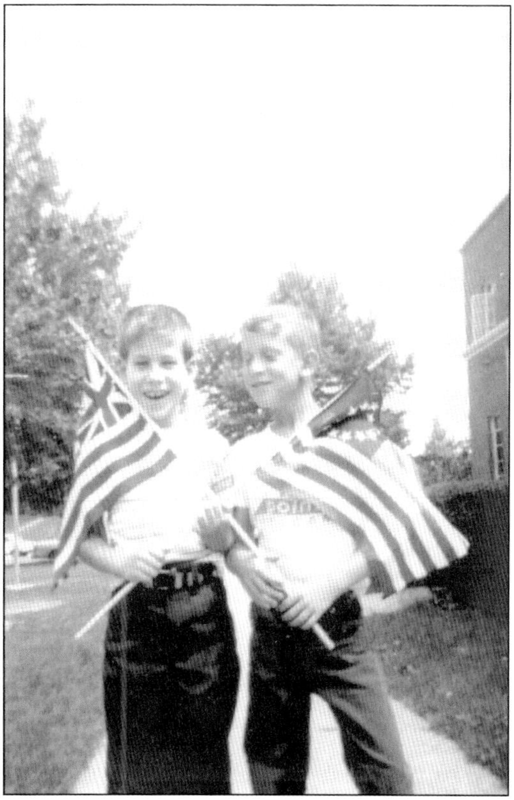

Independence Day brought celebrations as well. At left, Larry Saltzman and Marc Schneider are waving the British and US flags in 1962. The 1976 bicentennial celebration was the occasion for a parade along 71st Crescent. Tracey Hayes (center) twirls her baton alongside neighborhood girls. (Left, courtesy of Barry Schneider; below, courtesy of Tracey Hayes Justin.)

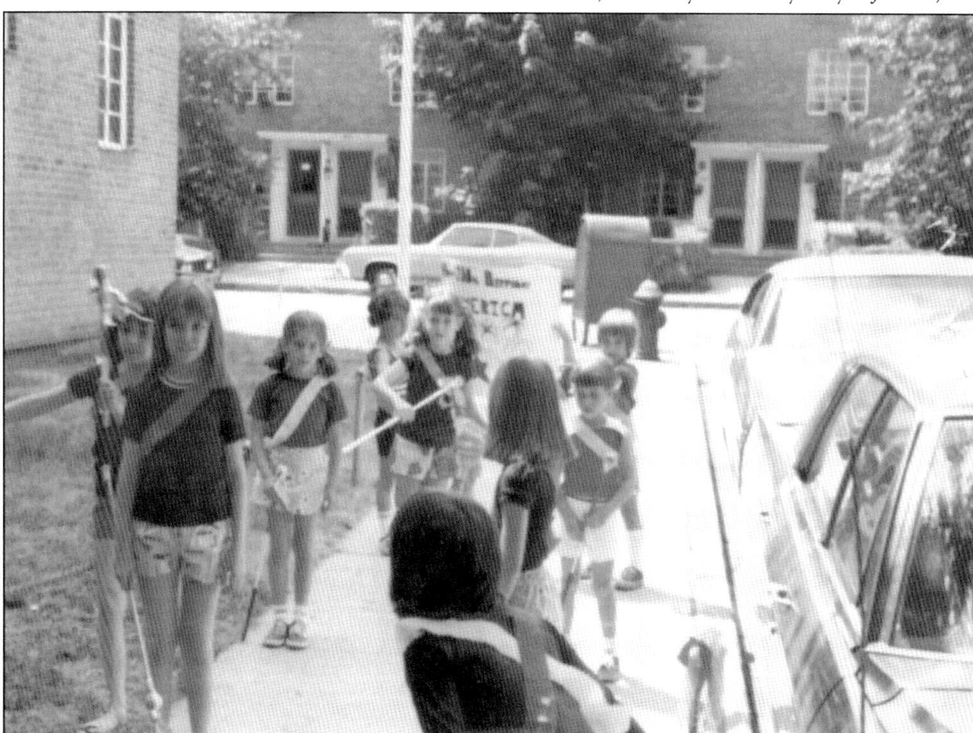

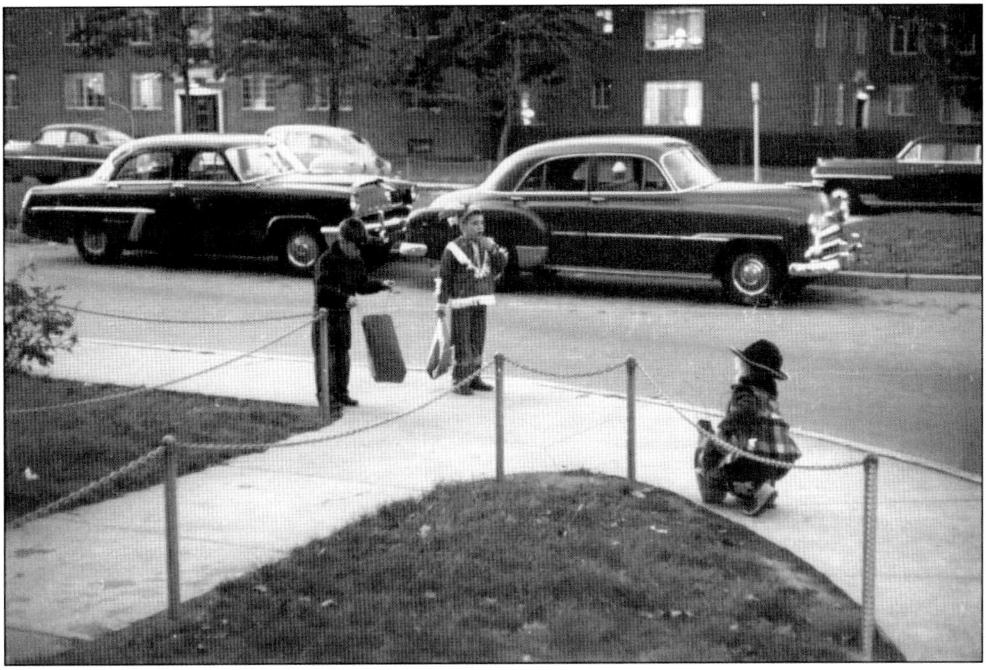

Any occasion to dress up in costumes was embraced by the children of Fresh Meadows. Former residents revel in Halloween memories of scores of children roaming every block with no adult chaperones needed. Above, from left to right, Mitchell Kaften, David Nimkin, and Scott Hewitt trick-or-treat near 64th Circle in the mid-1950s. Right, on 67th Avenue, Audrey Goldberg is dressed for the Jewish holiday of Purim, with her sister Erica, in 1959. (Above, courtesy of Mitchell Kaften; photograph by Douglas Kaften; right, courtesy of Erica Goldberg Blau.)

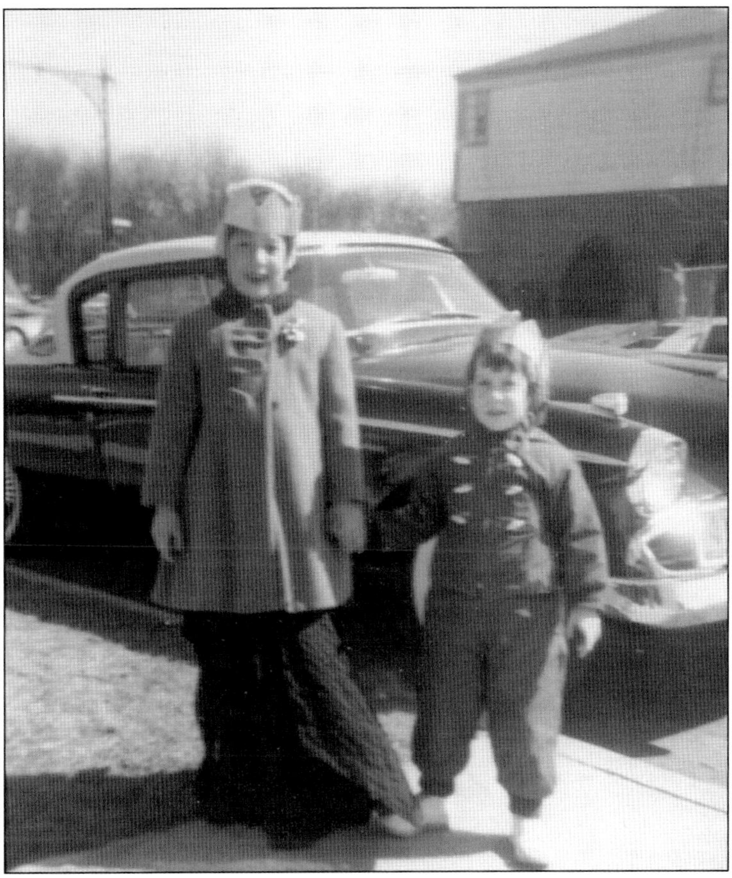

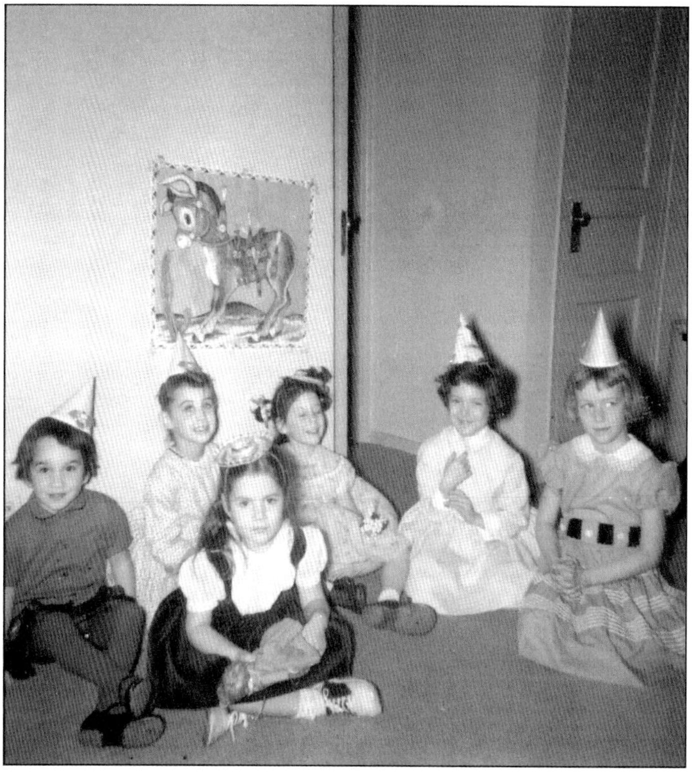

Birthday parties were simpler affairs in the 1950s, 1960s, and 1970s. At left, Erica Goldberg celebrates her fourth birthday in 1959 with a party at home that included the quintessential children's party game, Pin the Tail on the Donkey. Present are, from left to right, two unidentified, Cynthia Kahn, Erica Goldberg, Lynne Weinstein, and Linda Lee Wolfe. Below, Andrea Harris's backyard birthday party on 192nd Street off 73rd Avenue in the 1970s included a game of musical chairs. (Left, courtesy of Erica Goldberg Blau; below, courtesy of Edna and Bob Harris.)

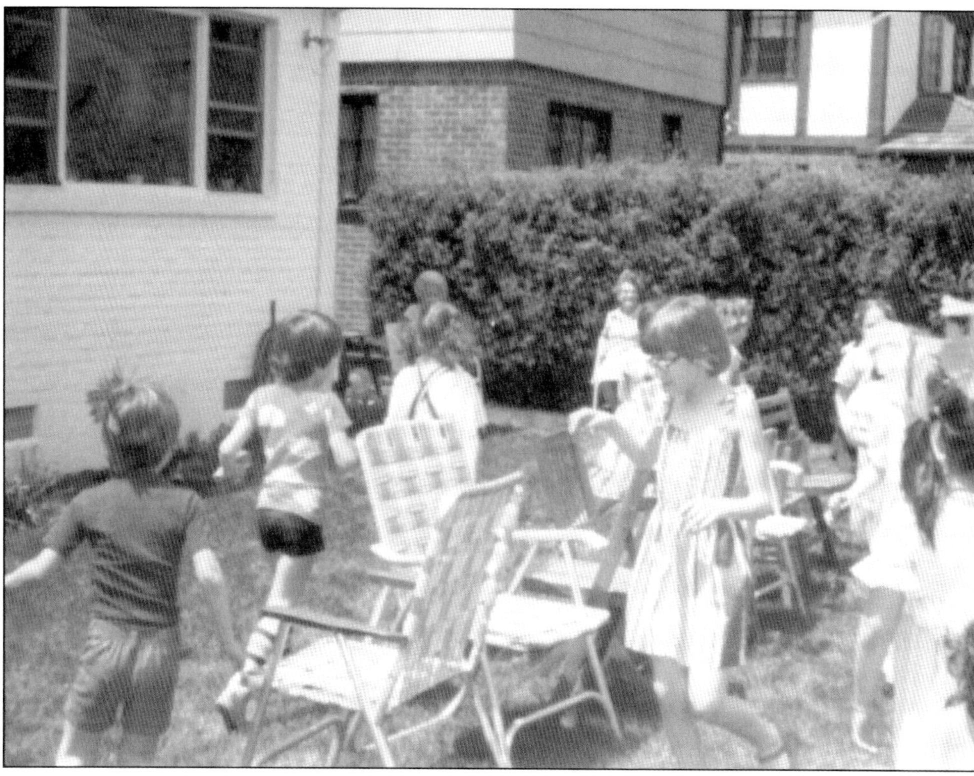

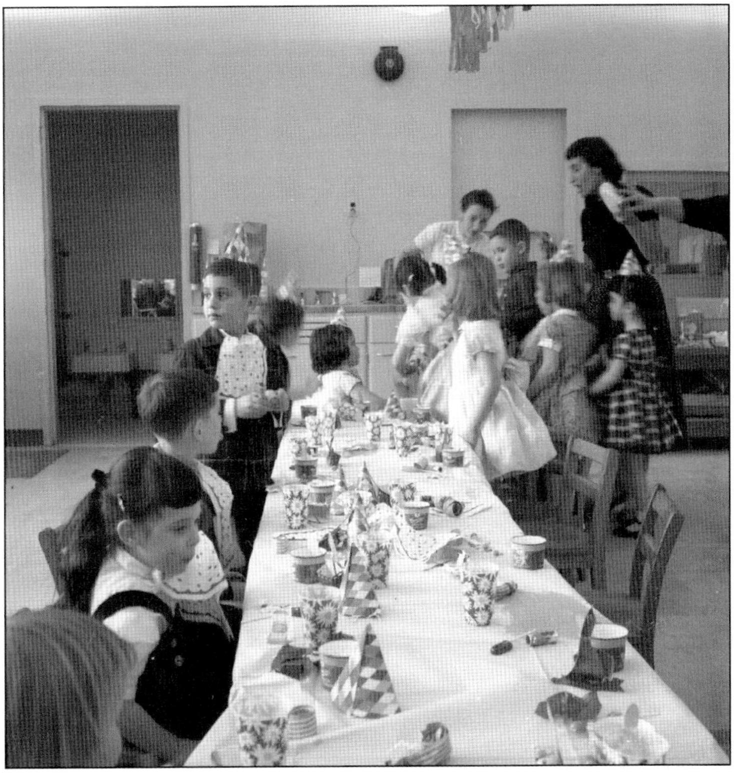

Jane Kaften, at the head of the table, celebrates her birthday in the mid-1950s with a party at the Fresh Meadows Nursery School. The entertainment included cartoon movies projected onto an easel. (Both, courtesy of Mitchell Kaften; photographs by Douglas Kaften.)

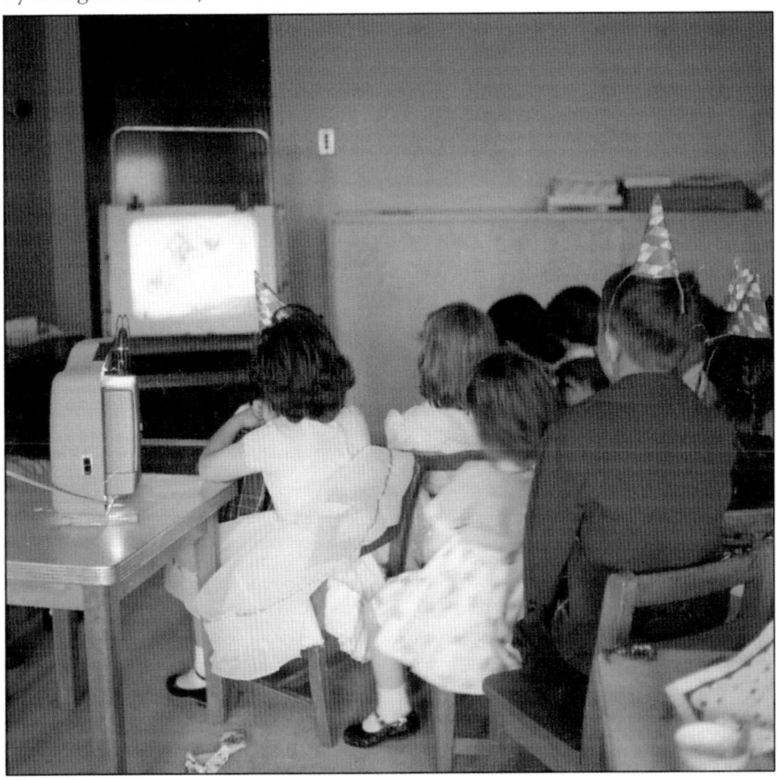

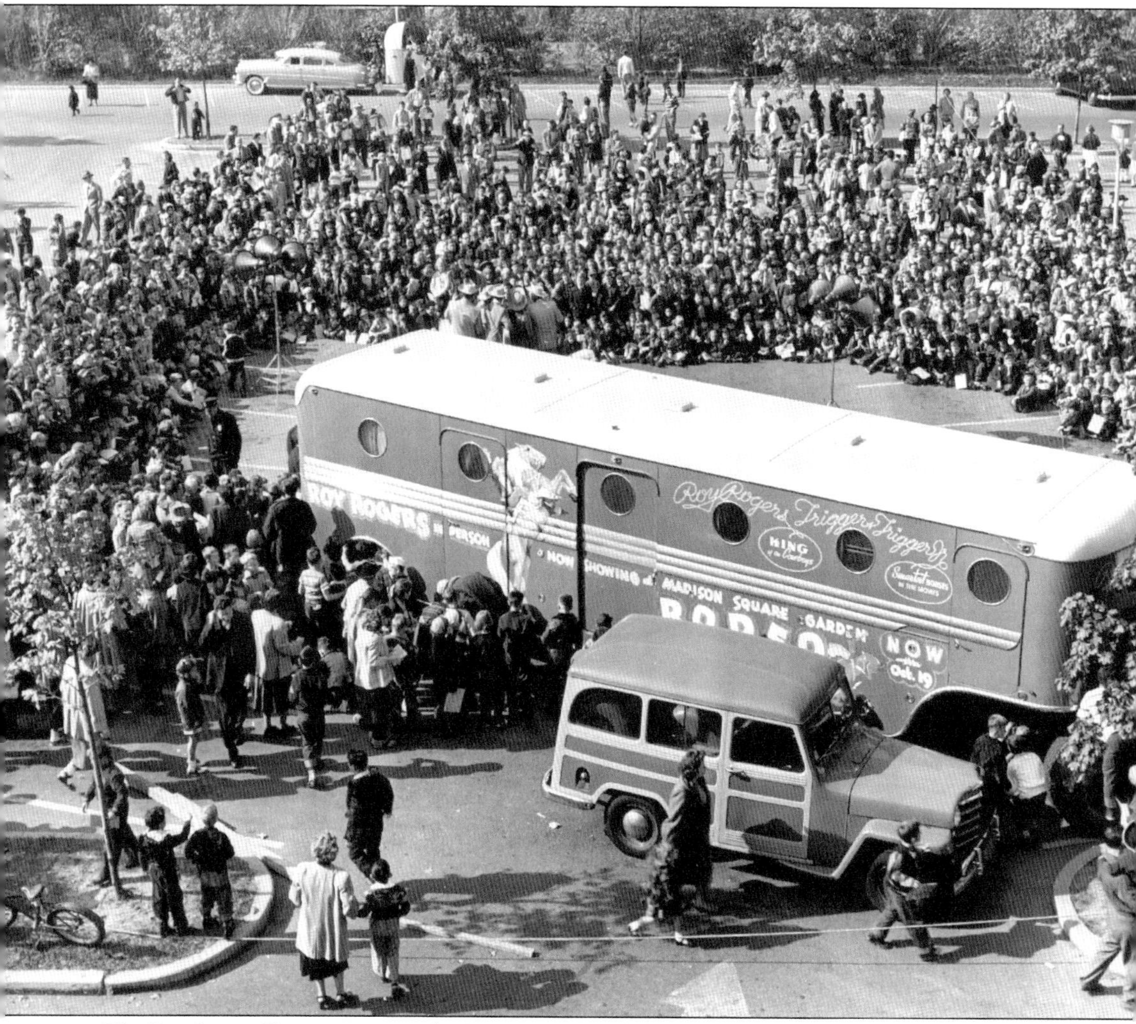

The Roy Rogers Show was a popular Western action/adventure series that was broadcast on NBC for six years beginning on December 30, 1951. In 1952, the 27th World's Championship Rodeo took place at Madison Square Garden in Manhattan during September and October. Roy Rogers and Dale Evans, the hugely popular "King of the Cowboys" and "Queen of the West," were among the stars of the show. They thrilled the adults and children of Fresh Meadows with a personal appearance and performance during the rodeo's run. (Courtesy of New York Life Insurance Company Archives; photograph by Jerry Saltsberg & Associates.)

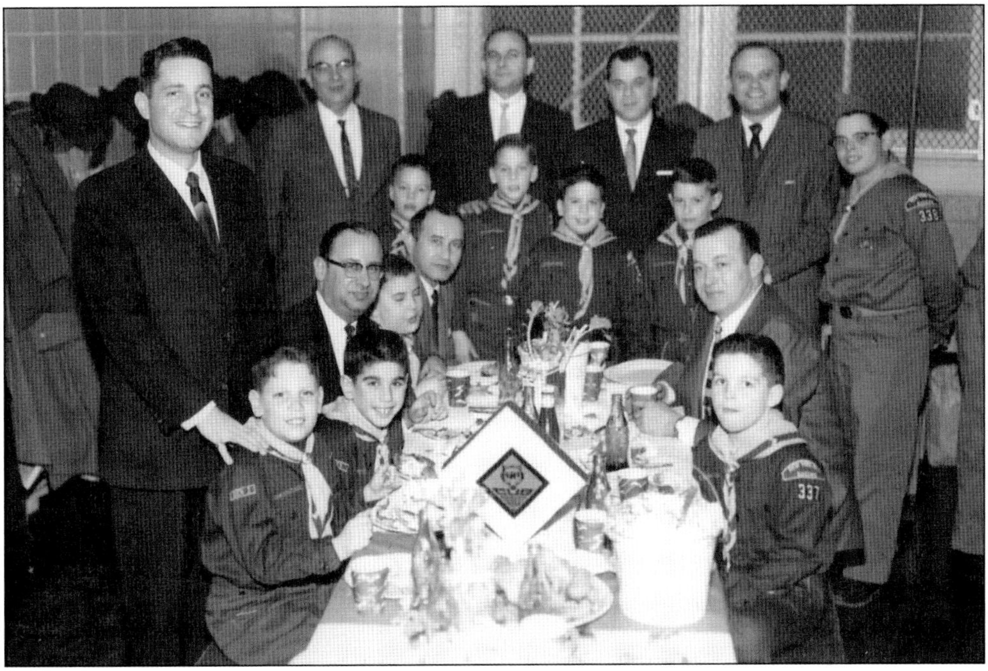

Scouting was enormously popular during the 1950s in Fresh Meadows. According to Ron Goldner, whose father, Ed Goldner, was the Cub Master in the 1950s, Pack 337 had, at its peak, 107 Cubs, making it the largest pack in New York City. Above is the annual Father/Son Dinner of Pack 337 held at PS 26 in 1957. The Cub Scouts are, from left to right, (sitting) Jimmy Weissman, Neil Daniels, Mark Kirmayer, and unidentified; (standing) Frank Lichtenberg, Neil Simon, Howard Mirsky, and Mitchell Gerber. Below, a captivated audience of Fresh Meadows youngsters listens to a special presentation about Native Americans at the nursery school on 188th Street. (Above, courtesy of Howard Mirsky; below, courtesy of New York Life Insurance Company Archives.)

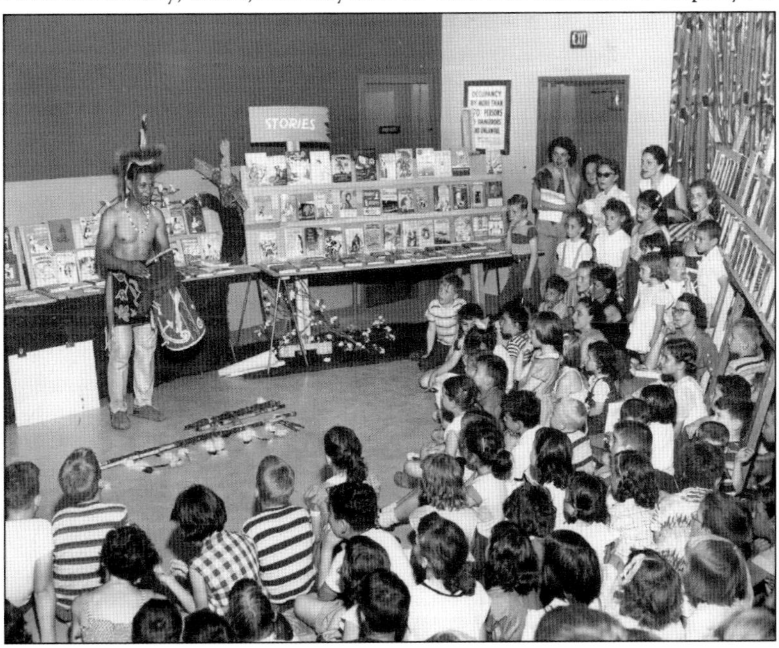

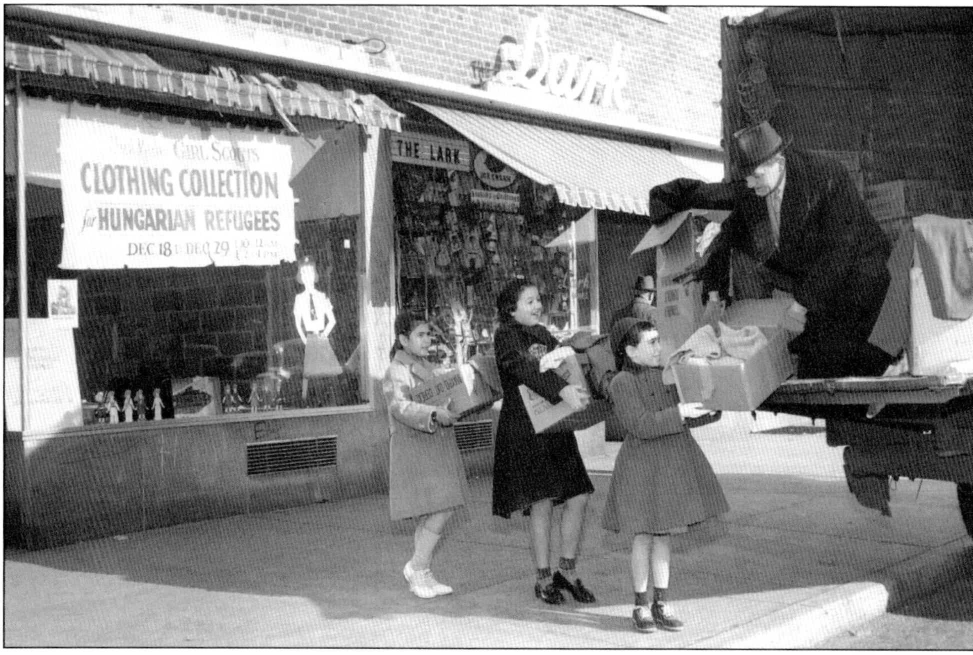

On November 4, 1956, Soviet forces launched a major attack on Hungary, crushing the revolution that had begun 12 days earlier. Hundreds of thousands of Hungarians fled, including 35,000 who made their way to the United States. On November 21, the first Hungarian refugees reached America, arriving at Camp Kilmer, New Jersey, as part of Operation Safe Haven. These Girl Scouts were participating in a clothing drive to benefit Hungarian refugees. (Courtesy of Queens Fresh Meadows LLC.)

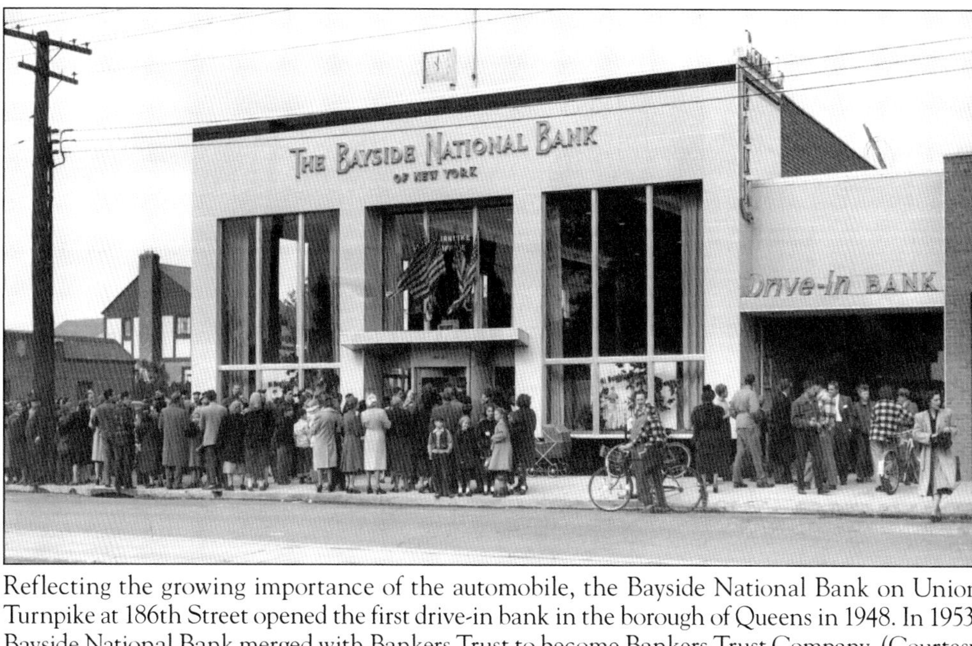

Reflecting the growing importance of the automobile, the Bayside National Bank on Union Turnpike at 186th Street opened the first drive-in bank in the borough of Queens in 1948. In 1953, Bayside National Bank merged with Bankers Trust to become Bankers Trust Company. (Courtesy of the Queens Borough Public Library, Long Island Division, Illustrations Collection—Queens Chamber of Commerce Collection.)

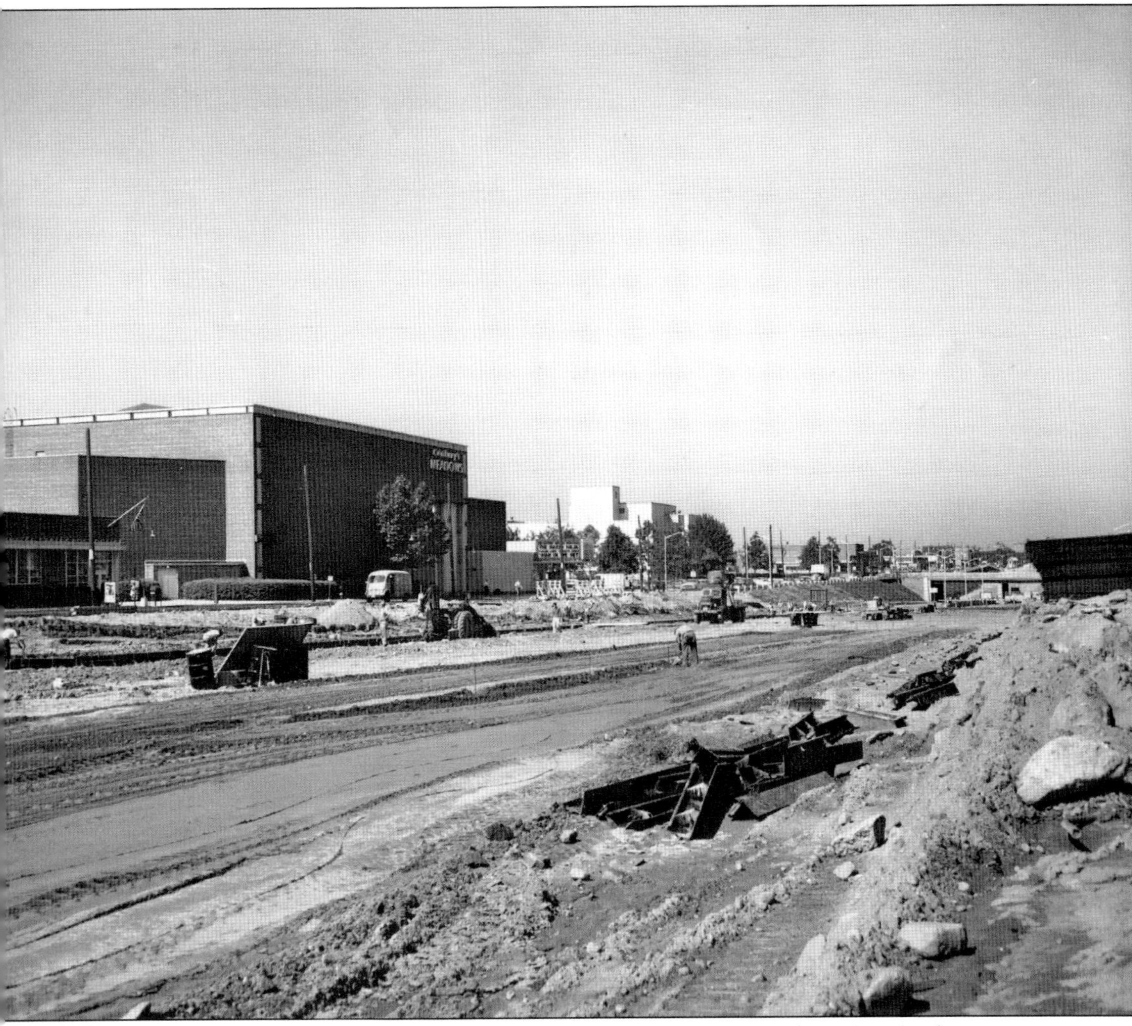

The Long Island Expressway was constructed in stages over the course of three decades, beginning in 1939. Initially known as the Midtown highway and then the Queens-Midtown Expressway, it was renamed the Long Island Expressway by 1956. Here, one can see the Expressway under construction just east of 188th Street. The huge construction site was a magnet for children, some of whom rode their bicycles down the entrance ramps in the days before the road was open to vehicular traffic. Richard Shepard, a resident of Fresh Meadows and writer for the *New York Times*, wrote, "When, in 1956, we moved to Fresh Meadows, I wheeled my older son to Horace Harding Boulevard, an extraordinarily broad highway with what appeared to be a dozen traffic lanes. In those days, Horace Harding was giving way to the Long Island Expressway, and we were absorbed in the spectacle of great earth-moving machines forging what would become one of the grand arteries (more often than not, choked) linking Long Island and Manhattan." (Courtesy of Queens Fresh Meadows LLC.)

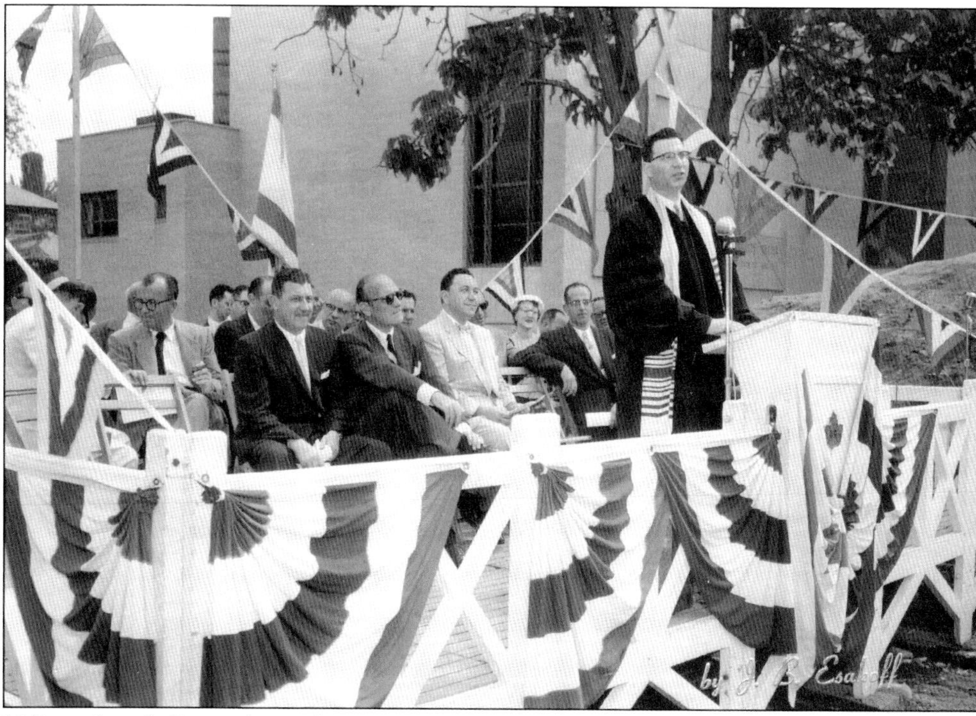

Hillcrest Jewish Center, located on Union Turnpike at 183rd Street, was one of several synagogues serving Fresh Meadows. In 1949, Israel Mowshowitz was appointed rabbi and served for 34 years until 1983 when he became rabbi emeritus. Respected by both the Conservative and Orthodox movements, Rabbi Mowshowitz rose to become one of the most influential rabbis in New York State. He was a close friend of Gov. Mario Cuomo, a Roman Catholic, who often called him "my rabbi." Above, in 1955, Rabbi Mowshowitz speaks at the ground-breaking for Hillcrest Jewish Center Youth Building. (Both, courtesy of Hillcrest Jewish Center; photographs by Jonah Esakoff.)

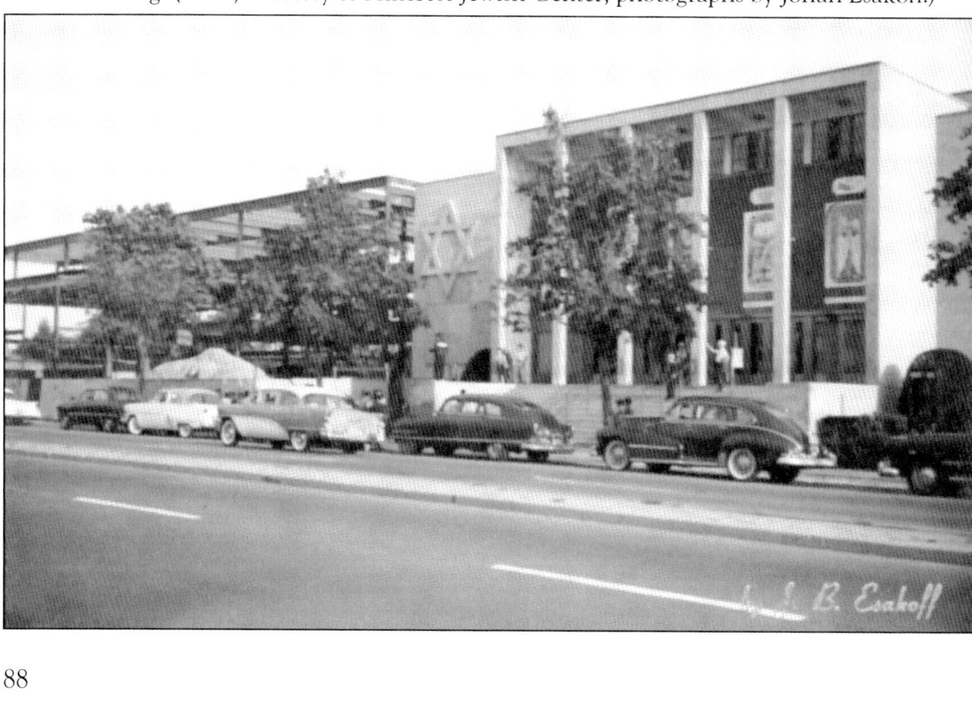

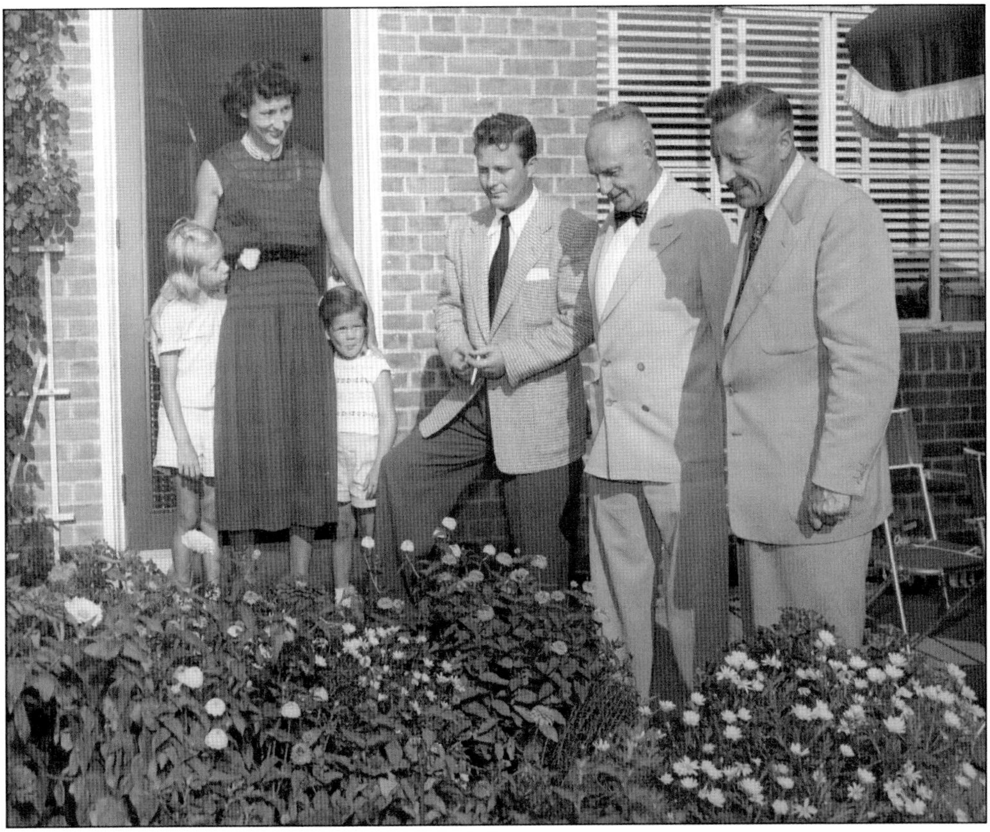

Beginning in 1950, an annual Tournament of Terraces contest was sponsored by the Fresh Meadows Garden Club in cooperation with the New York Life Insurance Company. Prizes of government bonds were awarded to the top two winners in each of two divisions. In addition to a representative of the management company, judges included representatives of the Queens Botanical Garden Society and the seed companies Peter Henderson & Co. and Stump & Walter Company. (Above, courtesy of Queens Fresh Meadows LLC; right, courtesy of New York Life Insurance Company Archives. Both, photographs by Jerry Saltsberg & Associates.)

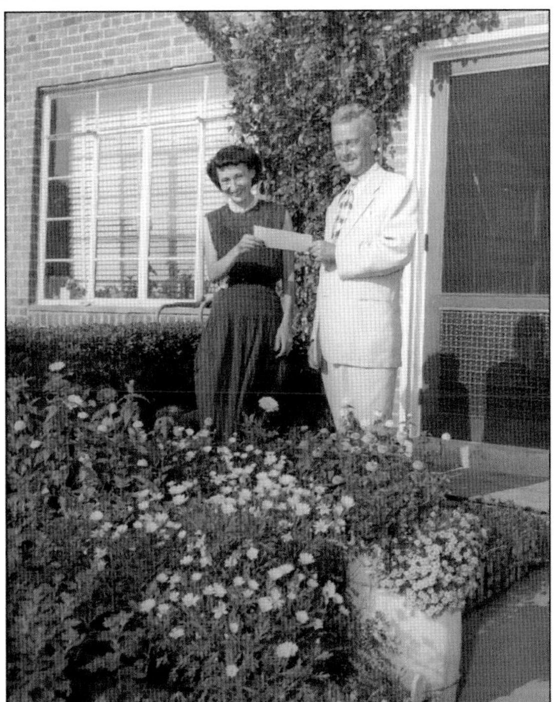

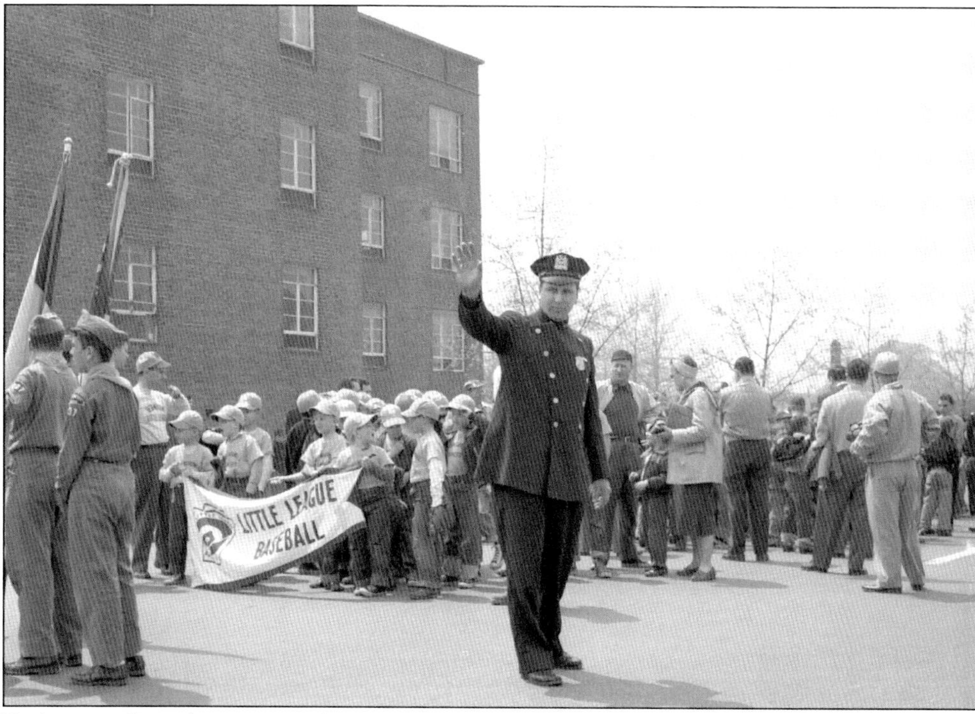

Each spring brought a new Little League season kicked off by a parade through Fresh Meadows. Little League was so popular in Fresh Meadows that in 1956, the *New York Times* carried a feature story about Kenny Ofshe, a 12-year-old player. The article described Ofshe's obsession with Little League as being so great that he would forsake watching *Sgt. Bilko* and *Wonderama* in favor of baseball practice. (Above, courtesy of Mitchell Kaften; photograph by Douglas Kaften; below, courtesy of Queens Fresh Meadows LLC.)

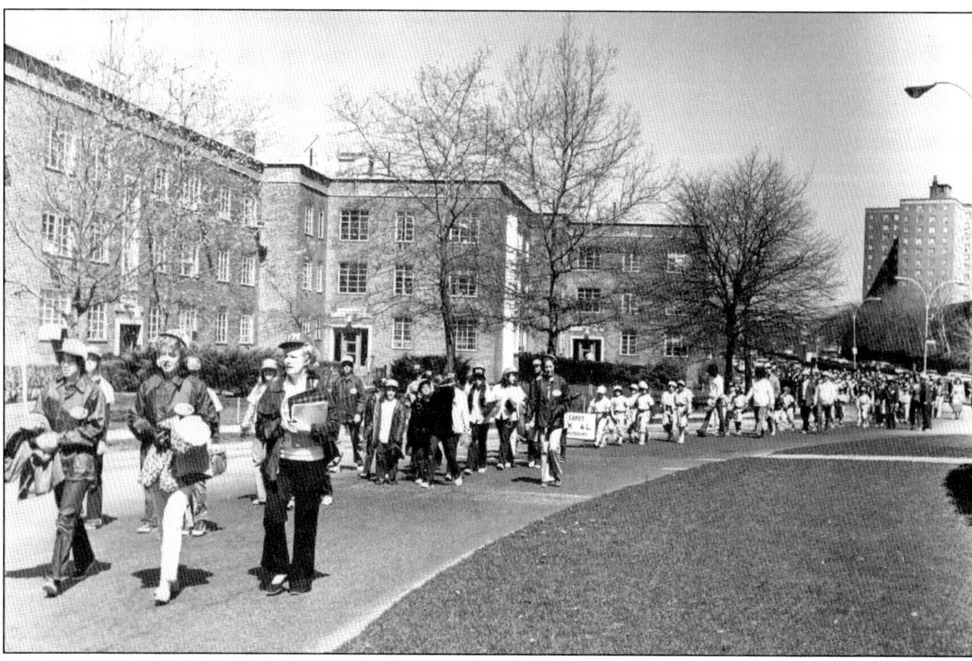

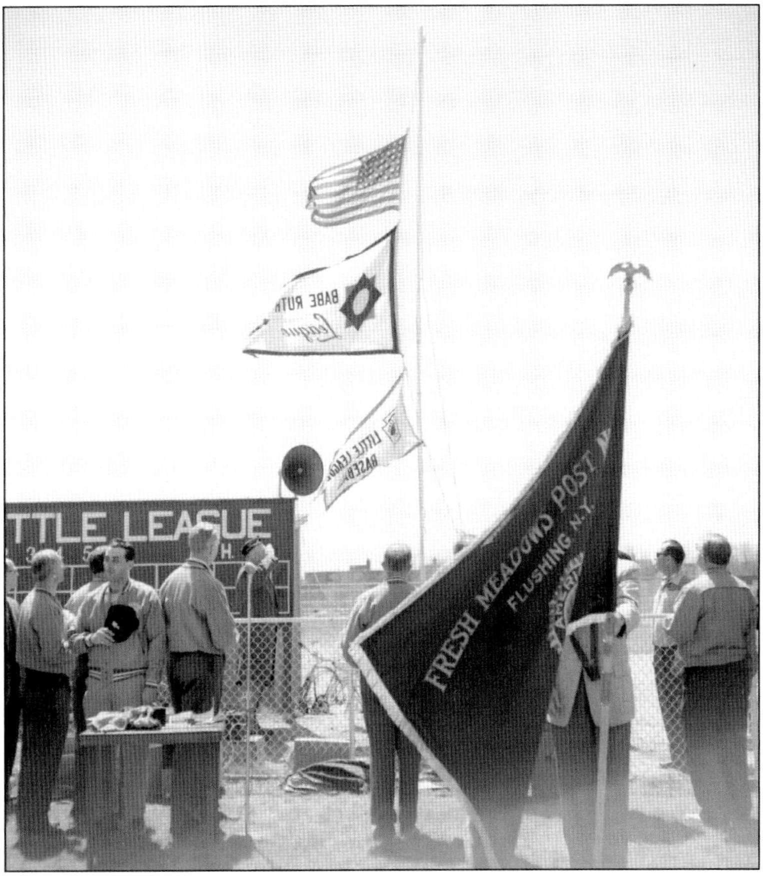

Opening day ceremonies were quite a spectacle with marching bands. Over the years, a variety of groups and organizations, ranging from the American Legion to the Brownies, participated in the Fresh Meadow Boy's Athletic League (FMBAL) parade and opening day ceremonies. (Both, courtesy of Mitchell Kaften; photographs by Douglas Kaften.)

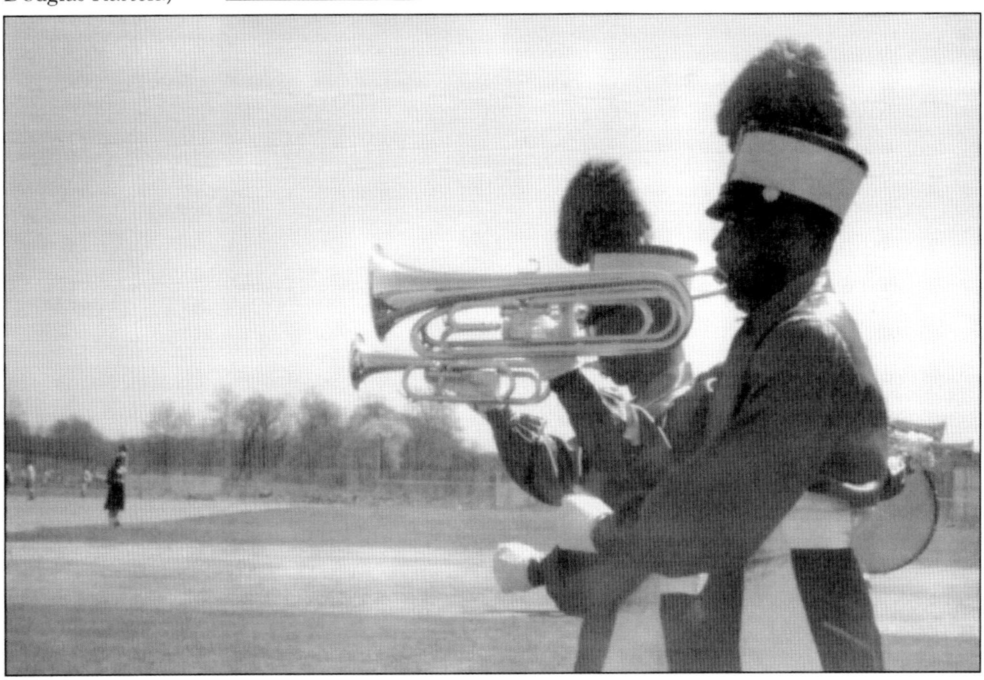

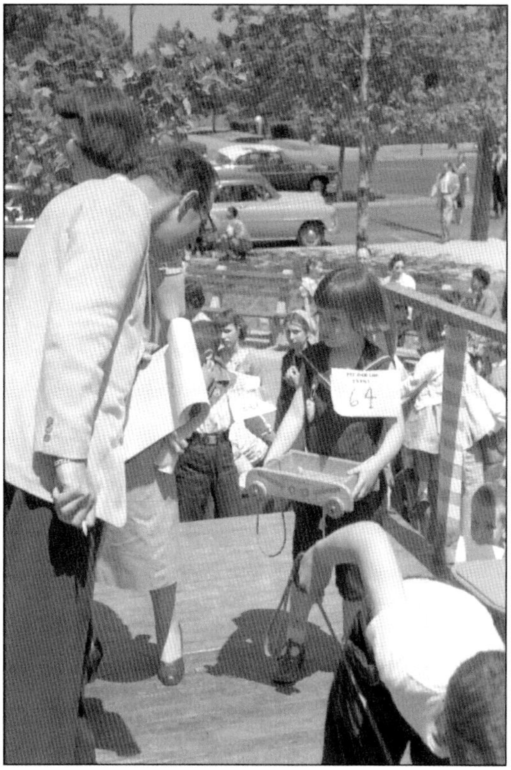

Another popular event for children was the Pet Parade, in which judges would award a prize to the most unusual pet. In the photograph at left, the judging took place on a grandstand in the park just east of Bloomingdale's. Visible in the background is the tree-lined Horace Harding Boulevard of the pre–Long Island Expressway days. (Both, courtesy of Mitchell Kaften; photographs by Douglas Kaften.)

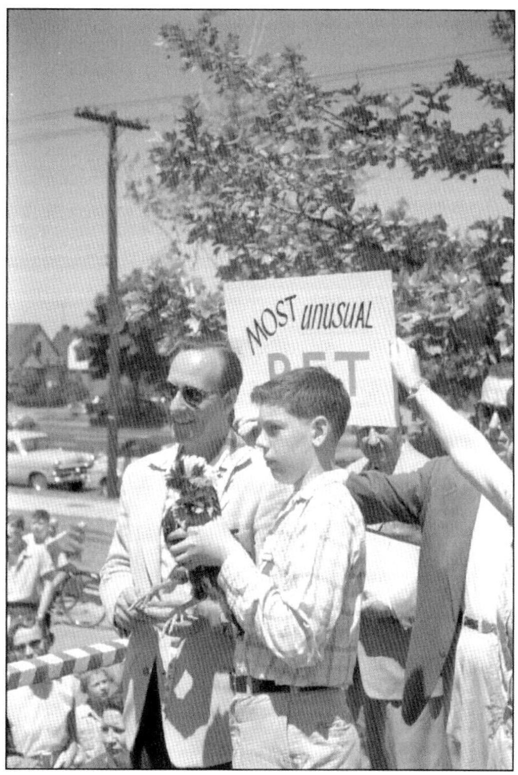

Of course, sometimes events meant to be fun can be stressful for young children. Here, a young boy has a meltdown when it all becomes too much for him. (Courtesy of New York Life Insurance Company Archives; photograph by Jerry Saltsberg & Associates.)

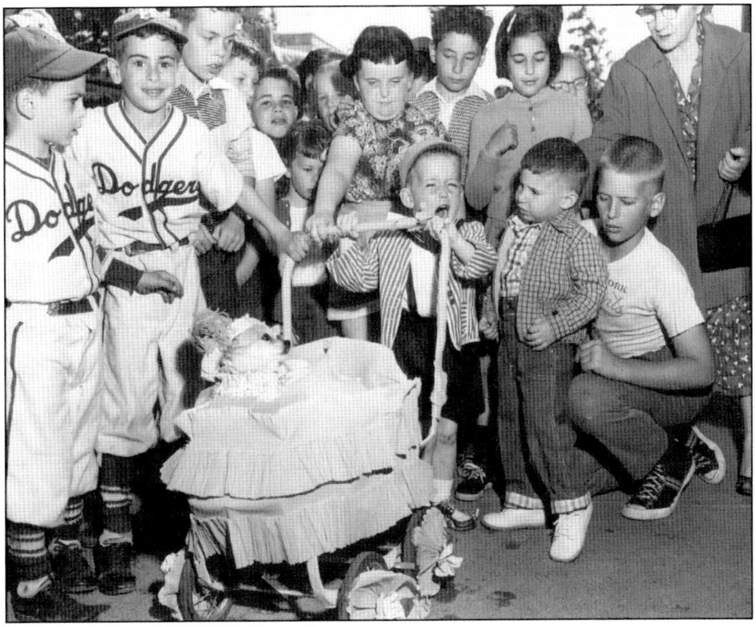

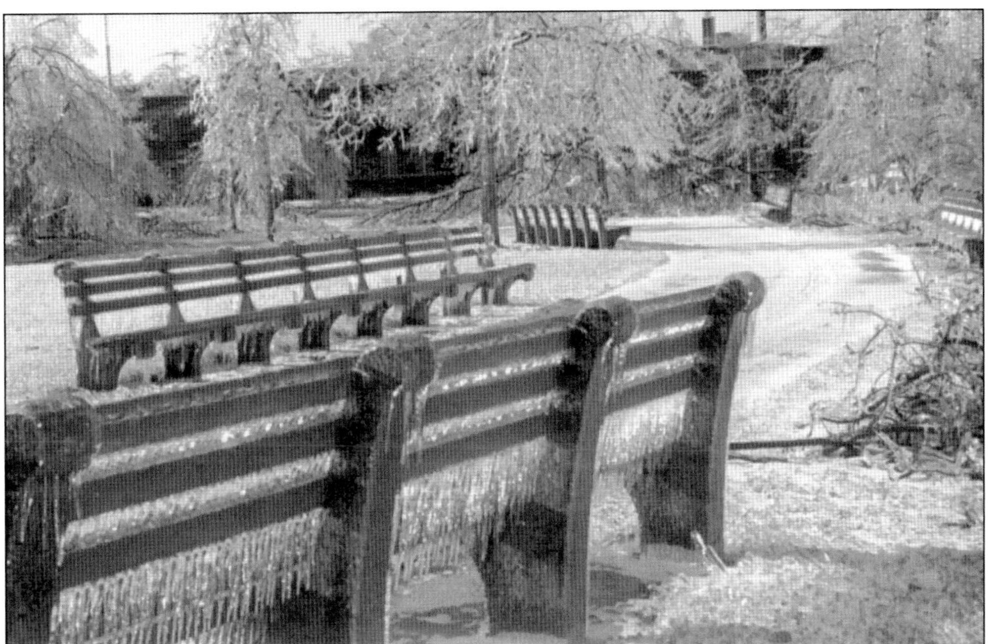

In 1973, shortly before Christmas, an unusual winter ice storm hit the New York metropolitan area. As residents woke up the next morning, according to the *Queens Tribune*, they saw "an incredible sight—a virtual crystal city. Some called it the day the world turned to glass." (Courtesy of Aina Balgalvis.)

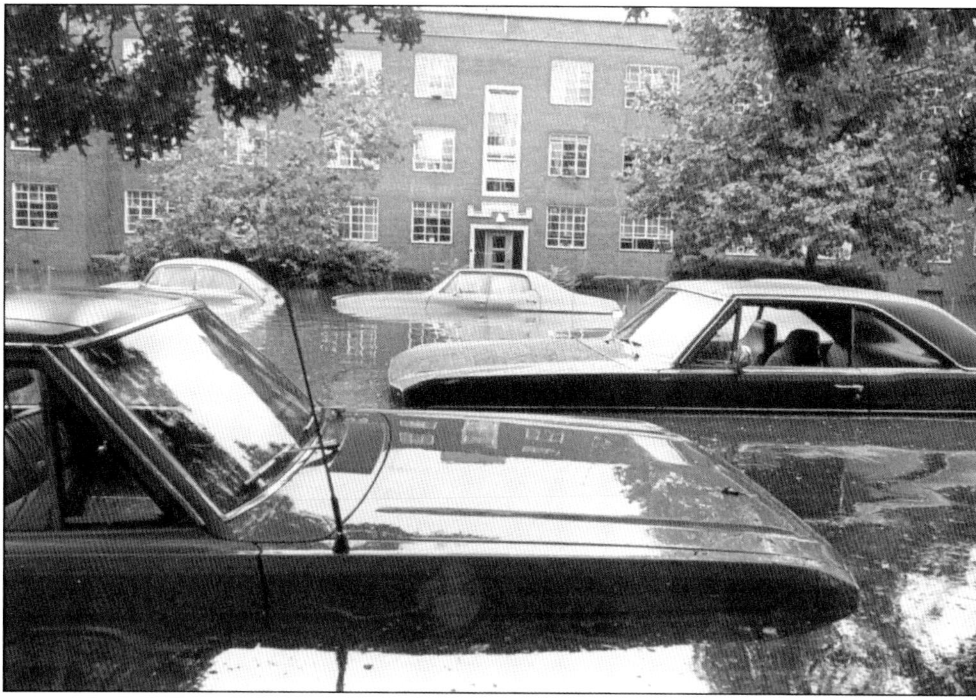

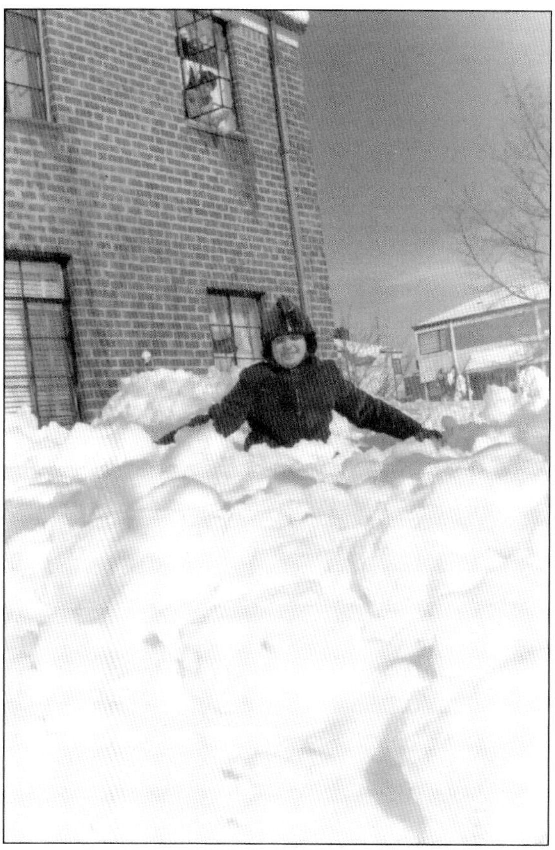

In September 1975, a storm spawned by Hurricane Eloise brought five days of rain to the New York metropolitan area, resulting in the worst flooding in years. Thousands of homes in Queens had flooded basements, and *the New York Times* featured a photograph of traffic stopped on the Long Island Expressway because of high water near Francis Lewis Boulevard. The *Times* also reported that homes along Utopia Parkway near 67th Avenue had six feet of water in their basements. Another memorable weather event was the New York Blizzard of 1969. While the weather bureau predicted snow turning to rain, 15 inches of snow fell on Sunday, February 9, catching the city off guard. At left, Gary Guttman demonstrates just how deep the snow is outside of his home. (Above, courtesy of Aina Balgalvis; left, courtesy of Judith Guttman.)

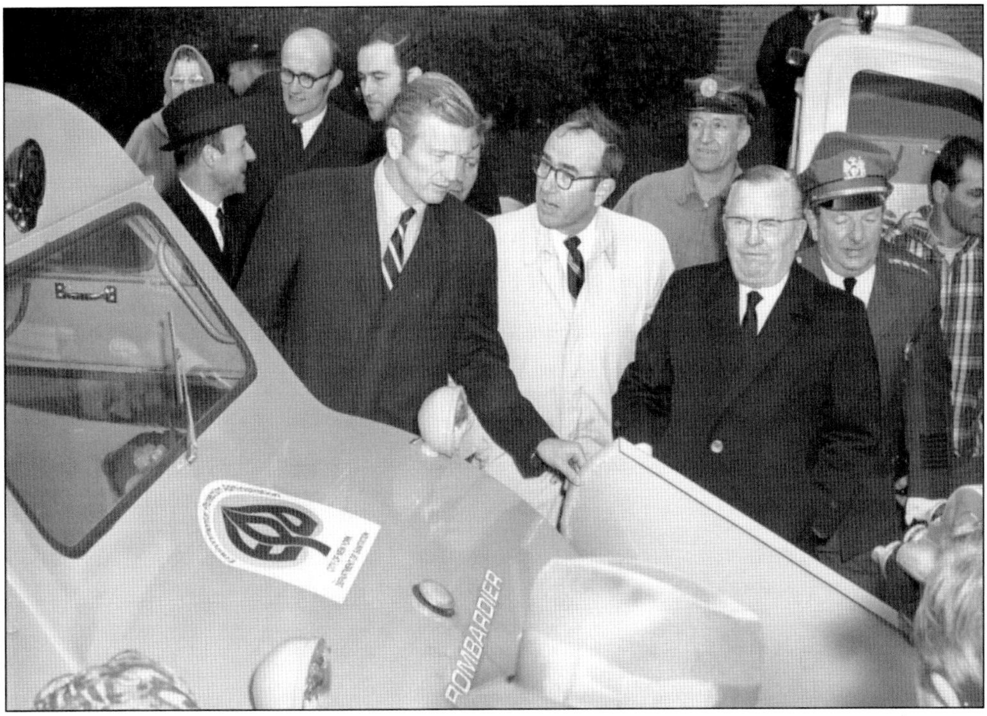

With much of the city's snow-removal equipment defective due to poor maintenance, the city's response to the storm was severely lacking. For three days, the city was all but paralyzed. In Queens, however, the recovery took even longer. In response to the enormous number of complaints, including, according to the *New York Times*, a telegram from Kew Gardens resident Ralph J. Bunche, the undersecretary general for the United Nations, Mayor John V. Lindsay visited Queens for a first-hand view. His limousine got stuck in Rego Park, "and even in a four-wheel-drive truck, he had trouble getting around. In Fresh Meadows, a woman told the mayor, 'Get away, you bum.' " Eight months later, Mayor Lindsay was back in Fresh Meadows demonstrating the city's new snow-removal equipment. (Both, courtesy of New York Life Insurance Company Archives; photographs by the Bayside Studio.)

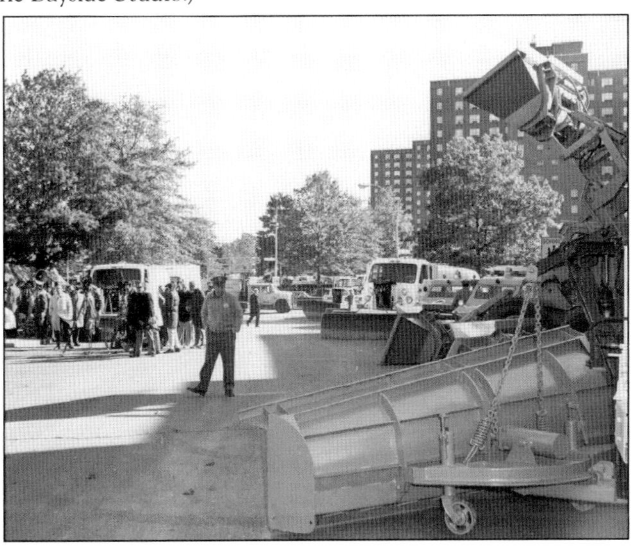

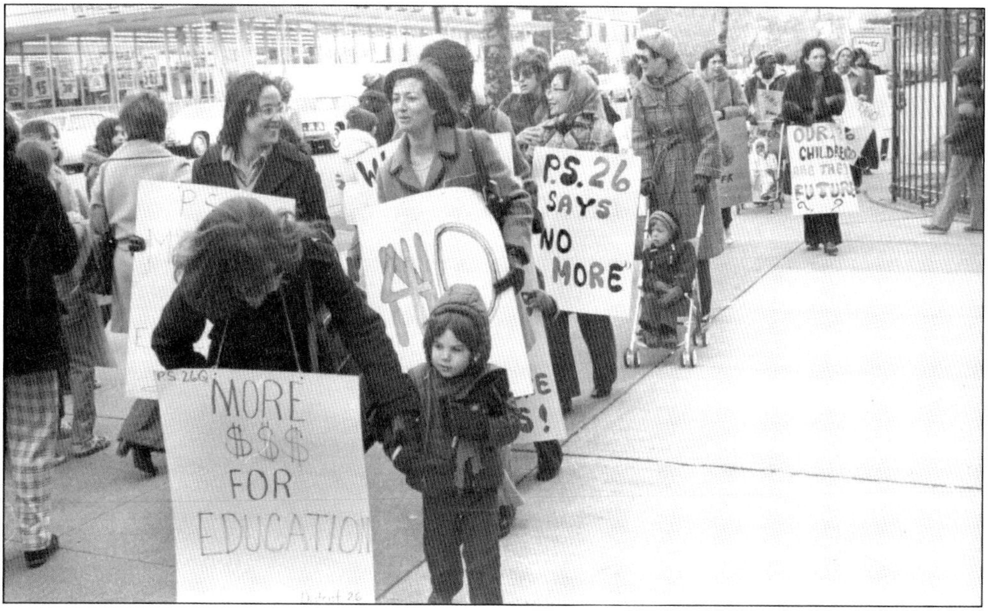

The 1970s brought a financial crisis to New York City that resulted in myriad labor and budget issues. Above, Fresh Meadow residents are seen protesting budget cuts at PS 26. Below, sanitation workers return to work after having staged a three-day wildcat strike in July 1975 after nearly 3,000 union members were laid off as a result of the financial crisis. (Both, courtesy of Aina Balgalvis.)

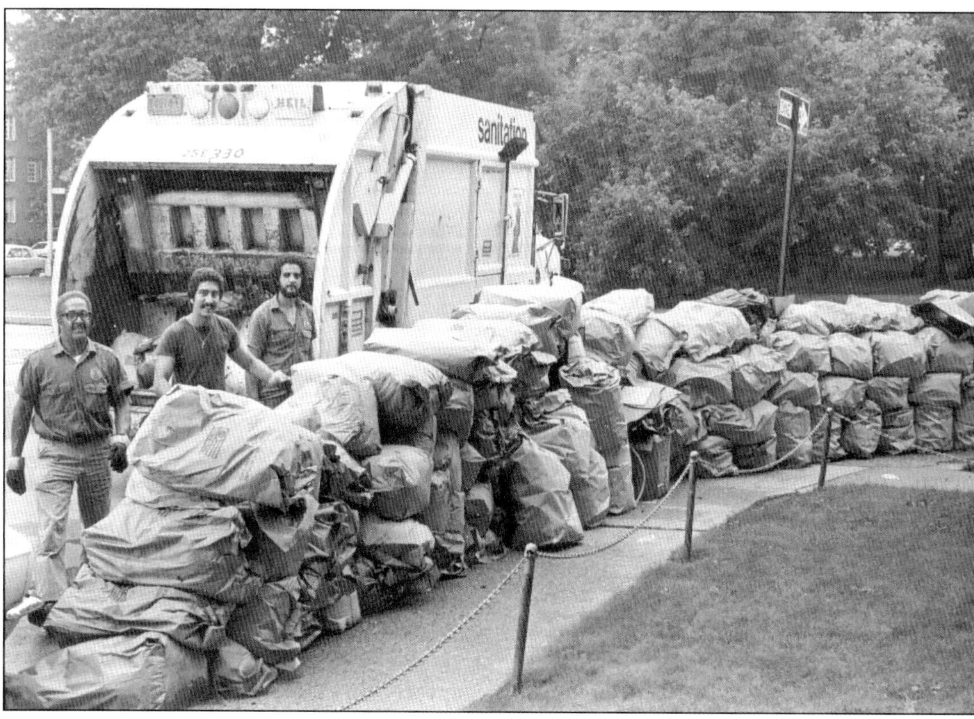

Four

Everyday Fun

Being a child in Fresh Meadows in the postwar years meant there was never an excuse for being bored. With the area populated almost exclusively by young families, Fresh Meadows was a mecca for children. With playgrounds at every turn for young children and schoolyards for older kids, there were plenty of places to gather and have fun. It was a time when the only scheduled activities a child would typically have would be Hebrew school, a weekly music lesson, or a ballet class. Those left lots of time to just enjoy the open areas and playgrounds.

The younger generation was not the only one to have fun. With a bowling center, a movie theater, and restaurants nearby, there was plenty to entertain adults. The New York Life Insurance Company also provided for meeting rooms and community spaces where one could take a class in acting, painting, or sculpting. Photography aficionados could join the Fresh Meadows Camera Club, and there were civic associations with a strong presence in the community.

And, of course, there were organized sports. The Fresh Meadow Boy's Athletic League (FMBAL) was hugely popular among both boys and their fathers, who often acted as coaches. The league sponsored both Little League baseball for younger boys as well as a basketball league for high school–age boys.

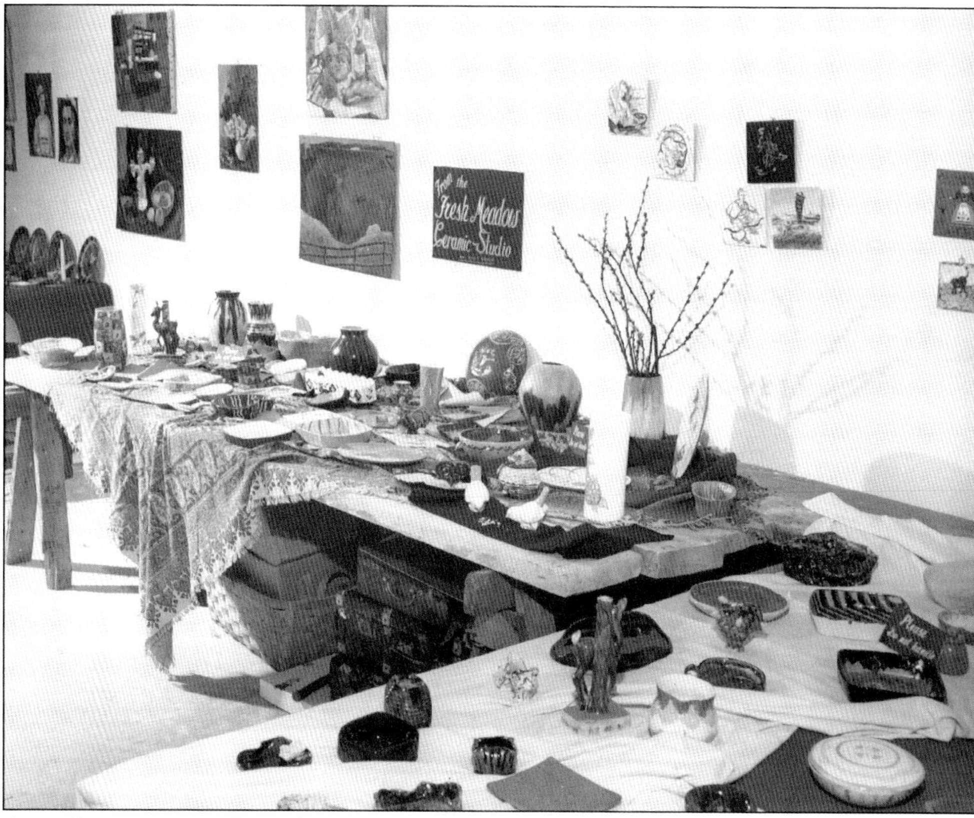

According to an article in the *New York Times* on July 19, 1949, "At Fresh Meadows, Eleanor S. Mullins, the company's community relations director, reported that numerous clubs have been organized in meeting rooms in the development." One of the organized activities was a ceramics studio. (Both, courtesy of Queens Fresh Meadows LLC; photographs by Jerry Saltsberg & Associates.)

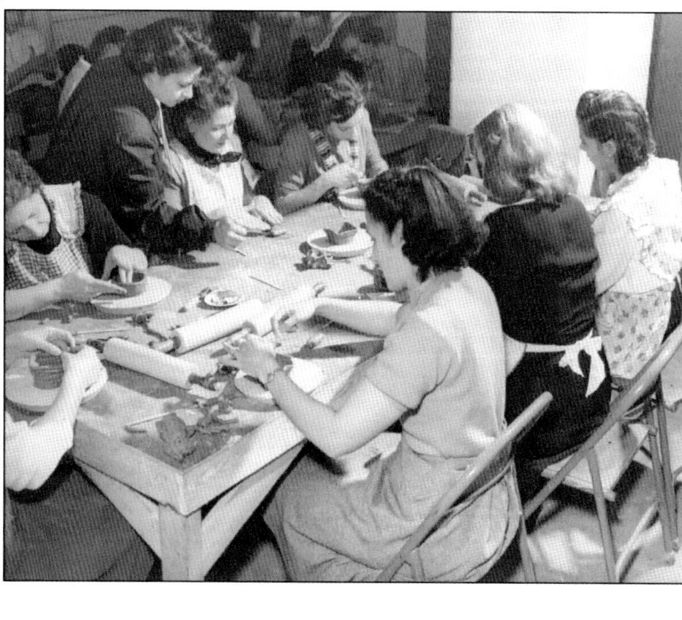

Activities were set up not only to accommodate a variety of interests, but also attract different age groups. These ranged from art classes and clubs for adults to Brownie and Girl Scout meetings for school-age girls. One club, the Fresh Meadows Art Group, hosted a yearly art exhibit. In 1959, the group held its 11th annual show in the lobby of the Century Meadows Theater. The *New York Times* reported that Gen. Otto L. Nelson, a vice president of the New York Life Insurance Company, viewed the Fresh Meadows development "as a 'family life' rather than a 'land use' trailblazer on the American scene." (Both, courtesy of Queens Fresh Meadows LLC; photographs by Jerry Saltsberg & Associates.)

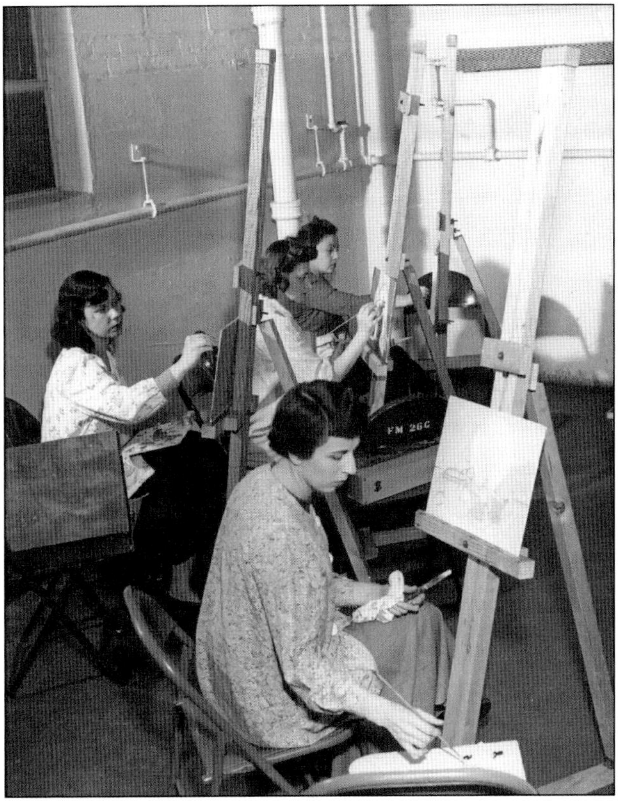

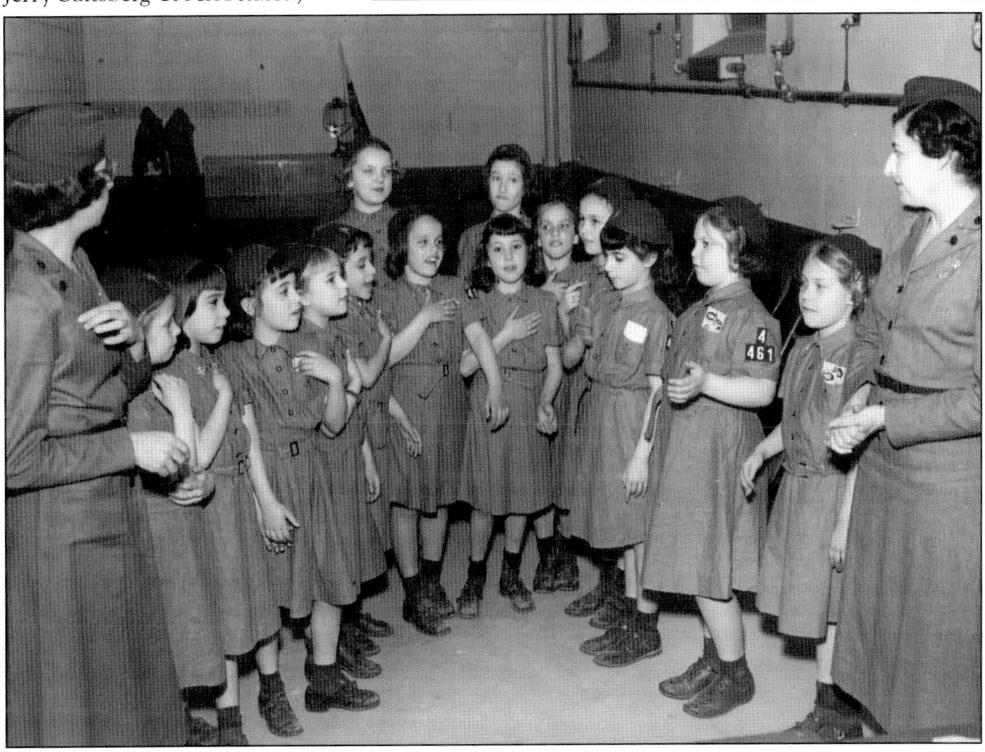

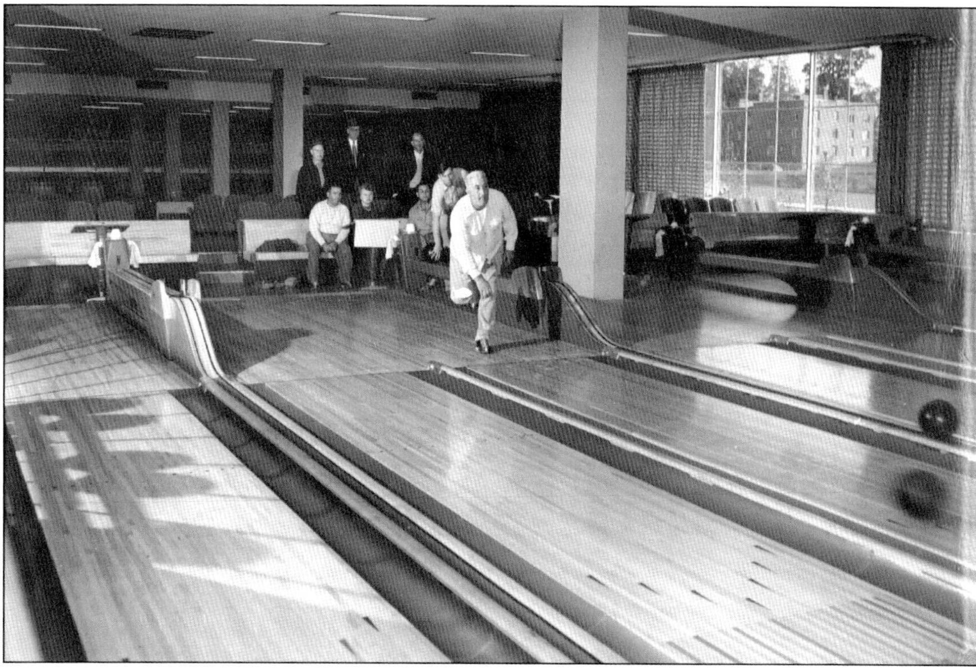

Bowling grew in popularity during the 1950s when television began featuring various bowling shows and tournaments, which ultimately led to the formation of the Professional Bowlers Association tour. The growing popularity was reflected by the existence of leagues in Fresh Meadows for both adults and children at the Bowling Center, located on the second floor of a commercial building situated between Bloomingdale's and Horn & Hardart. Saturday entertainment for kids during the winter consisted of walking to the bowling alley for a couple of games, to be followed by a matinee at the nearby Century Meadows Theater. (Both, courtesy of Queens Fresh Meadows LLC; photographs by Jerry Saltsberg & Associates.)

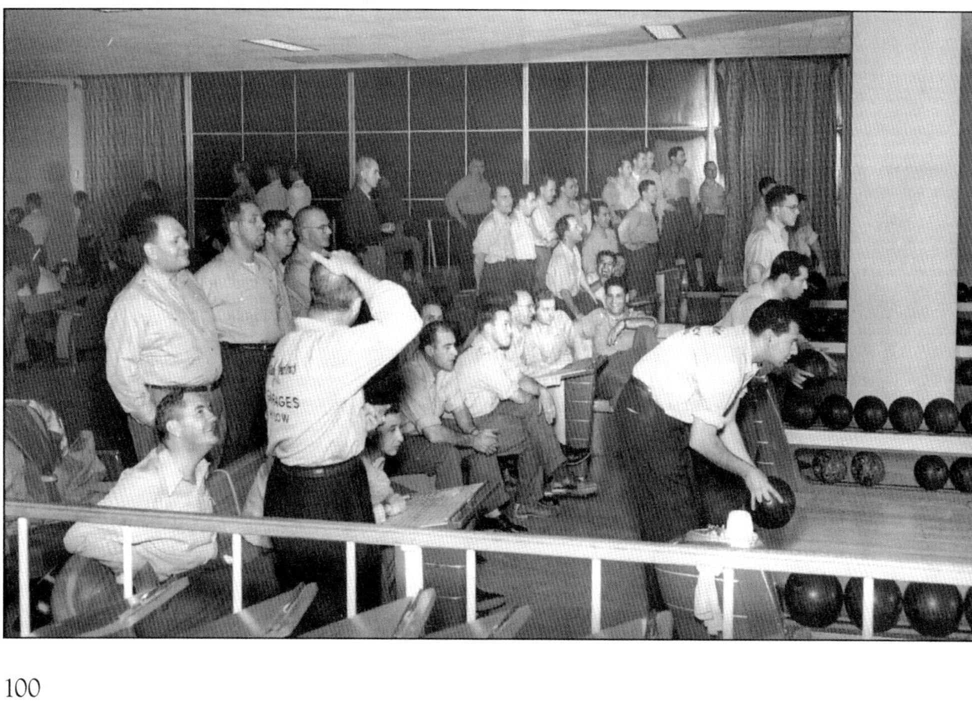

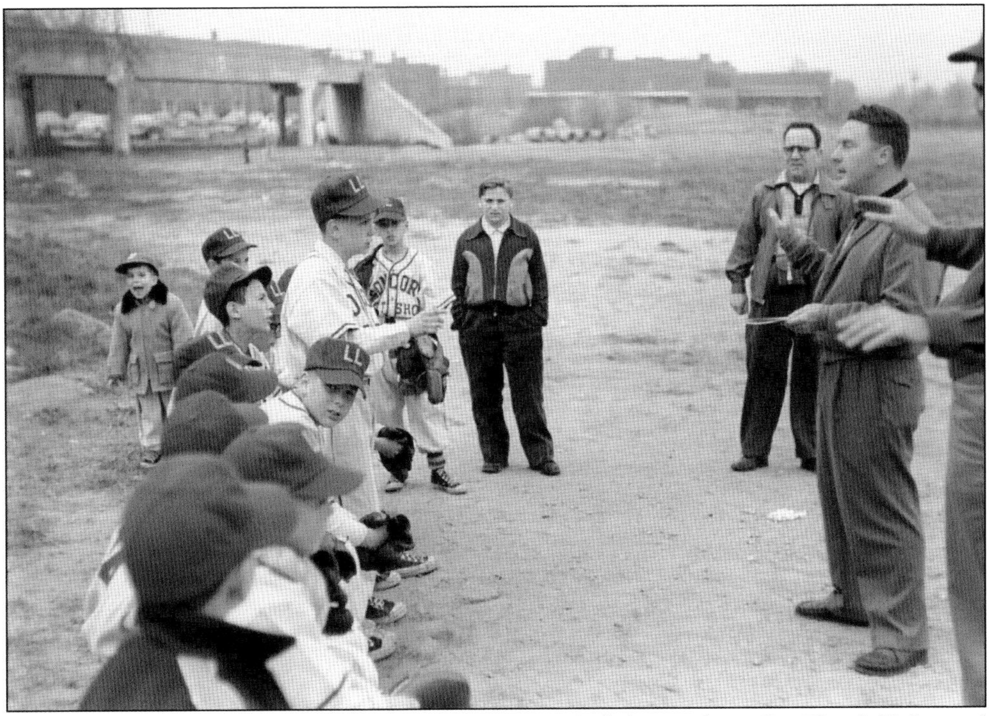

Many young boys also participated in Little League baseball during the 1950s. This field, located south of PS 179 (seen in the far background), was one of the earliest baseball diamonds used for Fresh Meadows Little League play. The bridge in the near background was part of the abandoned Long Island Motor Parkway; the road that ran underneath the bridge was part of the abandoned North Hempstead Turnpike. (Both, courtesy of Mitchell Kaften; photographs by Douglas Kaften.)

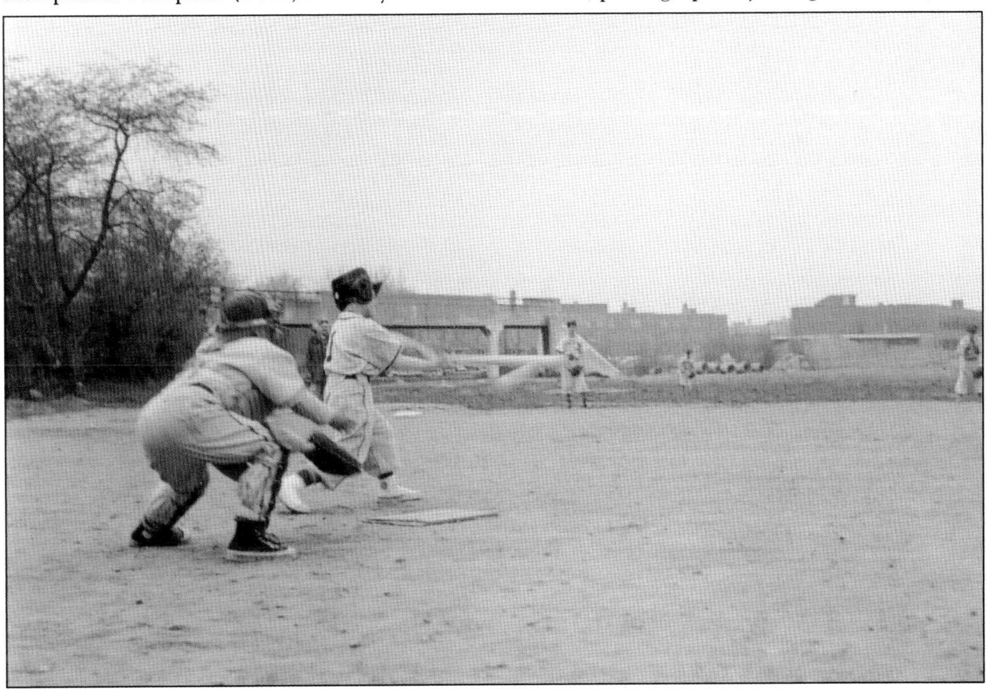

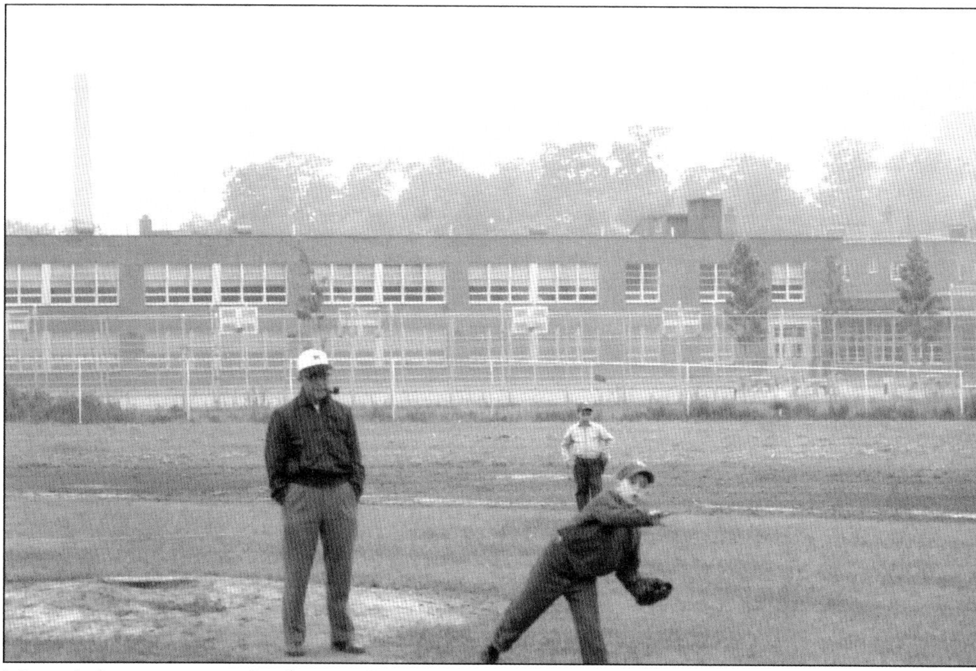

Many fathers were involved in Little League baseball as volunteer coaches. By the mid-1950s, the Fresh Meadows Boy's Athletic League was formed, and one of the FMBAL fields was located right behind PS 179, as seen in the photograph above. The boy pitching in this photograph is Mitchell Kaften. In 1956, the New York Life Insurance Company spent $7,000 on the installation of a link-wire fence and backstops for the FMBAL baseball diamonds. (Both, courtesy of Mitchell Kaften; photographs by Douglas Kaften.)

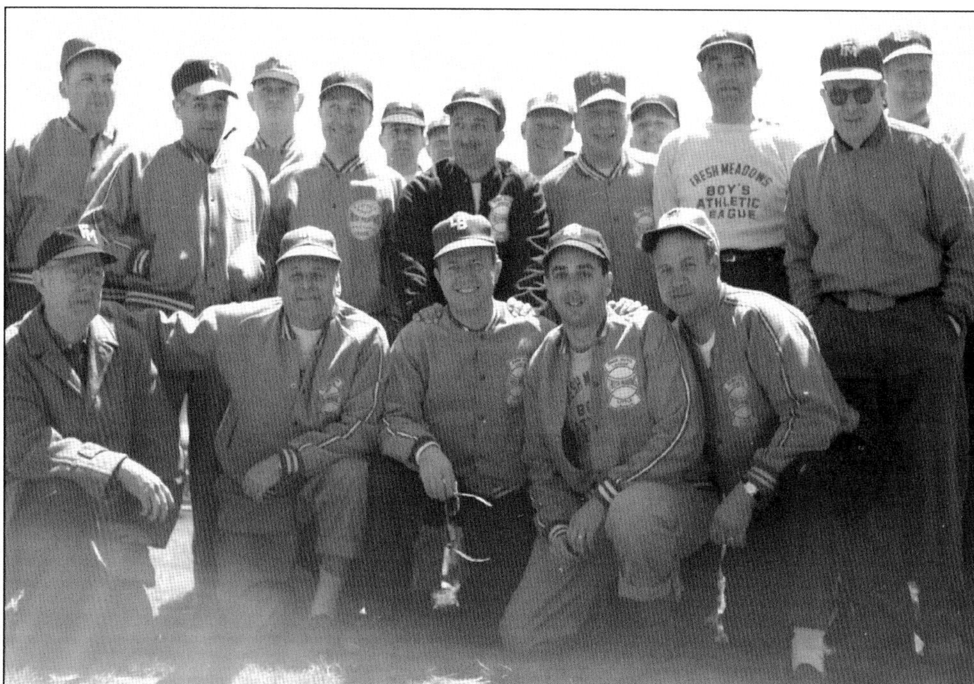

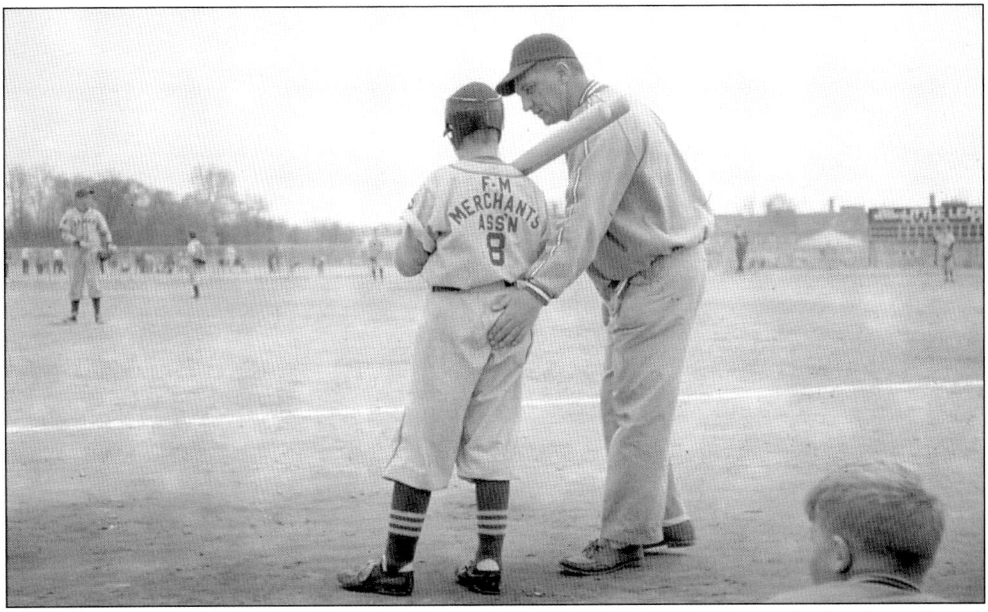

The Fresh Meadows Merchants Association and Carol Cleaners were among the local merchants who sponsored teams in the early years of the FMBAL. The cost of sponsorships typically ranged from $150 to $300. There were also more widely known sponsors, including the local branch of Bloomingdale's, as well as the local chapter of B'nai B'rith. According to an article in the *New York Times* on June 24, 1956, the B'nai B'rith team "incidentally, has a Protestant catcher, a Catholic pitcher, and a Jewish first baseman." (Above, courtesy of Mitchell Kaften, photograph by Douglas Kaften; below, courtesy of Fred Cantor, photograph by Gruber Photos.)

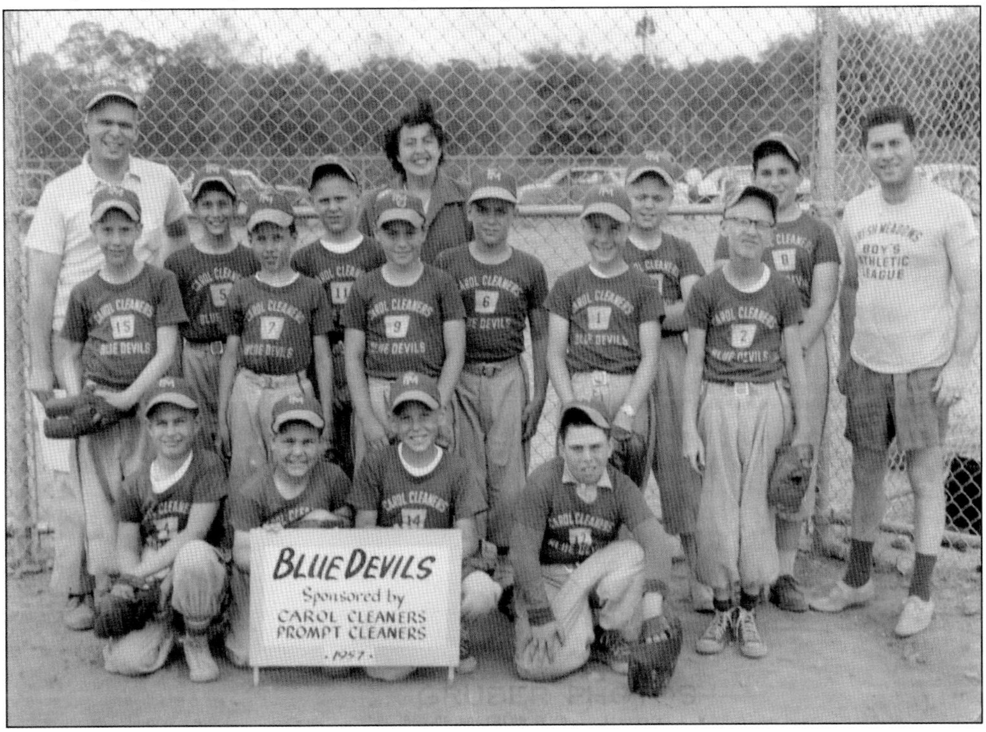

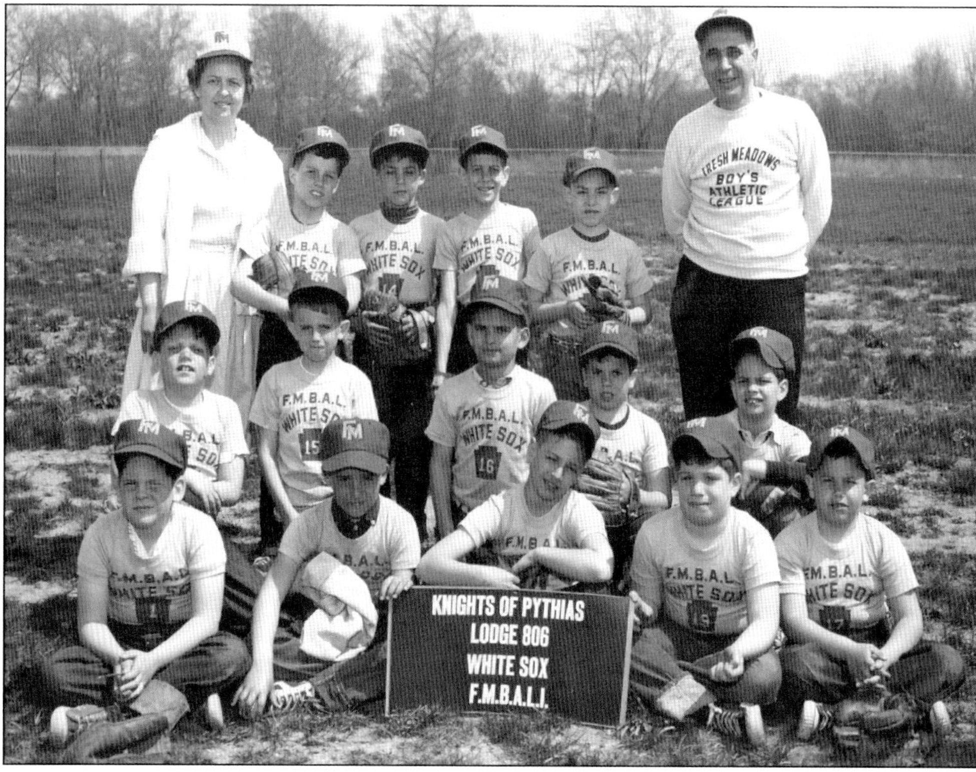

In the 1960s, the FMBAL also used fields in Cunningham Park near the intersection of Francis Lewis Boulevard and 73rd Avenue, seen in the above photograph, and on the east side of Francis Lewis Boulevard, between 73rd Avenue and the Long Island Expressway. While FMBAL teams typically adopted the names of clubs from major-league baseball (such as the White Sox), Marc Schneider, featured in the below photograph, played for a team that had one of the most distinctive FMBAL names: the Freddies. (Above, courtesy of Howard Mirsky; below, courtesy of Barry Schneider.)

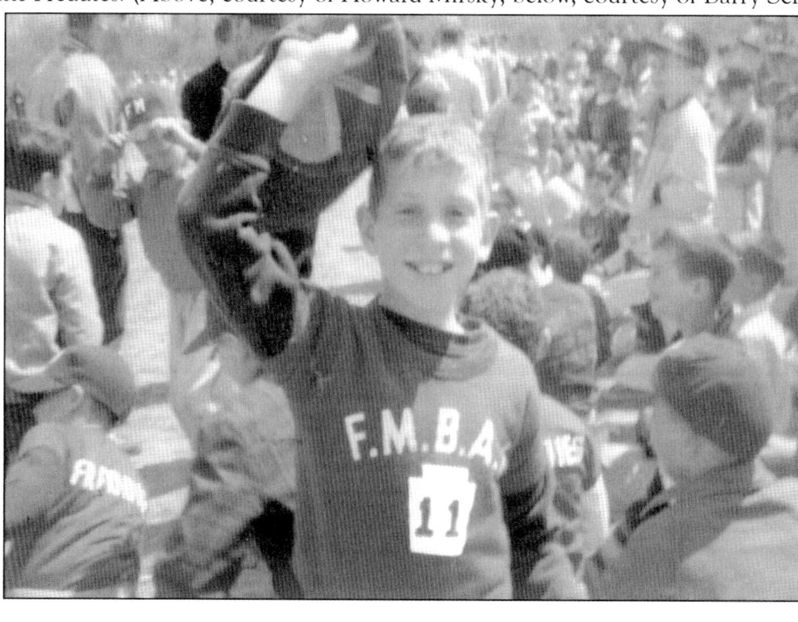

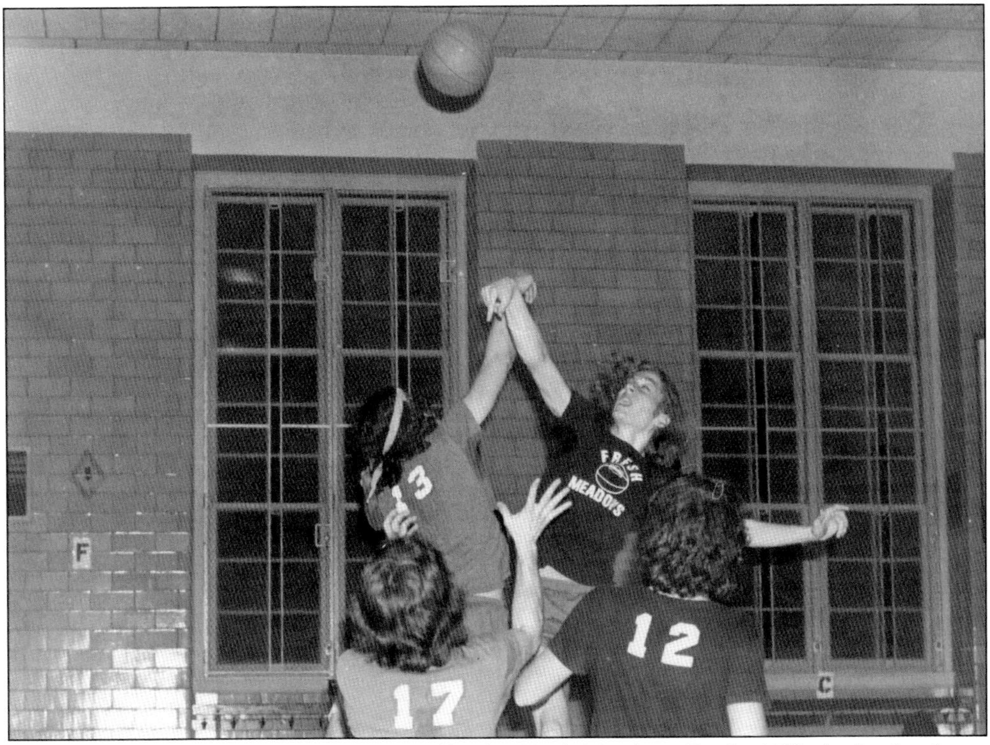

Baseball was not the only organized sport offered in Fresh Meadows. By the 1970s, high school–age youth were able to participate in a basketball league run by the FMBAL. Pictured above, Michael Hecht (No. 13) and Bill Sternberg are jumping center at PS 26. In the photograph below, also taken in the gymnasium at PS 26, a group of elementary school–age students wear jerseys with the name "Rufus King." (Above, courtesy of Steven Quat; below, courtesy of Aina Balgalvis.)

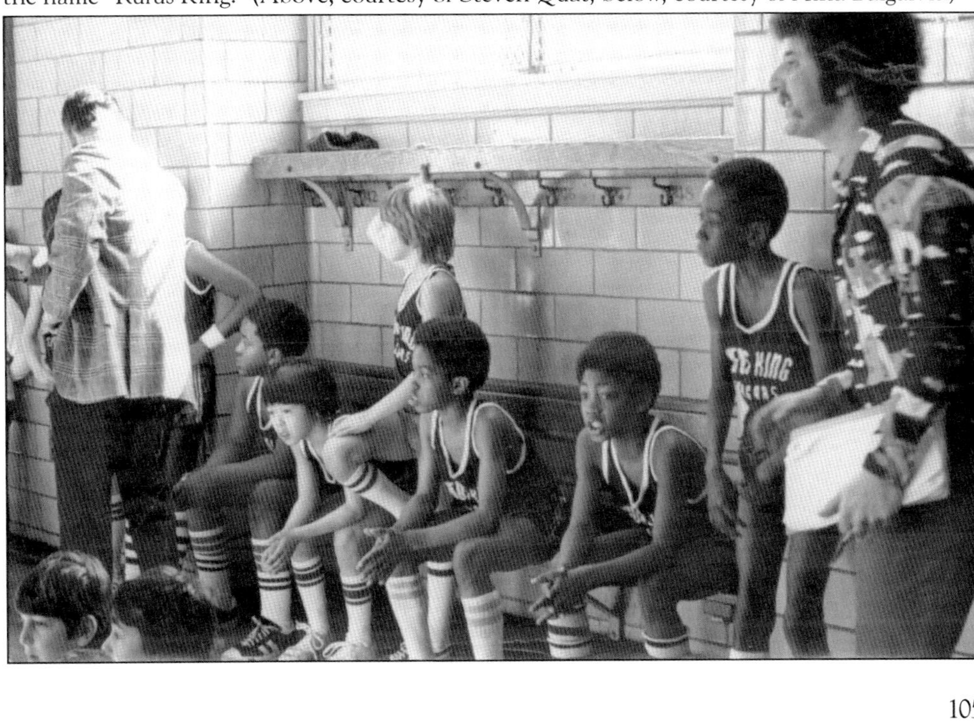

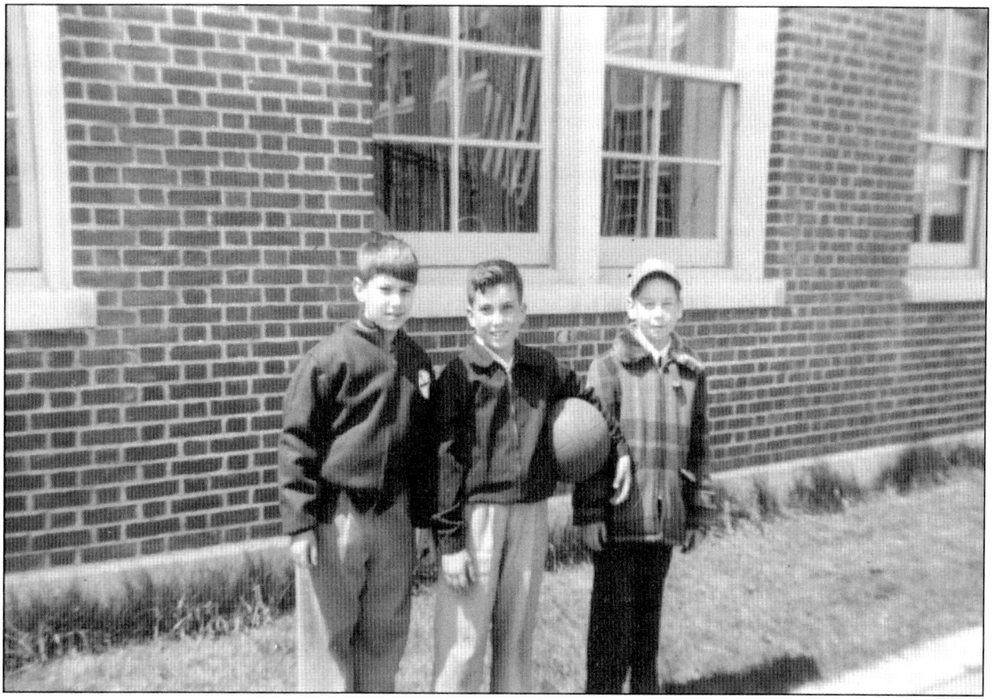

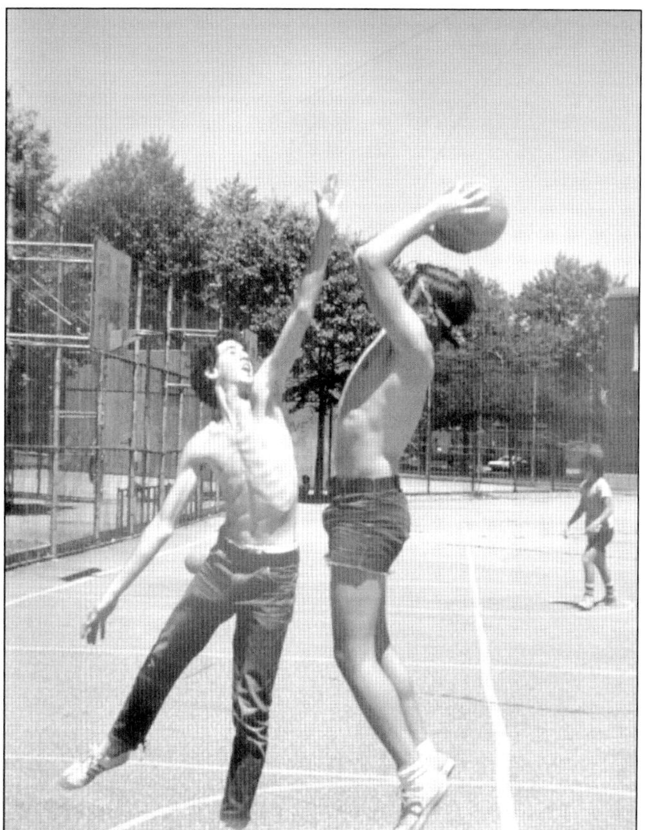

Of course, children in Fresh Meadows frequently played sports outside of organized leagues, and one tradition was pickup basketball in the schoolyards. In the image above, Harold Appel (left) and two friends are getting ready to play ball at PS 26 during the time period when Carl Braun was an all-star for the New York Knicks. Pictured at left, Daniel Wolkoff (left) and Jerry Infeld play one-on-one at PS 173 during the Willis Reed/Walt Frazier era. (Above, courtesy of Harold Appel; left, courtesy of Jerry Infeld, photograph by Martin Ehrlich.)

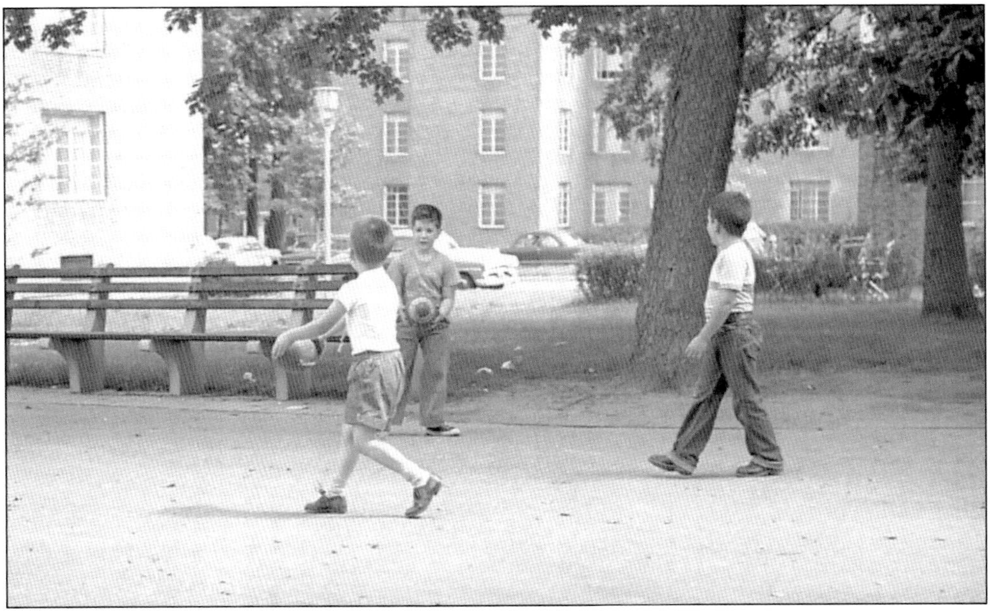

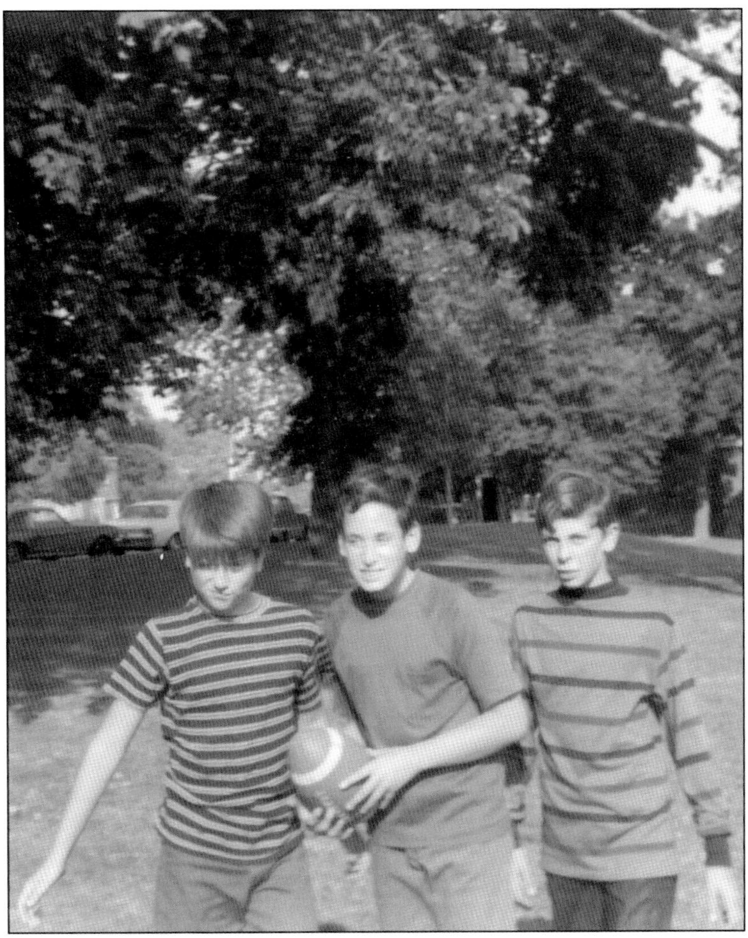

Touch football also was popular, going back to when Charlie Conerly and the New York Giants reigned as National Football League champions in the mid-1950s—the time period the above image was captured behind 192-24C 64th Circle—to the emergence of Joe Namath and the New York Jets in 1968, the date of the second photograph. In the picture at right, taken outside the 20-story building, are, from left to right, Tom Higgins, Lance York, and Jim Bercovitz. (Above, courtesy of Mitchell Kaften, photograph by Douglas Kaften; right, courtesy of Mitchell York.)

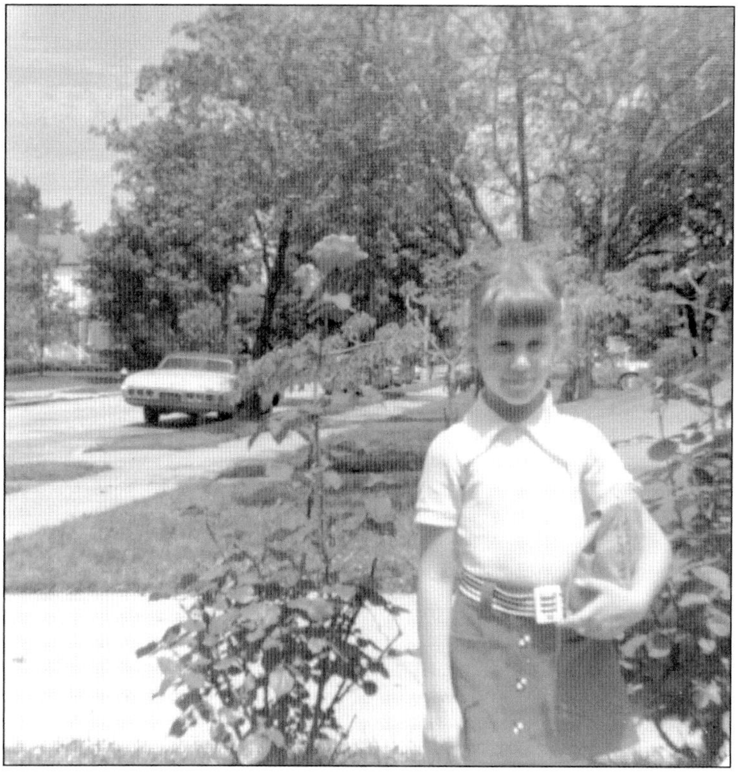

The love many Fresh Meadows children had for baseball was reinforced when Shea Stadium opened in 1964, which meant that a major-league game was now just a short ride from their homes. In this 1974 photograph, Andrea Harris stands in front of her home on 192nd Street with her baseball mitt as she gets ready to go to a New York Mets game to hopefully catch a foul ball. (Courtesy of Bob and Edna Harris.)

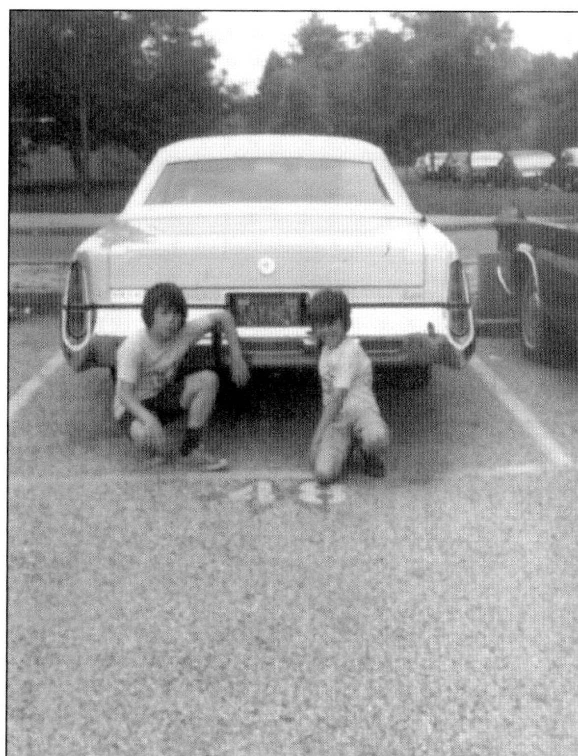

The Mets attracted considerable attention in 1972 when they acquired the legendary ballplayer and former New York Giant Willie Mays. Mays was a frequent visitor to Fresh Meadows at that time, and children were excited to see his pink Chrysler Imperial with its special "SAY HEY" license plate coming down the street. Jay Shelofsky (left) and his brother Scott are kneeling next to Willie's famous license plate in the parking lot adjacent to the 20-story building. (Courtesy of Jay Shelofsky.)

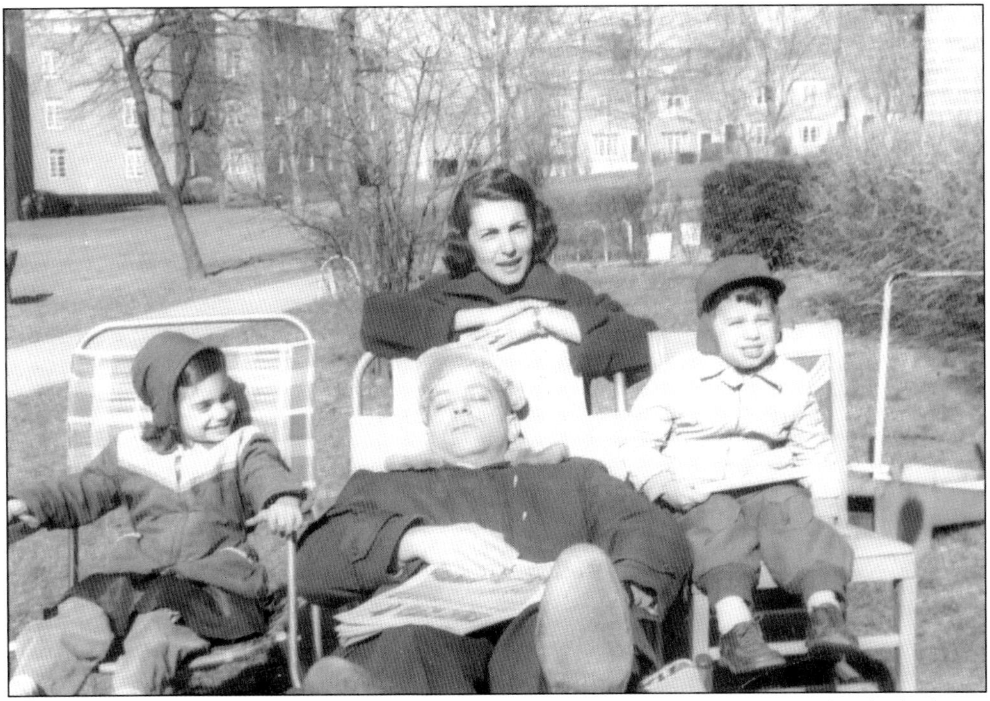

For many of the first wave of residents in Fresh Meadows, this was the first time they had a home with a yard right outside their door. A number of the newcomers had grown up and lived in apartment buildings in the Bronx, Brooklyn, or Manhattan. It was considered a real luxury to have grassy areas in front of or behind their apartments, and residents enjoyed taking advantage of this amenity with lawn chairs, even during the earliest hints of spring. Seen above, seated in the grassy expanse behind 190-19G 71st Crescent, are members of the Lager family. They are, from left to right, Anita, Ralph, Bernice, and Fred. Pictured below in their front yard overlooking Peck Avenue are Audrey and Emanuel Sternbach. (Above, courtesy of Anita Toby Lager; below, courtesy of Stephen Sternbach.)

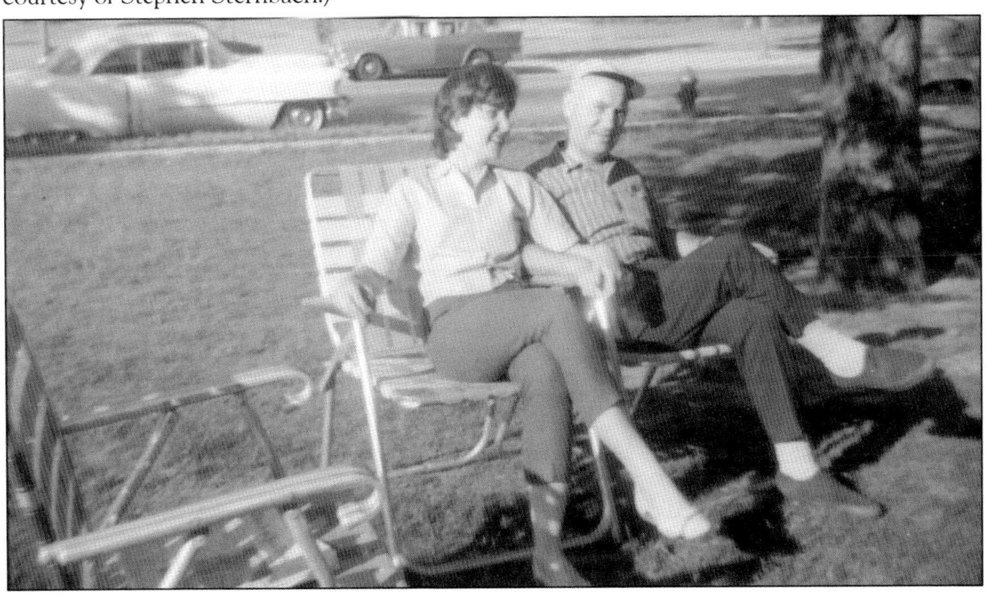

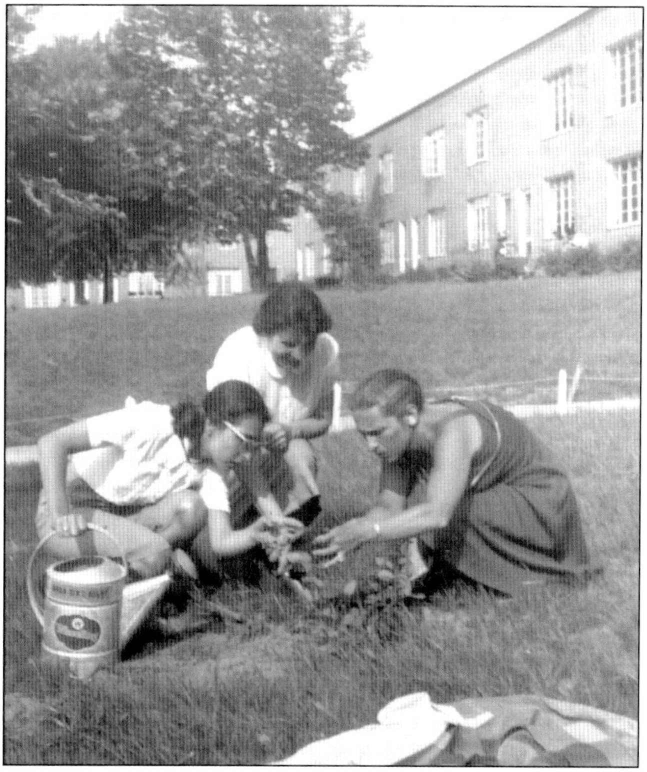

Of course, taking advantage of the yards also meant experimenting with gardening for the first time. In the photograph at left, taken in the spring of 1950, are, from left to right, Anita Toby Lager's mother, Bernice Lager; her grandmother, Beatrice Fried; and her aunt, Fannie Lager. And, in 1954, the *New York Times* reported on a new development in the use of front and back yards—the increasing use of plastic, aboveground pools. Part of this trend was the proliferation of mini-inflatable pools for tots. Seated in the pool, which overlooks Peck Avenue (with PS 179 in the background), are Neil Simon (left) and his brother Robert. (Left, courtesy of Anita Toby Lager; below, courtesy of Robert Simon.)

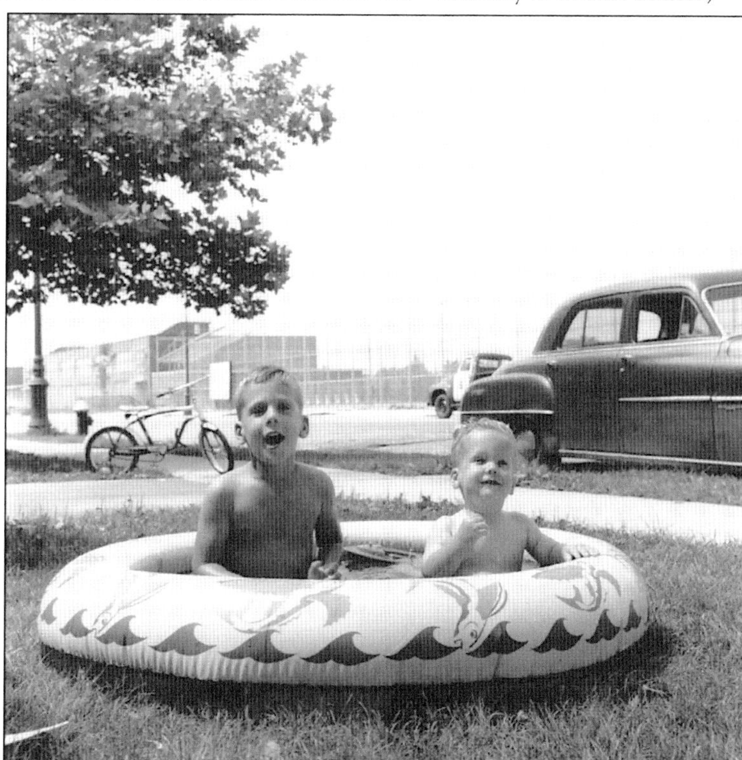

A child's fascination with cars and trucks began at a very young age. Toddlers typically embraced little red fire trucks, as exemplified in the photograph at right that shows Mark Weissler (right) with his cousin Ann Merson. Older children would sometimes follow the events of the soap box derby, which reached new heights in media coverage and attendance in the 1950s. A soap box–type vehicle was also featured in an episode of a popular television series that ran in syndication at that time—*The Little Rascals*. The picture below was taken in 1958 in the playground behind 65th Crescent. Aris Nitsos is in front, and in back are, from left to right, Laurie Bernstein, Susan Cohen, Jay Mirsky, Howard Mirsky, and Richard ? (Right, courtesy of Doris Weissler; below, courtesy of Howard Mirsky.)

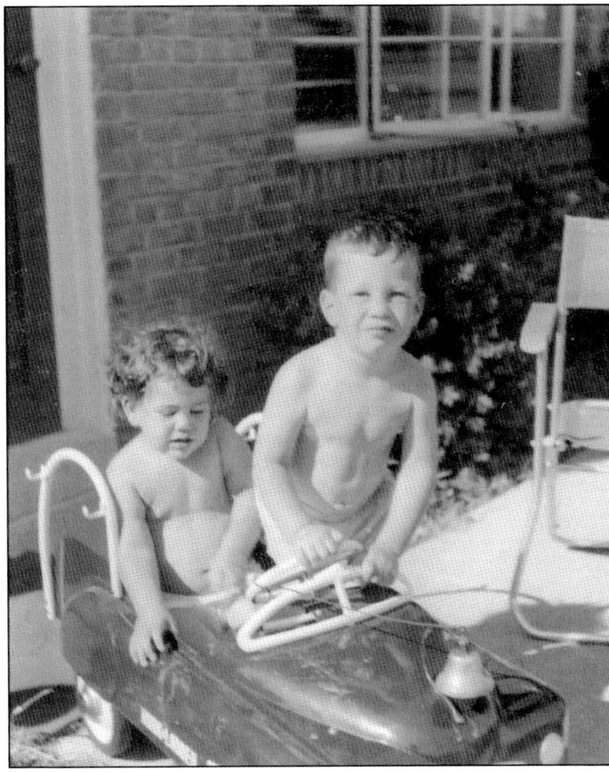

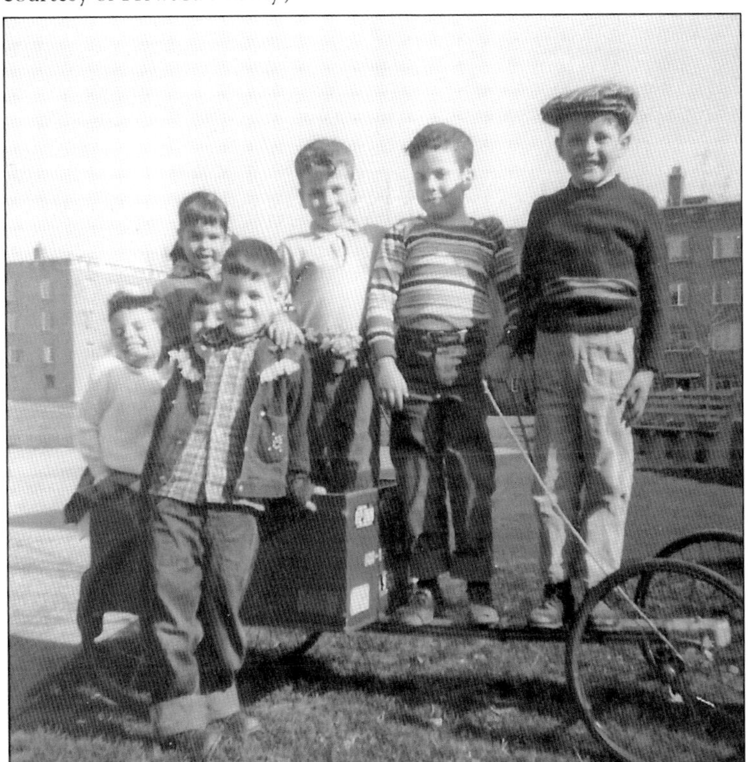

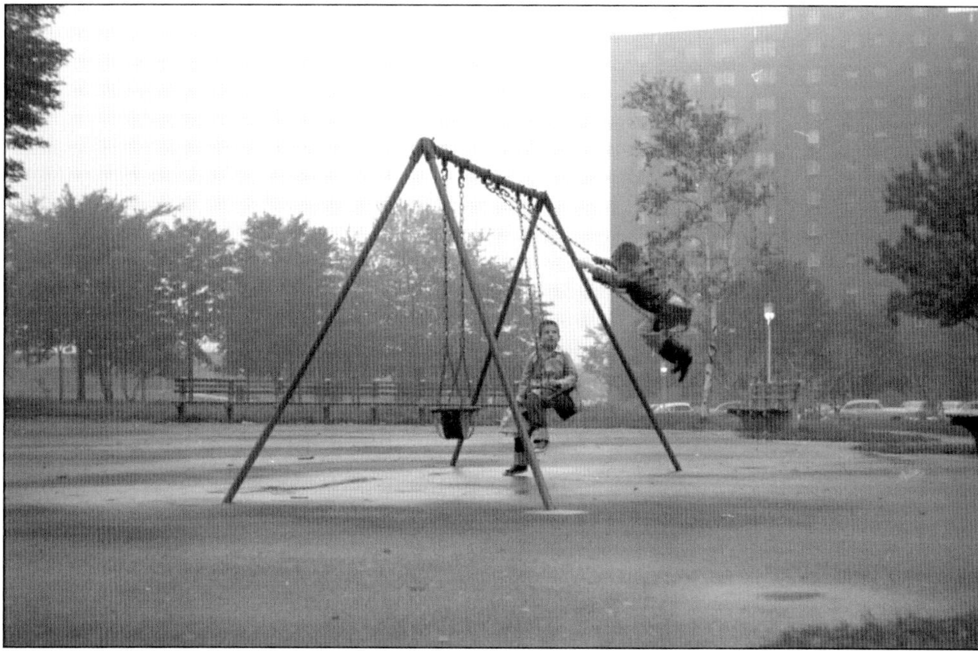

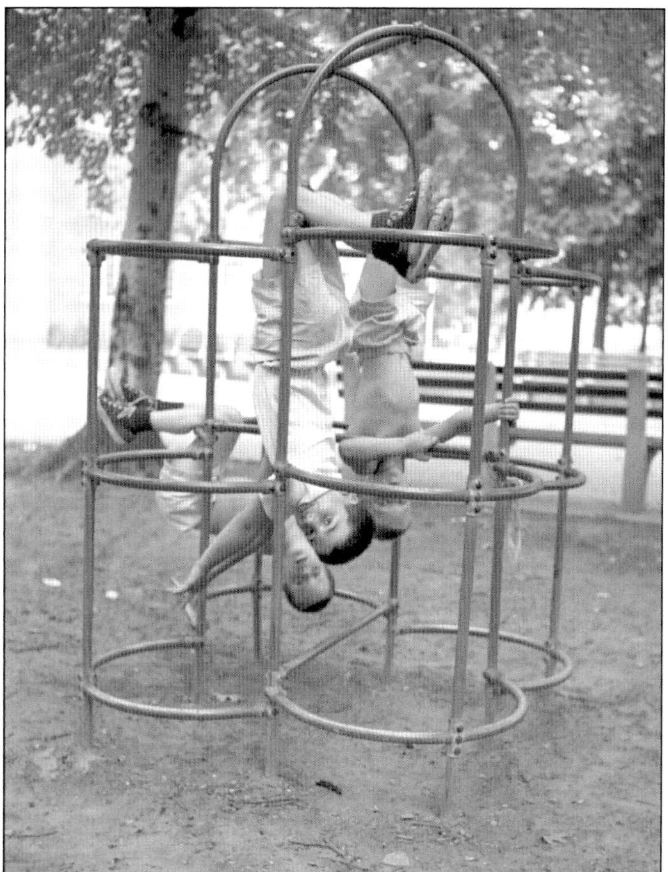

The playgrounds located throughout the Fresh Meadows development provided a range of equipment for children to enjoy, and even the prospect of rain did not deter kids from going out to meet some friends. The swing sets were very popular with younger children. Older children liked to climb and hang from the jungle gyms, which, as can be seen in the picture taken in the playground behind 192-24C 64th Circle, frequently offered nothing more than hard dirt as a landing zone. Certain safety features that are common today, such as impact-absorbing material at the base of the jungle gym, were not even on the radar screen back in the 1950s. (Both, courtesy of Mitchell Kaften; photographs by Douglas Kaften.)

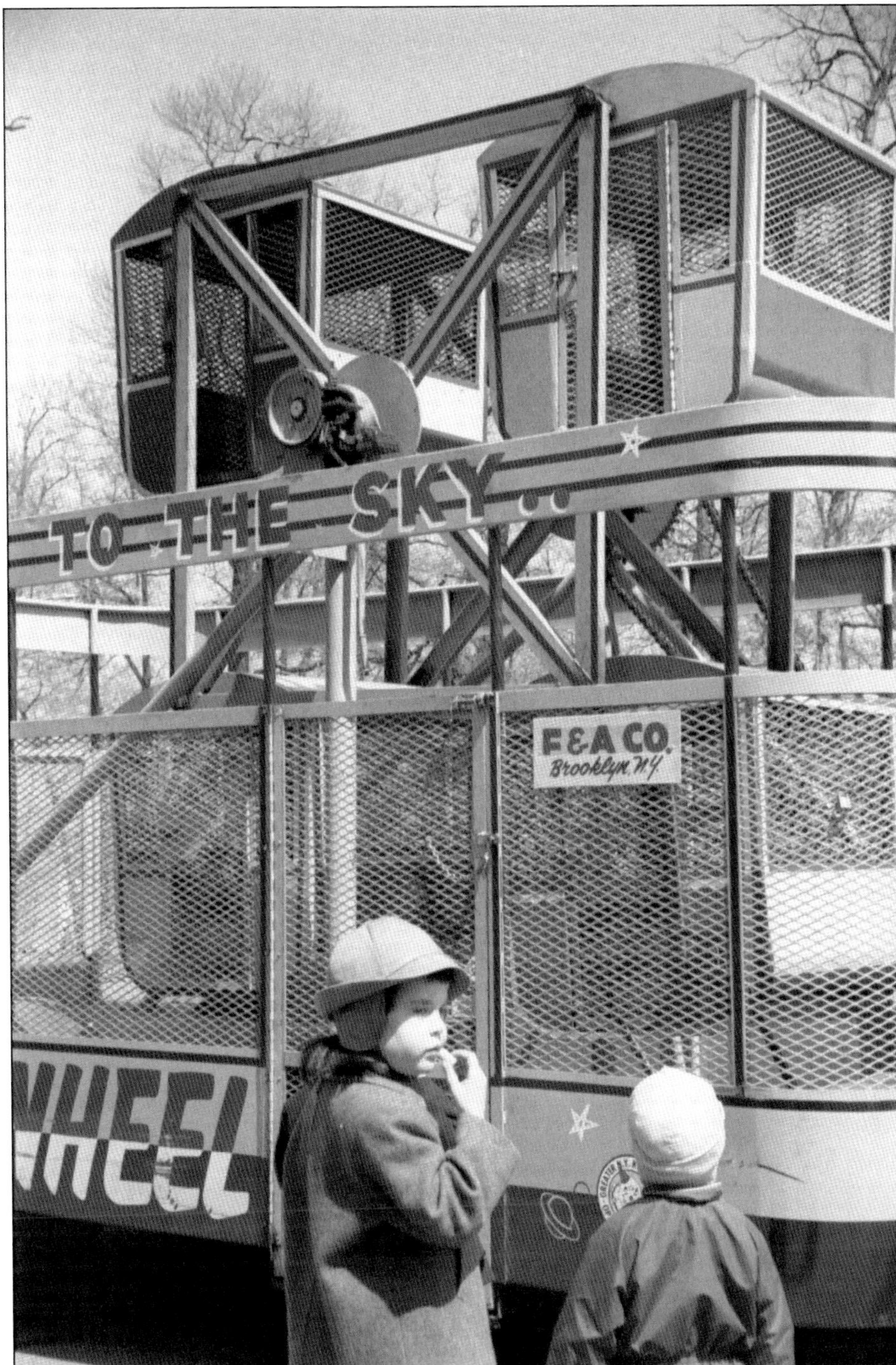

The first signs of spring and warm weather signified that it was the time of year for the arrival of mobile amusement rides in Fresh Meadows. One such ride was a miniature Ferris wheel. Young children would be quick to gather at the first sighting of these trucks. And once the rides started to appear, children knew it would not be long before the Good Humor truck would be around. (Courtesy of Mitchell Kaften; photograph by Douglas Kaften.)

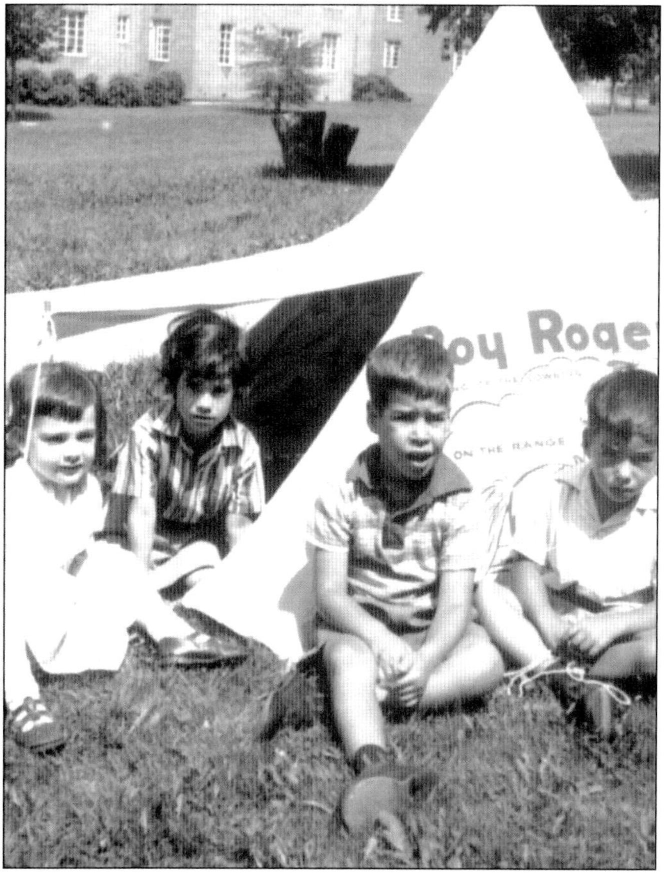

Summers naturally offered large blocks of free time to engage in a variety of activities with friends. One such activity was setting up a tent and just hanging out. As with a number of products bought for or by children in the 1950s, the tent pictured at left was a merchandising tie-in with an iconic pop culture figure in 1956. From left to right are unidentified, Anita Toby Lager, Ken Winthrop, and Andy Dancis. Trying to catch butterflies was also a popular summertime activity. After dinner, it was not uncommon to see a number of children running about with their butterfly nets. Pictured below with their nets are, from left to right, Rhonda Uziel and Karen Marmer. (Left, courtesy of Anita Toby Lager; below, courtesy of Rhonda Goodman.)

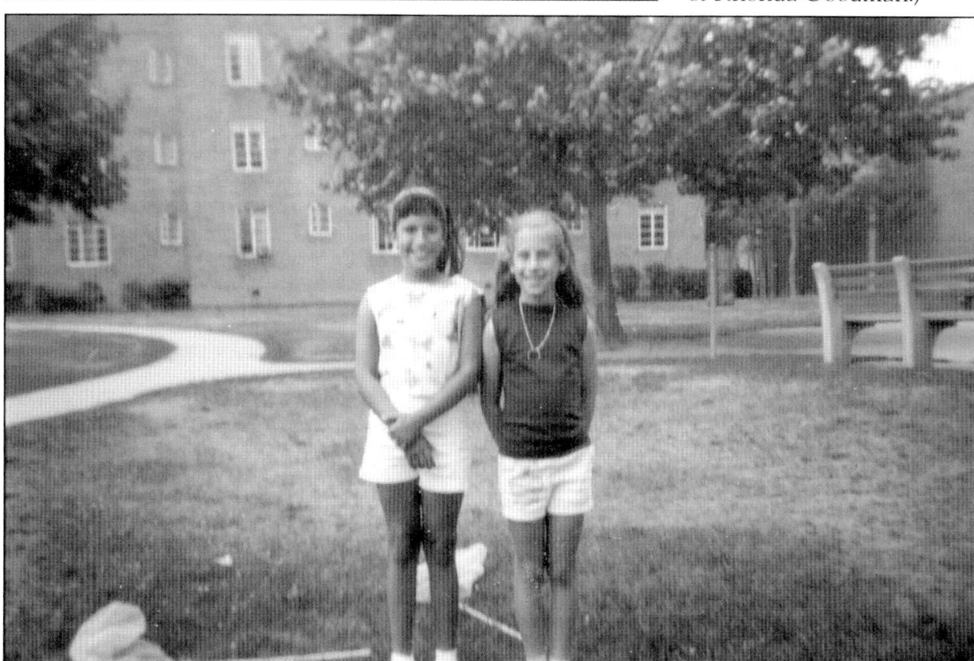

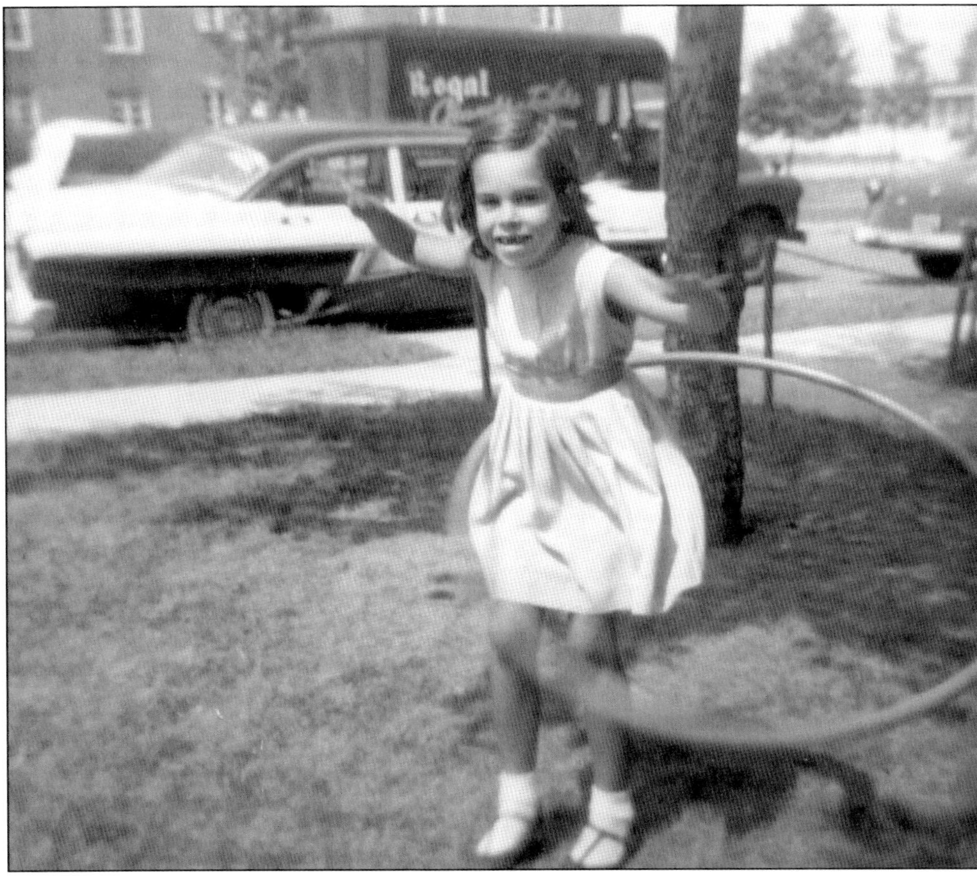

One activity that exploded into the national consciousness during the summer of 1958 was the hula hoop. It started out as a fad in California before spreading to the rest of the country. In the spring and summer of 1958, twenty-five million hula hoops were sold in the United States. Pictured above during the summer of 1959, in the yard in front of 194-40A 64th Avenue, is Carole Gerstenhaber. For some, summertime meant going to day camp. In the photograph at right, Peter Guttman and his brother Gary (standing) relax while waiting for the bus that will pick them up and take them to the Hillcrest Jewish Center Day Camp. (Above, courtesy of Carole Gerstenhaber Thomasco; right, courtesy of Judith Guttman.)

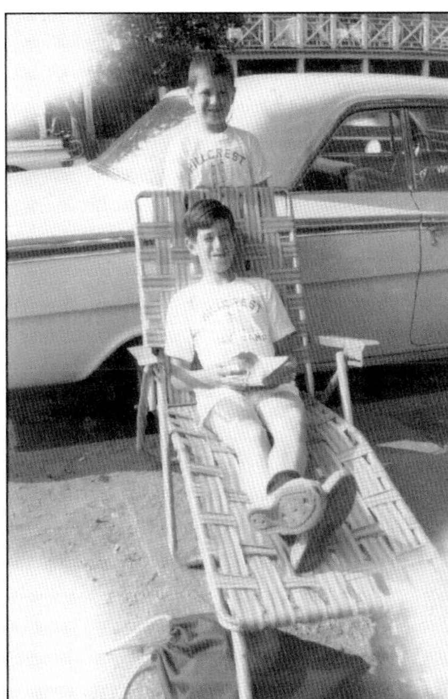

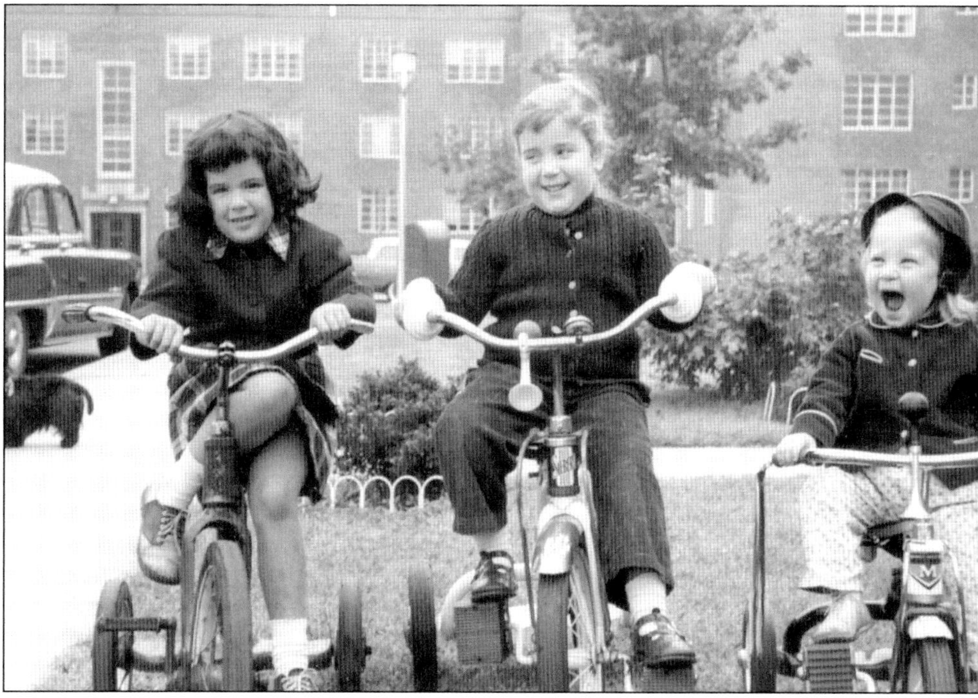

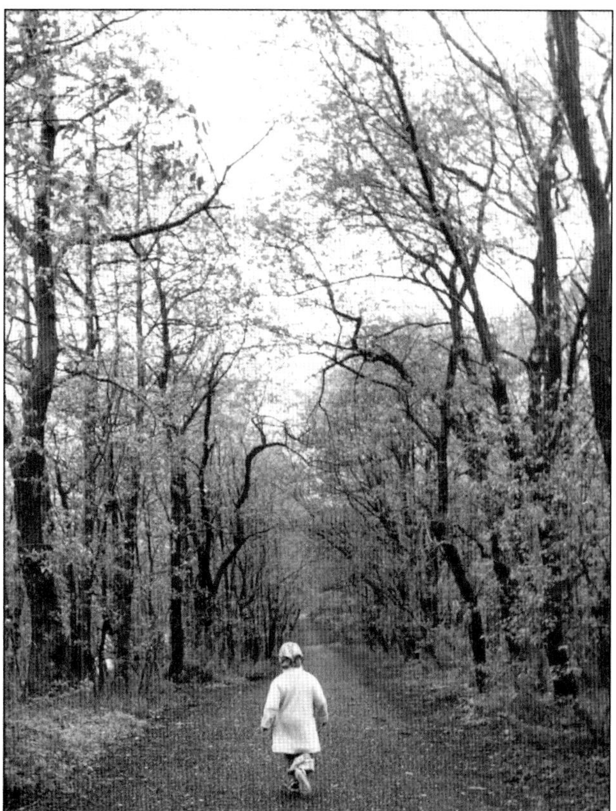

Younger children naturally started down the road to bicycling by learning how to ride tricycles. And one of the roads children would play on was the abandoned Long Island Motor Parkway, as seen in the photograph at left, which ran parallel to 199th Street, with an entrance just beyond the southern side of the PS 179 playground. The Long Island Motor Parkway was a toll road that opened in 1908, closed down in the 1930s, and in the Fresh Meadows vicinity, ultimately became part of Cunningham Park. Pictured above on the far right is Louise Covitt with two unidentified friends. (Above, courtesy of Louise Covitt; left, courtesy of Aina Balgalvis.)

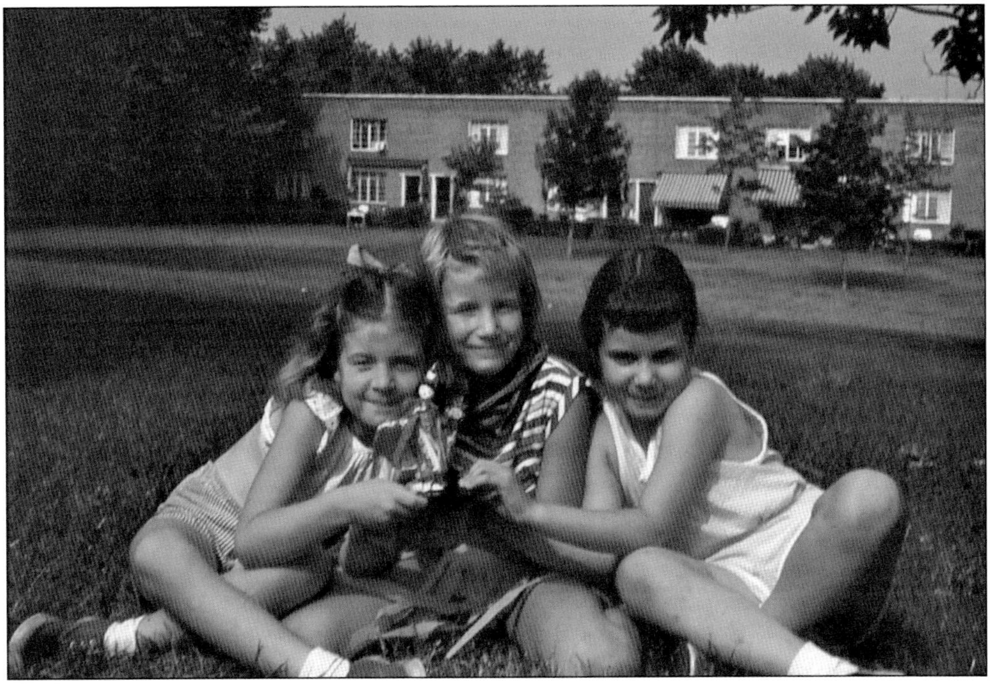

The common open space behind apartment buildings was conducive to kids getting together with friends and engaging in activities, such as playing with dolls or simply hanging out on the park benches. In the center of the above photograph is Laura Ostrow with two of her friends. Pictured below, Eytan Fichman (left) hangs out with his older brother and his friends (from left to right) Richard Perlman, Mark Fichman, and Bob Feigenbaum. (Above, courtesy of Laura Ostrow George; below, courtesy of Eytan Fichman and Mark Fichman.)

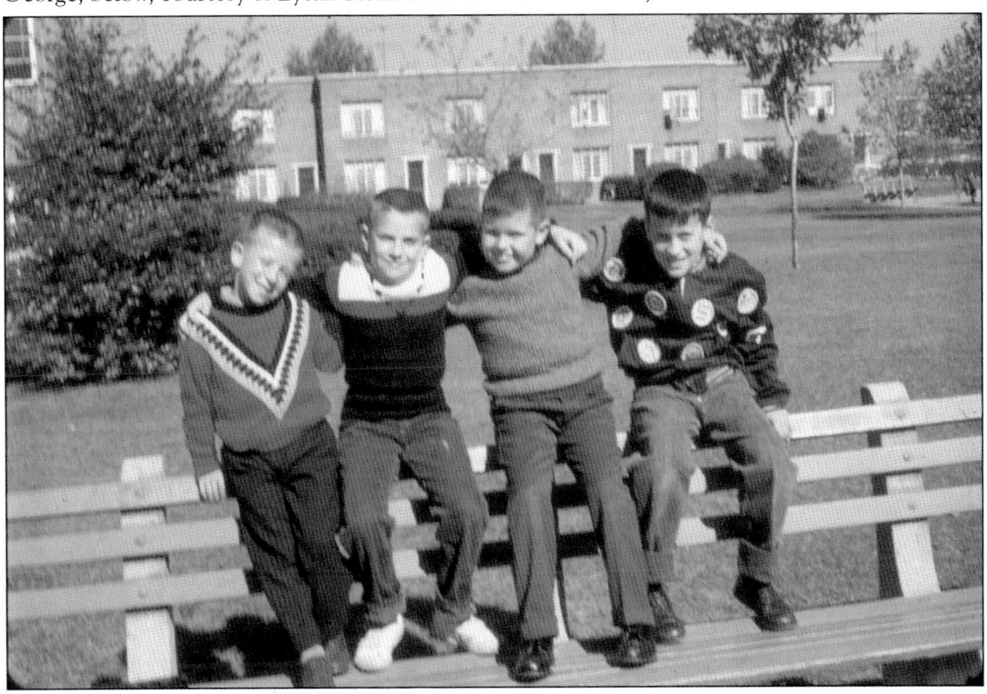

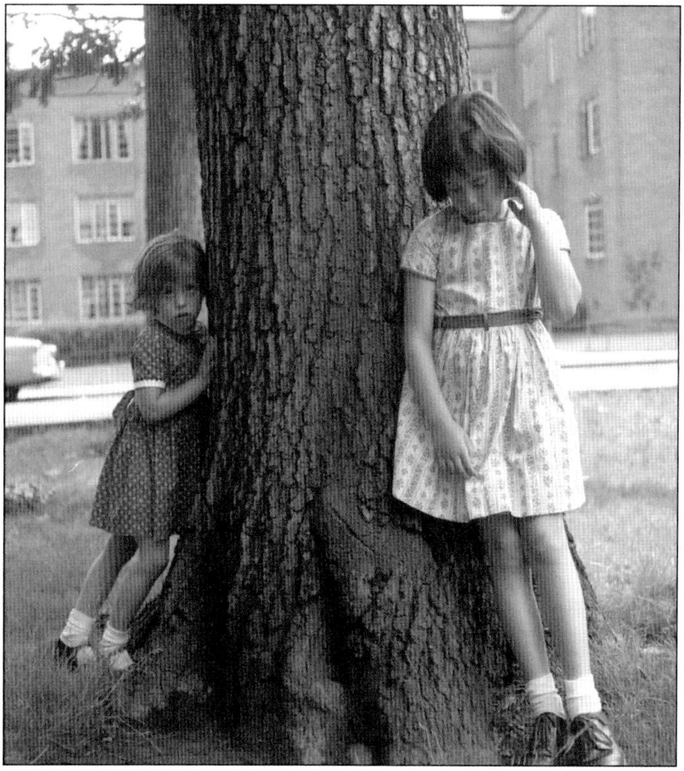

The Oak Grove offered almost six acres of wooded area to walk about in or play games, such as hide-and-seek. The large tree trunks provided wonderful places to hide behind. In the photograph at left are Sandy Kaften (left) and her sister Jane. Alternatively, younger children could simply walk outside the front door of their apartment building and enjoy the simple pleasure of jumping off the front steps, as the three boys in the photograph below are doing. In this image are Mitchell Kaften (wearing the sailor's cap) and David Nimkin, on the right. (Both, courtesy of Mitchell Kaften; photographs by Douglas Kaften.)

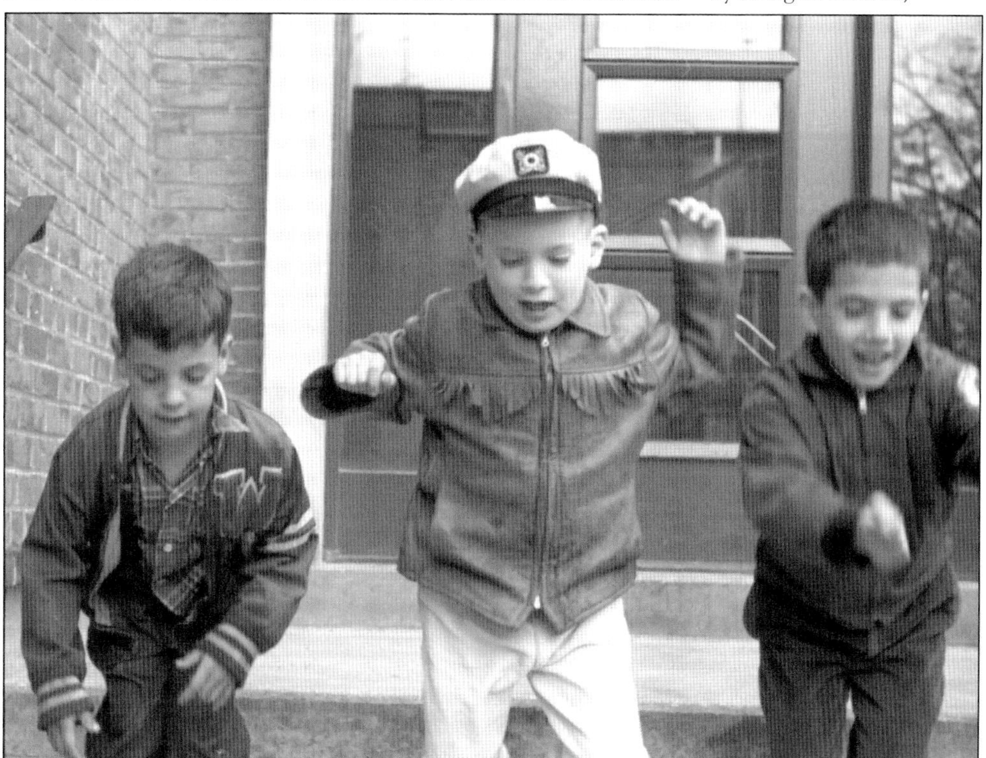

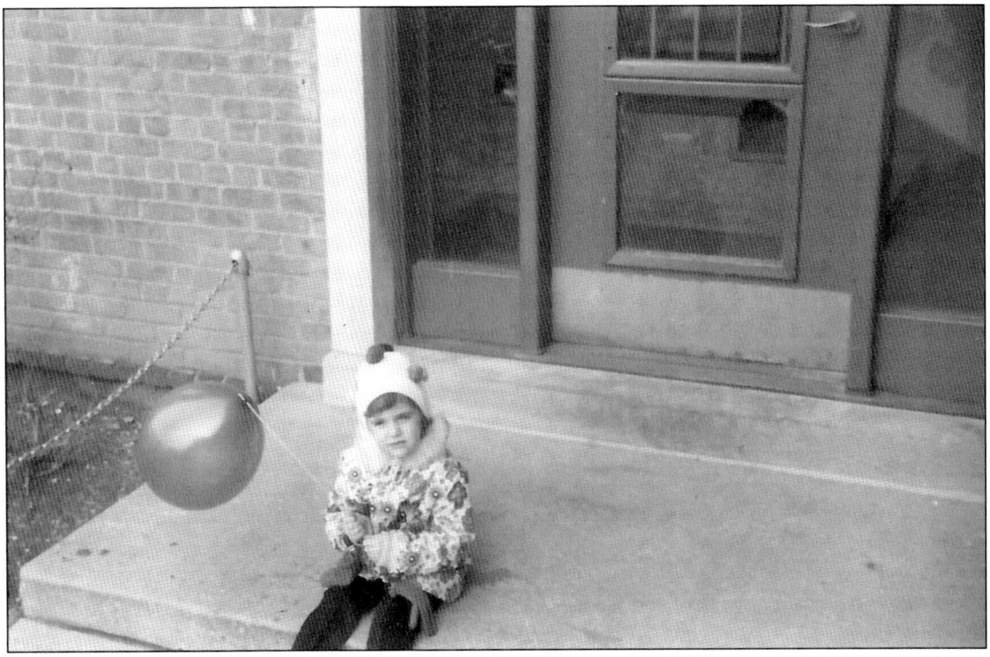

On occasion, the front steps provided a resting place for a young child to enjoy holding a balloon, as can be seen in the photograph above. Pictured here is Paula Fortgang in front of 194-60B 64th Avenue. The front stoop also offered a place for dads to get together while watching their youngest children. The image below was captured in front of adjoining entrances at the Meadowlark Gardens complex. From left to right are (first row, young children) Sandra Furstman, Robin Meisel, and Laurie Seiden; (second row, men sitting) Harold Hochstein, Hank Seiden, and Harold Furstman; (third row, standing) Len Meisel holding his son Steven. (Above, courtesy of Howard Mirsky; below, courtesy of Sandra Furstman.)

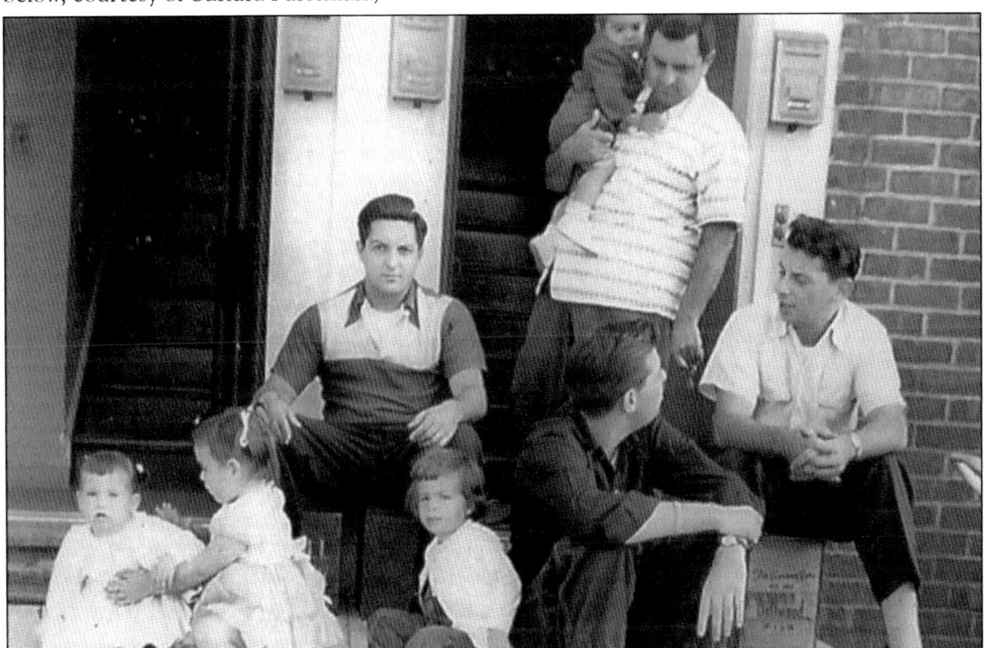

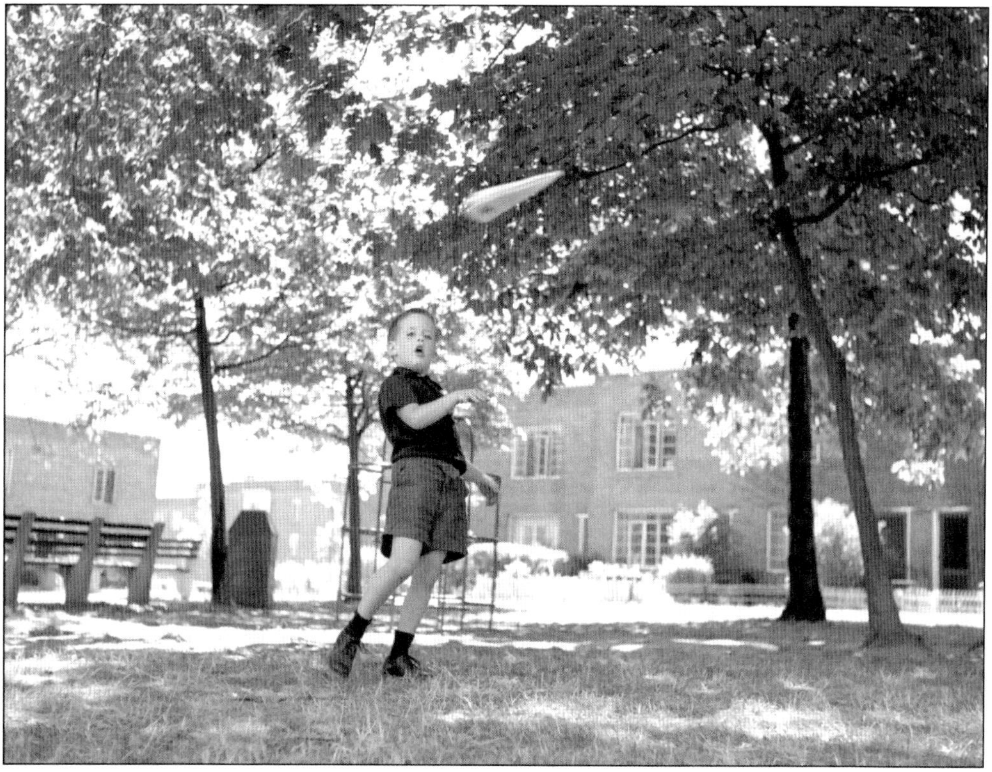

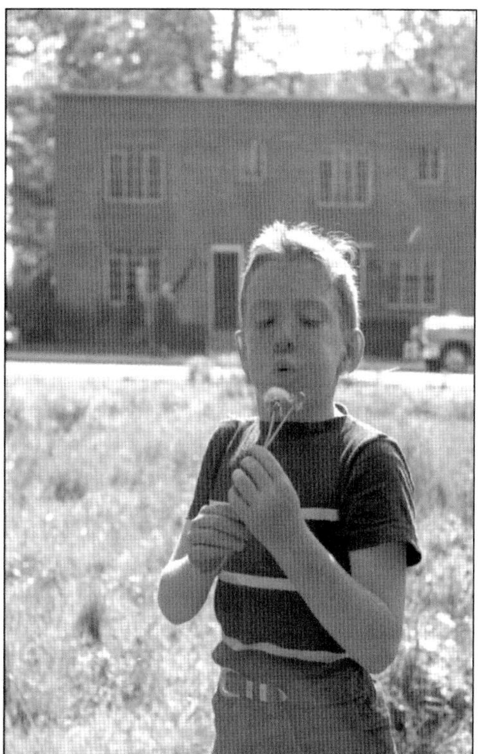

While children in Fresh Meadows would often play with friends in a variety of outdoor games such as stoop ball and skully, there were also times when they would go outside and enjoy simple, solitary activities. One such example is seen in the above photograph with the launching of a paper airplane in the playground. Another instance can be seen at left, as Len Leighton blows the seeds of a dandelion (and unknowingly spreading weeds) in the Oak Grove. (Both, courtesy of Mitchell Kaften; photographs by Douglas Kaften.)

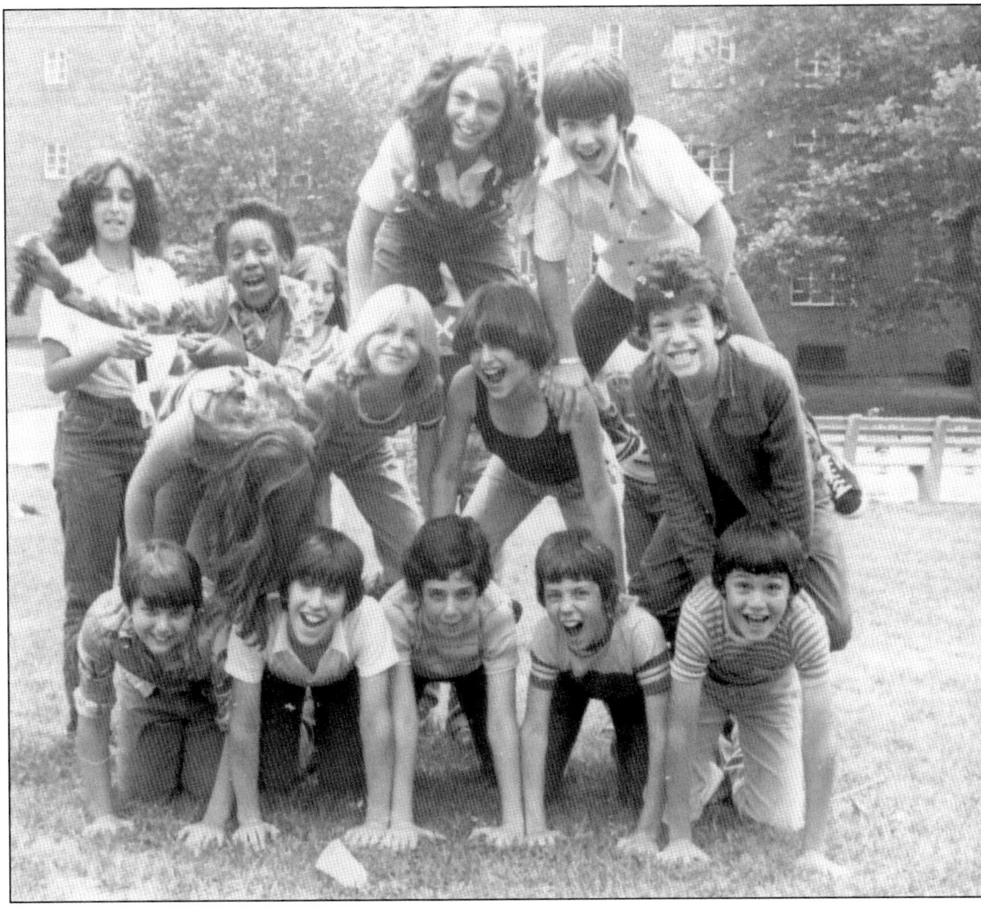

Celebrating the end of the school year might result in something like this. In this photograph, taken in 1978 are, from left to right, (first row) Stuart Levine, Joseph Farkas, Brian Shapiro, Bryan Moore, and unidentified; (second row) unidentified, Inta Balgalvis, Jill Bloom, and Eric Ancharoff; (third row) Sandy Packer, Laci McDowell, Heather Pascal, Pamela Dein, and Joseph De la Viesca. (Courtesy of Aina Balgalvis.)

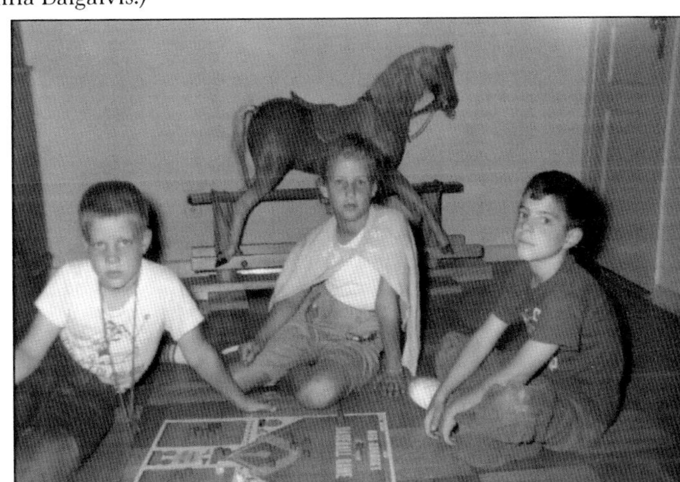

Of course, not all play took place outdoors. It was not uncommon to invite a couple of friends over who lived across the hall or in a neighboring building. One popular indoor activity was playing board games. Pictured here, playing Red Barber's Baseball Game, are, from left to right, Christopher Faas, Laura Ostrow, and Marc Cantor. (Courtesy of Fred Cantor.)

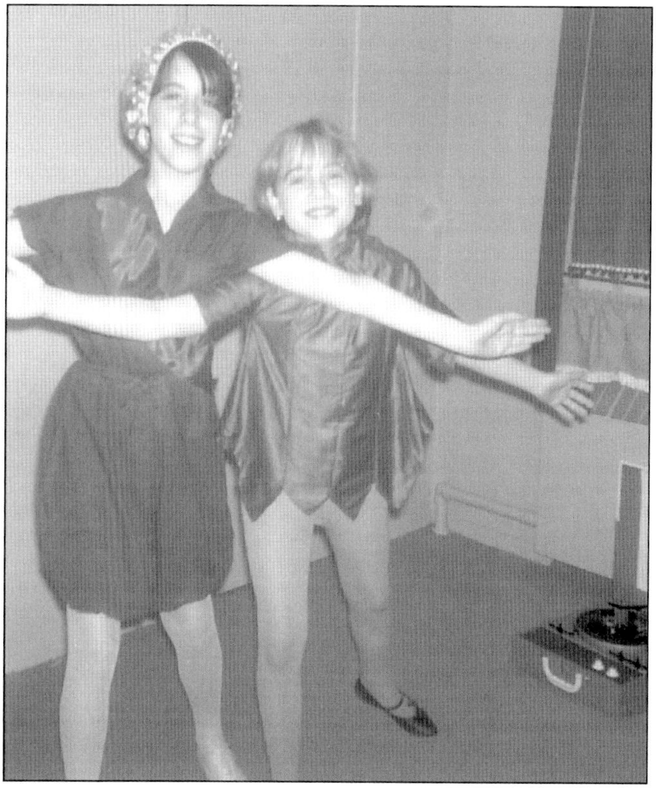

Another indoor pastime, especially with the growing popularity of rock music in the 1950s and 1960s, was listening to 45-rpm records on a portable record player. And for a 12-year-old, what could possibly be more fun than having a costume party with your friends, listening to music, and mimicking the go-go dancers from the television show *Hullabaloo*? At left are, from left to right, Erica Goldberg and Lori Herskowitz at Barbara Reiss's 12th birthday party in 1967. In the photograph below are, from left to right, (first row) Randi Abrams, Bonnie Reiss, and Barbara Reiss; (second row) Loretta Nitsos, Joan Berenson, Amy Gottlieb, Lori Hershkowitz, and Erica Goldberg. (Both, courtesy of Barbara Reiss Congemi.)

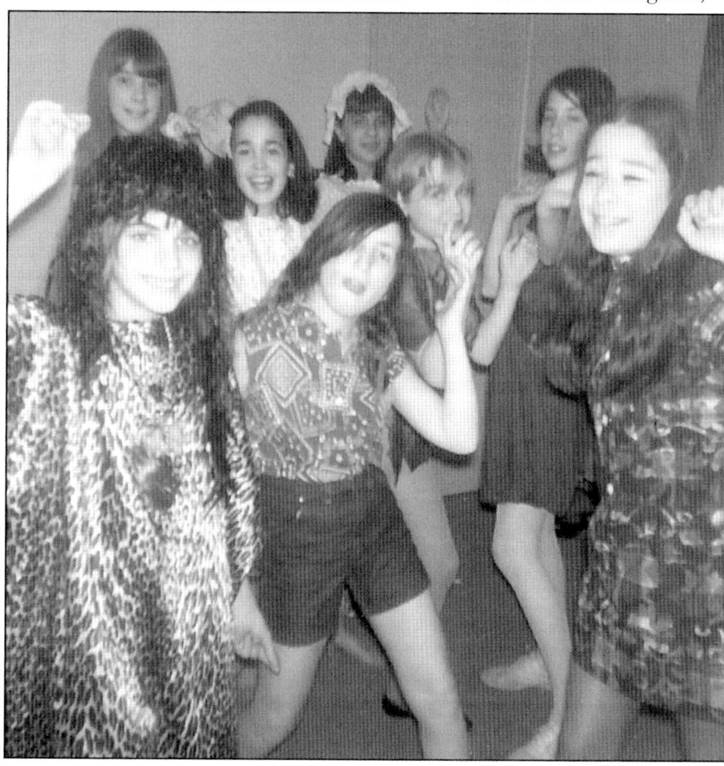

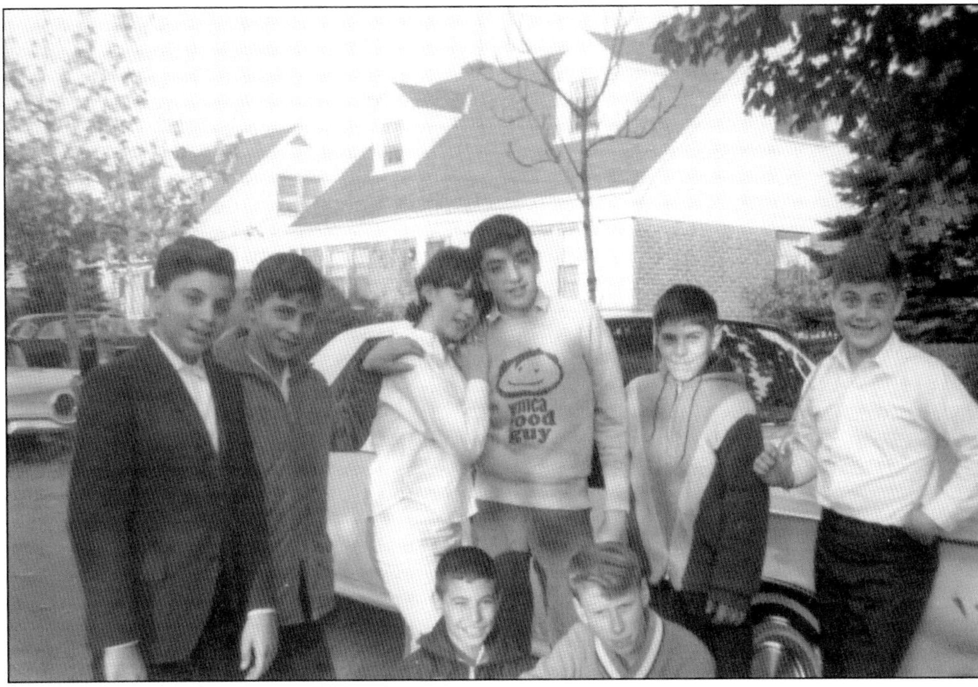

For teenagers, just hanging out with friends was an activity in itself. Above, Sheila Kupersmith and a group of friends gather on her block near Ryan JHS. WMCA was a leading pop music radio station in the 1950s and 1960s, and its disc jockeys were known as the Good Guys. Sweatshirts bearing the WMCA logo were frequently part of the radio station's promotional giveaways. Pictured above, are, from left to right, (sitting) Barry Davis and Allen Filiberti; (standing) George Lucas, Jerome Davis, Sheila Kupersmith, David Levy, Philip Davis, and unidentified. In the photograph at right, Debra Davidson and Susan Schwartz enjoy a beautiful spring day on 180th Street between 67th and 69th Avenues. (Above, courtesy of Sheila Kupersmith Soriano; right, courtesy of Debra Davidson.)

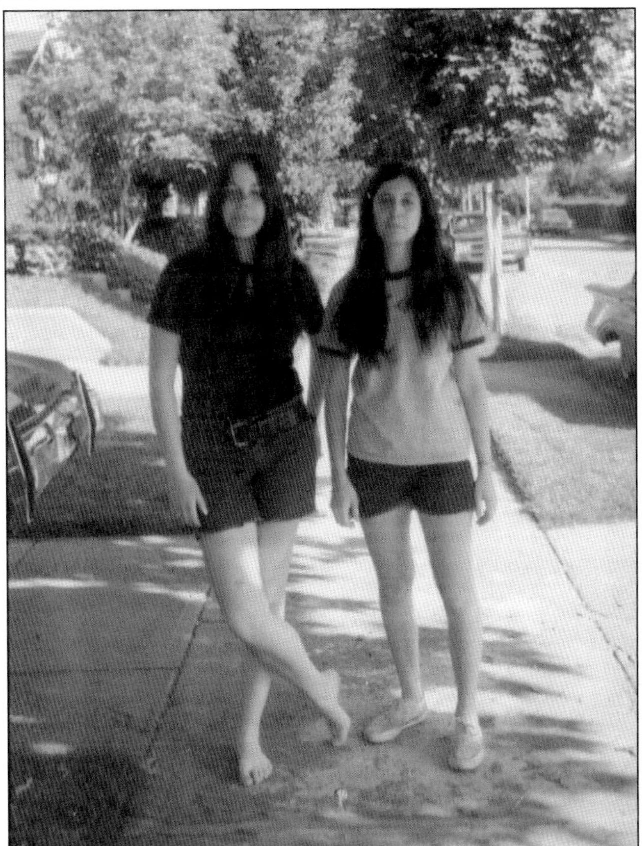

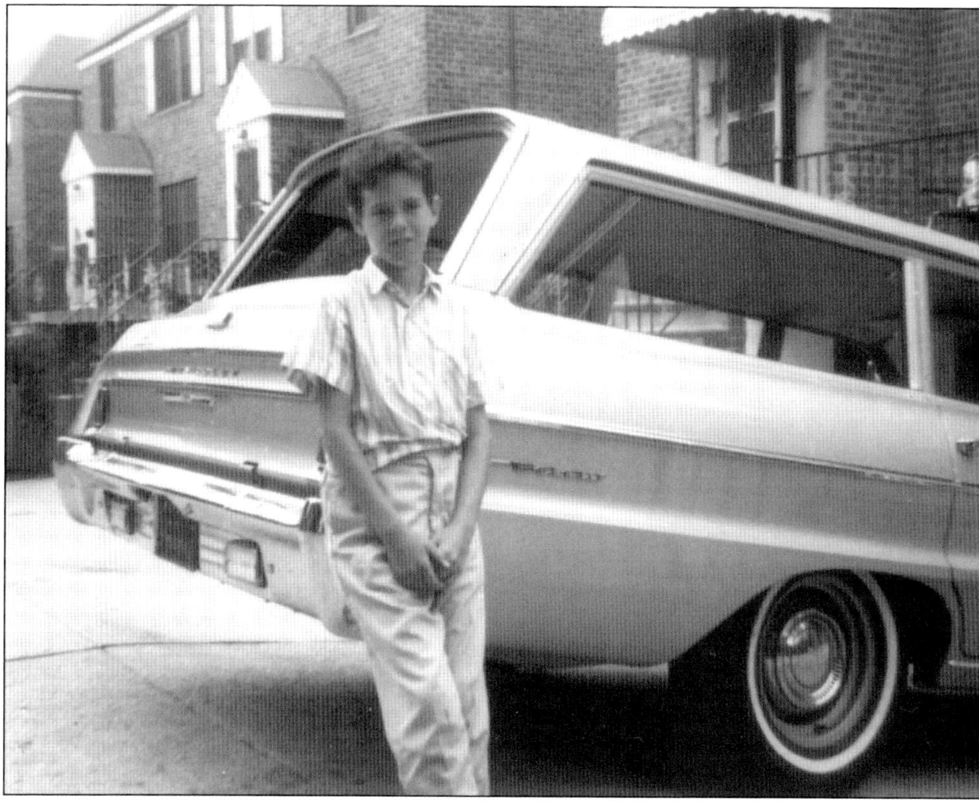

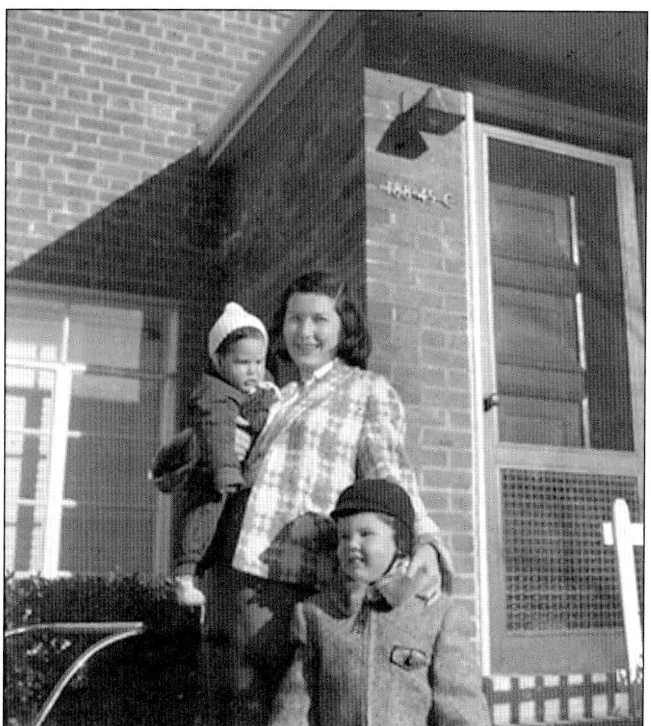

The baby boom was one of the contributing factors making station wagons so popular in the 1950s and 1960s. Daniel Wolkoff is leaning against his family's 1964 Chevy Belair station wagon in his driveway on Fresh Meadow Lane, directly across from PS 173. The homes on this block were semi-attached, two-family houses with raised front porches, which provided a comfortable place to relax on hot summer evenings. Naturally, getting dressed up for a car ride to visit relatives was also a regular occurrence. Pictured at left in 1955 are Beatrice Richman and her sons Steve (left) and Mark. (Above, courtesy of Daniel Goldon Wolkoff; left, courtesy of Steve Richman.)

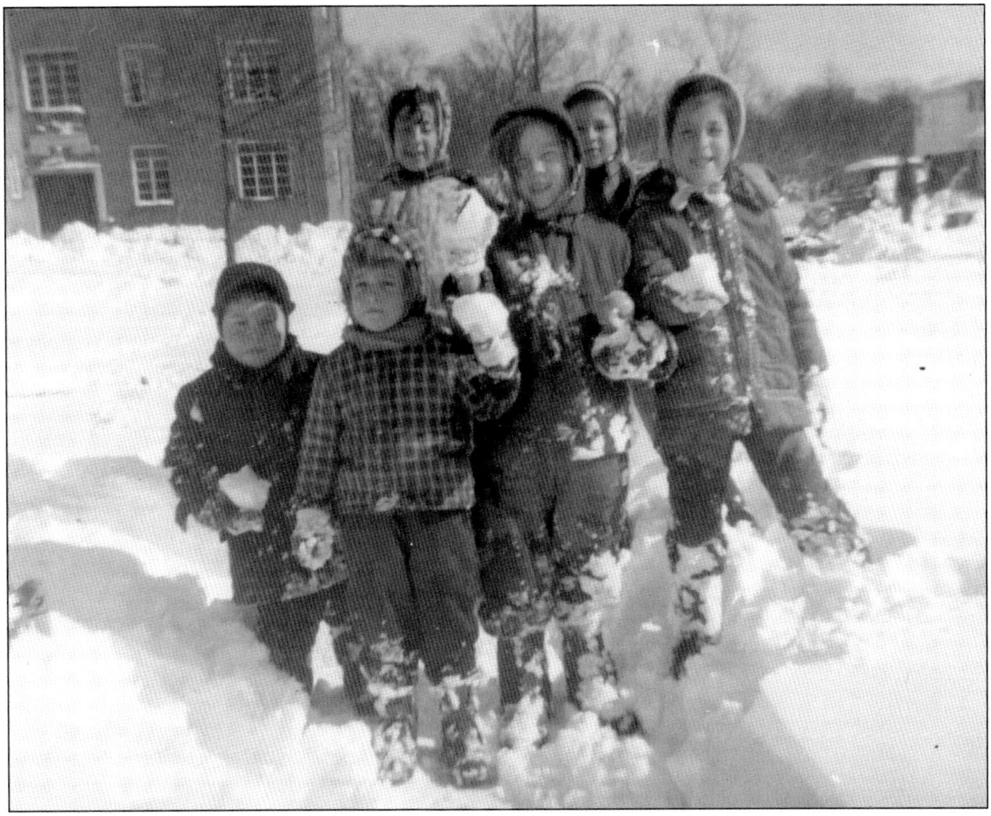

Snowstorms in Fresh Meadows provided lots of possibilities for fun right outside one's apartment. One option was getting together for a giant snowball fight. In the photograph above, taken near the corner by 198-01A 67th Avenue, are, from left to right, (first row) two unidentified, Linda Lee Wolfe, and Erica Goldberg; (second row) Audrey Goldberg and unidentified. Another popular snow activity was sledding. For younger children, sledding would take place on the smaller inclines that could be found behind some of the apartment buildings. Older children would typically head for the larger hill that existed south of the 13-story buildings before the 20-story building was constructed in the early 1960s. (Above, courtesy of Erica Goldberg Blau; right; courtesy of Queens Fresh Meadows LLC, photograph by Jerry Saltsberg & Associates.)

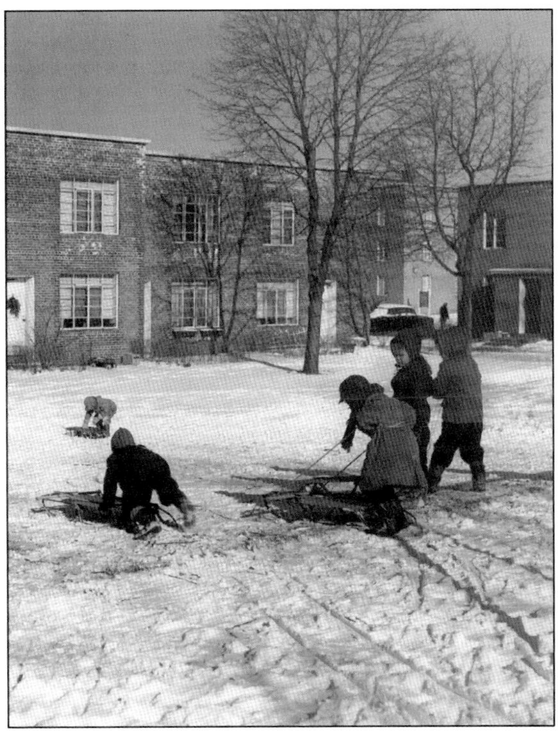

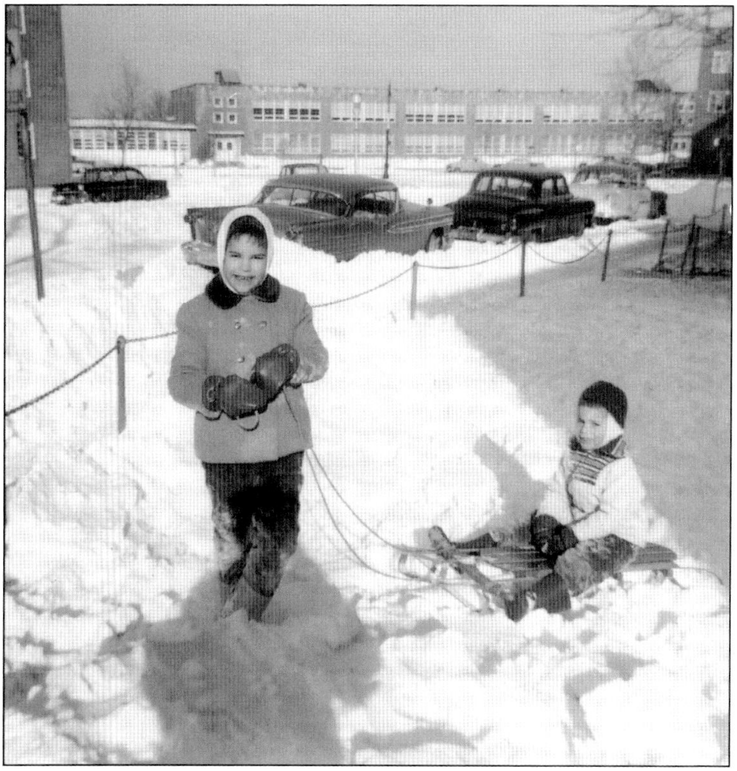

The sled would sometimes be used for taking out younger siblings on a snow day when school, such as PS 179 in the background, was closed for the day. In the photograph at left are Carole Gerstenhaber and her brother Robert next to 64th Avenue. In the photograph below, taken in January 1961, Ellen Schechter, bundled up after a large snowfall, is standing near the 13-story buildings. (Left, courtesy of Robert Gerson; below, courtesy of Ellen Schechter.).

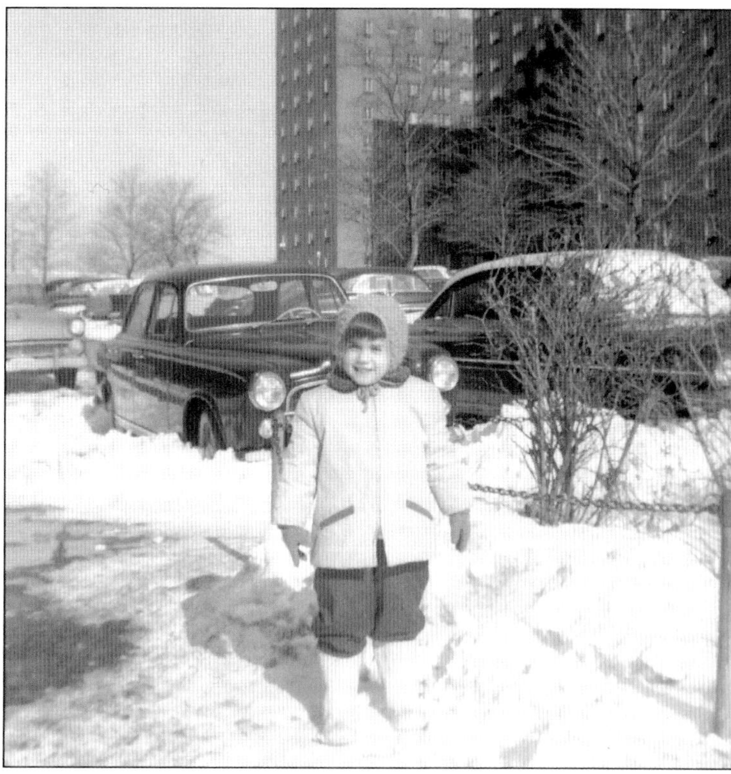

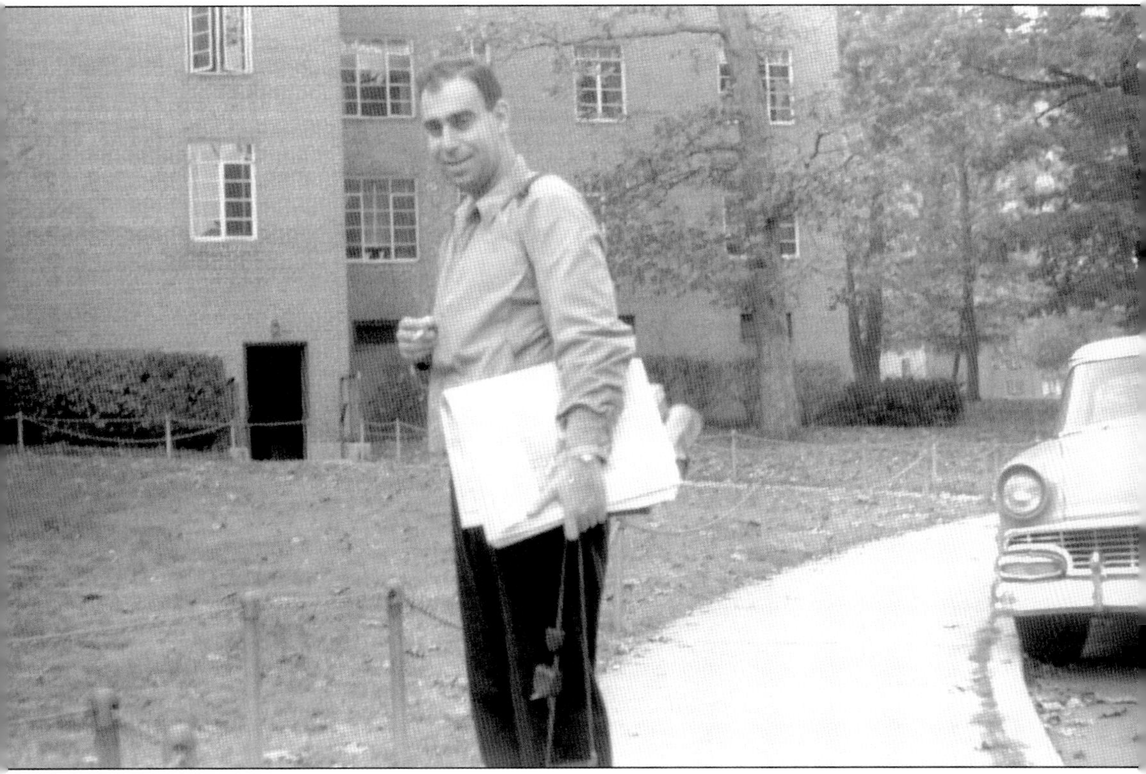

Douglas Kaften, with his camera always at hand, was one of the earliest members of the Fresh Meadows Camera Club, the oldest ongoing camera club in Queens. Thanks to his photographs, those of Jerry Saltsberg and others, there is ample documentation of why in 1949, Lewis Mumford wrote, "But a hundred years from now, Fresh Meadows will, unless it falls into less conscientious hands, still be as spacious, handsome, and 'sweet'—a green island in the midst of Queens—as St. John's Wood, which long remained an island in the growing welter of London." (Courtesy of Mitchell Kaften.)